Mount Fuji and N

Mount Fuji and Mount Sinai

A Pilgrimage in Theology

KOSUKE KOYAMA

SCM PRESS LTD

334 01054 3

First published 1984
by SCM Press Ltd
26–30 Tottenham Road, London N1

Typeset by CK Typesetters Ltd
and printed in Great Britain at
The Camelot Press Ltd
Southampton

To the memory
of Herbert G. Brand (1865–1942)
an English gentleman,
through whose preaching, in broken Japanese,
my grandfather was converted
to Jesus Christ

Contents

Preface

This book has four parts; each part has been assigned a biblical theme. The four biblical themes are; 'All its cities were laid in ruins before the Lord, before his fierce anger' (Jer. 4.26); 'My help comes from the Lord who made heaven and earth' (Ps. 121.2); 'You shall not take the name of the Lord your God in vain' (Ex. 20.7); and 'My mind is turning over in me. My emotions are agitated all together' (Hos. 11.8).

These biblical passages have gradually become central to my Christian life since 1945, the year of Hiroshima. With my own eyes I saw Tokyo become wilderness by the constant bombings. This seeing the wilderness of Tokyo has become, over the years, a 'theological' experience. My reflection on the Japanese cities that were laid in ruins before the fierce anger of the Lord is the theme of Part I. As I reflected on the destruction of Japan I was led to evaluate critically my own nature-oriented culture, focussing on emperor worship and sun worship. Out of this critique arose the intriguing challenge of the Bible that 'my help comes from the maker of heaven and earth', not just from 'heaven and earth'. Theological investigation of this theme is the subject of Part II. In Part III, I have attempted to provide a historical background to the discussion of idolatry in Japanese culture. Have the Japanese people taken the name of the Lord God in vain? In what way can it be said they did? Part IV focusses on the meaning of our faith in the God who is passionately involved in history. Behind our history is the agitated mind of God because of God's love for us. 'My mind is turning over in me. My emotions are agitated all together.' Does this not point to the spirit of 'the word of the cross' (I Cor. 1.18)?

All these four biblical themes are deeply 'disturbing' to the spiritual orientation of the East. For a son of the East to dialogue historically, culturally and religiously with the tradition of Mount Sinai has been a strange and moving experience. The slow assimilation of the traumatic events of 1945, which only gradually yielded their theological implications, has moved me towards the emotive region of the cross of Christ. The theology of the cross, at the core of the gospel message, gives me the fundamental orientation in which to engage in theology while living in a world dangerously fragmented by violent militarism, racism and nuclearism. This book, then, is a report of my personal pilgrimage, how I have brought together my historical experience and my confession of faith, or, more truly, how I have been brought, by grace of God, to dialogue between my own historical experience and the theology of the cross. I came to realize gradually that it is the theology of the cross that can really level a sharp and, at the same time, helpful critique against idolatry.

I have written this book with a keen awareness of the global peril of nuclear war. Wars are waged 'in the name of God', that is, with 'theological' justification. Such justification is idolatry. All nations are busy in quoting the names of their gods to justify what they are doing. I have had my personal knowledge of this during the time of the emperor worship cult of Japan. In the name of our own Solar Goddess we appointed ourselves to be the Righteous Nation that possessed the fullness of morality! One of the fundamental functions of theology is to expose idolatry. Theology that does not expose idolatry is not worthy of its name. However, this simple remark involves a painful difficulty. It may involve an application of the words of Jesus, 'Why do you see the speck that is in your brother's eye, but do not notice the log that is in your own eye?' (Matt. 7.3) to ourselves and not to someone else.

New York City   Kosuke Koyama
Christmas 1983

PART I

All its Cities Were Laid in Ruins before the Lord, before his Fierce Anger

(Jeremiah 4.26)

1
Let Us go up to
the Mountain of the Lord

Come, let us go up to the mountain of the Lord,
...For out of Zion shall go forth the law and the word
of the Lord from Jerusalem.
(Isa. 2.3)

1. Introduction and perspective

The subject of this book is not new. It is a study of idolatry. What, then, is idolatry? To this question answers will be attempted in several ways in the course of the discussion. A psalmist described it picturesquely as 'exchanging the glory of God for the image of an ox that eats grass' (106.20). 'Put to death ... covetousness which is idolatry', says Paul in his letter to the Colossians (3.5). In more philosophical language idolatry is a violent misuse, or even a usurpation, of centre symbolism. It is related to a deeper sense of human insecurity and spiritual restlessness which can become a malignant growth, boundless egocentric self-glorification.

> Idolatry is the elevation of a preliminary concern to ultimacy. Something essentially conditioned is taken as unconditional, something essentially partial is boosted into universality, and something essentially finite is given infinite significance.[1]

My interest in the subject of idolatry, I now know, began in 1945, the year of Hiroshima, when as a young boy I stood in bomb-devastated Tokyo. From where did this terrible destruction come upon Japan? Was the fate of Japan in some way related to the violent growth of the cult of emperor worship? What began as a vague feeling in that tragic moment has become a preoccupation with the mysterious destructive power of idolatry in history. The memory of war refuses to disappear.

While this subject is subtly different from that of the East-West dialogue in religions, I take it up in the context of the dialogue between Mount Fuji and Mount Sinai, between Asian spirituality and biblical spirituality. As an Asian Christian this is the theological context to which I am responsible. It is my understanding that this context is critically important for understanding the global human situation, full of bombs and genocides, in which we find ourselves today.

In my cultural and theological investigation of idolatry, the words of Abraham Heschel have been with me as a guiding inspiration.

What concerns the prophet is the human event as a divine experience. History to us is the record of human experience; to the prophet it is a record of God's experience.[2]

Hiroshima in 1945 and the Nuclear Freeze Movement in 1983 are indeed human experience. But their deep meaning will be revealed to us when we try to understand them as experienced by God. This is the secret and glory of theology in spite of our misuse and distortion of theology. Against the Nuclear Freeze Movement in Europe and America President Reagan expressed his view:

I know that the paradox of peace through a credible military posture may be difficult for some people to accept. Some even argue that if we really want to reduce nuclear weapons we should simply stop building them ourselves. That argument makes about as much sense as saying that the way to prevent fires is to close down the fire department.[3]

The President is making this remark in the world whose 'stockpile of nuclear weapons is equivalent to 16,000 million tons of TNT. In World War II, 3 million tons of munitions were expended, and 40–50 million people died'.[4] Does this describe the 'credible military posture'? Humanity lives in an extremely dangerous world today. The extinction of all living beings on this planet earth is possible by our own doing. We are experiencing this ultimate threat. According to the theological insight of Heschel, we must try to see how God experiences this threatening situation. Dorothee Solle says that the nuclear weapons are aimed at God! It is not enough merely to point out that the experience of history by us and by God is qualitatively different. The famous words of Samuel; 'For the Lord sees not as man sees; man looks on the outward appearance, but the Lord looks on the heart' (I Sam. 16.7) intimates the dimension of 'history as a record of God's experience', giving the basis for the difference in experience of history by God and by us.

The theological illumination I received from Heschel means briefly three things. First, in an unexpectedly refreshing manner the thought of history as a record of God's experience defined for me the dynamic character of theology. In the light of this perspective I am able also to find the critical importance of human history. Secondly, I realized that theology is almost by definition open to the temptation of itself falling into idolatry. There is only a perilously thin distinction between saying 'history is a record of God's experience' and 'taking the name of God in vain'. This difficult situation is reflected in the conflict between true prophets and false prophets. And thirdly, my awareness of the importance of history which has been enriched by Heschel convinced me of the importance of the meaning and value of human cultures. Human history is always cultural. A denuded a-cultural history is an impossibility. That history is a record of God's experience implies an interrelatedness that is present between theology and culture.

I was baptized into the Christian faith in 1942, as the war was gaining momentum. In the light of the events of that time, my becoming a Christian was an unusual occurrence, to say the least. Japan was at war with the United States, a 'Christian' nation, and I, a young Japanese boy, born to a Christian family but moulded by the Japanese imperial cult in the schools, was being baptized into the religion of the enemy.

On 18 April 1942, only five months after the 'victorious' beginning of the war, American Army planes staged their first raid on Tokyo, Nagoya and Kobe. This incident shook the people of Japan. For me the memory of this raid has a particular theological association. On the day of the air raid I was reading the Bible. I came upon the story of Abram giving Lot the first choice of the land. I was surprised and impressed with the generous personality of Abram.

> So Abram went up from Egypt, he and his wife, and all that he had, and Lot with him, into the Negeb. Now Abram was very rich in cattle, in silver and in gold. ... And Lot ... also had flocks and herds and tents, so that the land could not support both of them dwelling together. ... and there was strife between the herdsmen. ... And Abram said to Lot, 'Let there be no strife between you and me, and between your herdsmen and my herdsmen; for we are kinsmen. Is not the whole land before you? Separate yourself from me. If you take the left hand, then I will go to the right; or if you take the right hand, then I will go to the left'. And Lot ... saw that the Jordan valley was well watered everywhere like the garden of the Lord. ... So Lot chose for himself all the Jordan valley, and Lot journeyed east; thus they separated from each other. Abram dwelt in the land of Canaan (Gen. 13.1–12).

It struck me at that time, as I read the story, that not to insist upon having the first choice is a mark of being 'religious'. Such non-insistence suggests a life style expectant of an open-future. There is a hint of spiritual beauty in non-insistence. This encounter with Abram was my first vivid introduction to the land and culture of Mount Sinai. I still find it significant that it is

Abram, later Abraham, who could give up the Jordan valley, 'well watered everywhere like the garden of the Lord', who became patriarch of three great religions, Judaism, Christianity and Islam. I still feel, as I felt then, that Abram fits into the image of the 'religious person' in the Asian tradition which portrays renunciation as a central symbol for religious life. Abraham was not a European, of course! I now understand why I felt 'at home' with Abraham, even though I may not be able, as he was, to give up such good land. Unfortunately, in human community people of non-insistence will be exploited by the people of insistence. Religion has been used widely and cleverly by the exploiters because often it makes people accepting and non-insistent. I understand this cruel arrangement without any difficulty. But there is something in non-insistence, if it is an expression of our trust in God, that goes beyond such discussion of exploitation. In a way Lot exploited the 'meek' Abram's religiosity. Yet it was not Lot but Abram who 'inherited the earth' (Matt. 5.5).

I retain one other theological association with the first bombing of Tokyo. At the time I was reading an abridged Japanese translation of John Bunyan's *Pilgrim's Progress*. I could not understand this very complicated book, but was impressed by the struggle of Christian, who in spite of all obstacles pressed toward his ultimate goal. This first experience with a Christian classic left me with an impression which I later found significant for my understanding of the theological terrain of Mount Sinai. Upon my young mind was imprinted then the notion that history is full of obstacles, the works of demonic powers, and we must struggle against these forces if we want to live a life of faith in God. I saw, too, that such a life of struggle is not without a goal at which point we can genuinely feel fulfilled, just as this man called Christian finally arrives at his destination where he is saved. John Bunyan introduced me to the image of history as linear progression.

When I was baptized I sensed that I was moving from the cultural world of Mount Fuji to that of Mount Sinai. Was it a simple transition, as one abandons one's former cultural life and resolutely moves to another, this move from the land of Prince Shotoku (one who is comparable to Moses in Japanese history) to that of Moses? Did I so separate myself from the heritage of Prince Shotoku that I can now completely identify myself with Moses? No, such a thing is not possible at all. I confessed, at my baptism, before the people of the believing community, that Jesus Christ is 'the Lamb of God who takes away the sin of the world' (John 1.29). Mount Calvary is more central than Mount Sinai for me as a Christian. It is in the name of Jesus Christ that I received a new self-identity both spiritual and cultural. With this new identity I began to appreciate the tradition represented by the name of Moses. When I came to Mount Calvary I brought my Japanese language, culture and psychology to Jesus Christ. No matter what I do, 'Prince Shotoku' is within me, just as Moses is found in every Jew. It is true that I moved from a polytheistic, cosmological world (fertile nature orientation) to a monotheistic, eschatological world (critical time orientation), from cyclical culture to linear culture, and from a relaxed culture to a tense culture. Yet there are elements of the polytheistic cosmological world, the cyclical, relaxed culture, which are too rich and precious to be lightly discarded, and which can make very significant and positive contributions to the Christian faith, such as loyalty, filial piety to lord and community, and self-negation. The worlds of Moses and of Prince Shotoku are different, but there is a Christian possibility for a creative two-way traffic between them.

My baptism provoked a radical appraisal of my own culture and religion which involved both critical yes and no. This criticism was not generated within my own culture and religion. It came to me over the years as I pondered the meaning of Mount Calvary and Mount Sinai. In this process there developed an active conversation between my perceptions of Mount Calvary and Mount Sinai. I listened to the tradition of the 'Old Testament' as I endeavoured to understand the message of the New Testament, and vice versa.

In my student days I came across the following words of Martin Buber.

I live not far from the city of Worms, to which I am bound by a tradition of my forefathers; and, from time to time, I go there. When I go there, I go first to the cathedral. It is a visible harmony of members, a totality in which no part deviates from perfection. With consummate joy I walk about the cathedral, gazing at it. Then I go over to the Jewish cemetery. It consists of crooked, cracked, shapeless, random stones. I station myself there, gaze upward from the jumble of a cemetery to that glorious harmony, and it is as though I were looking up from Israel to the Church. Below, there's not a lot of form; there are only the stones and the ashes under the stones. The ashes are there, no matter how thinly they are scattered. There is the corporeality of men, which has turned to this. There it is. There it is for me. There it is for me, not as corporeality in the space of this planet, but as corporeality in my own memory, far into the depths of history, as far back as Sinai. I have stood there, have been united with the ashes, and through them with the patriarchs. That is a memory of the transaction with God which is given to all Jews. From this the perfection of the Christian house of God cannot separate me, nothing can separate me from the sacred history of Israel. I have stood there and have experienced everything myself; all this death has confronted me: all the ashes, all the ruins, all the wordless misery is mine; but the covenant has not been withdrawn from me. I lie on the ground, fallen like these stones. But it has not been withdrawn from me.[5]

In the Jewish cemetery consisting of 'crooked, cracked, shapeless, random stones' Buber experiences his fundamental identity in terms of the sacred tradition of Mount Sinai with the memory of all that happened there. A gentile and Japanese, I stand outside of that corporeality of sacred memory. But I do not find my spiritual home base in the tradition of the Christian cathedral either. The graveyard – consisting of crooked, cracked, shapeless, random stones – in which I find my identity would be that of Mahayana Buddhism. I am proud of this great tradition. It's memory reaches back to the Enlightenment of Gotama Buddha. Born in a land which has embraced Mahayana Buddhism for thirteen centuries, I am invited to achieve Enlightenment in emulation of this great son of Asia. This profound memory is not to be scorned.

I have been to several synagogues in New York City, particularly the one on the Fifth Avenue. 'It is a visible harmony of members, a totality in which no part deviates from perfection. With consummate joy I walk about the synagogue, gazing at it.' Then I go over mentally to the Mahayana Buddhist graveyard outside Tokyo. ...Each one of us has 'the graveyard consisting of crooked, cracked, shapeless, random stones' which signifies a sacred memory. The Indians, Chinese, Tibetans, Cambodians and others have their own ancient sacred memories. My theology begins with a deep sense of respect for these memories. In this respectful approach to the ancient memories I find something 'different' in the memory of which Buber speaks, from the others. In the years since my baptism gradually I have come to appreciate the difference as my respect to the Jewish memory of Mount Sinai and other peoples' memories has grown. I am saying 'different', not 'better'. In my theological reflection, engaged in the contest between Mount Fuji and Mount Sinai, I find myself hesitant to say easily that the memory of Mount Sinai is 'better' than other memories. If I say that it is 'better' I must be able to substantiate what I say with careful studies.

When I became a Christian I joined myself to the memory of Mount Calvary. Because of my fascination with the thought world of Mount Sinai, it might be said that I approached Mount Calvary from the perspective of Mount Sinai. On the other hand, what happened at Calvary was certainly important for me. In that sense I may have approached Mount Sinai from the perspective of Mount Calvary. I am not sure in my own mind whether it is possible, or even necessary, to untangle chronologically the influence of these two 'semitic' mountains on my thinking. In terms of my Christian experience of faith in Jesus Christ, I can say that I have come to appreciate the gospel of Christ in proportion to my understanding of the cultural and theological world of Mount Sinai. And this appreciation, I have found out, does not come to me apart from my interest in other 'memories', particularly one of my own, Mount Fuji. How can I appreciate the thought world of Mount Sinai without bringing it into a dialogue with the culture world native to myself?

Mount Fuji is a beautiful symmetrical mountain, the subject of many poems throughout the centuries.

> When going forth I look far from the Shore of Tago
> How white and glittering is
> The lofty Peak of Fuji
> Crowned with snows![6]

Mount Fuji can be a dangerous mountain if we try to climb up to the top in the bad weather. Otherwise, it is basically a safe mountain. Mount Sinai is a dangerous mountain.

> Then Moses brought the people out of the camp to meet God and they took their stand at the foot of the mountain. And Mount Sinai was wrapped in smoke, because the Lord descended upon it in fire; and the smoke of it went up like the smoke of a kiln, and the whole mountain quaked greatly. And as the sound of the trumpet grew louder and louder, Moses spoke, and God answered him in thunder. And the Lord came down upon Mount Sinai, to the top of the mountain, and Moses went up. And the Lord said to Moses, 'Go down and warn the people, lest they break through to the Lord to gaze and many of them perish. And also let the priests who come near to the Lord consecrate themselves, lest the Lord break out upon them' (Ex. 19.17–22).

My Japanese mind has been puzzled about this mountain for many years. '... the whole mountain quaked greatly. ... God descended upon it in fire, ... God answered him in thunder...'. What is the matter with this mountain? What kind of God is this? I find it difficult to engage in conversation in the noisy New York subways. My sympathy goes out to Moses who had to understand the voice of God in such a thunderous atmosphere. This God would make people nervous and overwhelmed. This is not a therapeutic arrangement. I would naturally prefer a situation in which Moses spoke and God answered him in a quiet, peaceful environment. Mount Sinai is a 'theological' mountain. It becomes a special mountain not because of itself but because of the appearance of God that takes place on it. What happens in and around this mountain symbolically expresses the character of God. The whole mountain becomes a symbol for the 'descending' God. No wonder that the mountain shook! The people trembled. Mount Fuji is a 'spiritual' mountain in the sense that it can go back to the ancient Japanese religious tradition of mountain-spirit cult which some scholars trace back as far as to the Jomon period before the period of rice cultivation.[7] The spirits dwell in mountains. Later, the mountains began to have graves and temples. Valleys were called 'hells' and sunny peaks looked upon as 'paradise'. When I speak of Mount Fuji I am referring to this ancient tradition of mountain-religion in Japan.

The critical word about Mount Sinai is that 'the Lord descended ... in fire'. In contrast, in the tradition of Mount Fuji the basic orientation is that we 'ascend' the mountains to do our own spiritual exercise. In this tradition certain portions of the mountain are thought to be 'beyond' this world, and it is into these sacred spaces that the experienced practitioners of the mountain religion stepped for their salvation. The mountain represents religious space for spiritual and physical disciplines. The Japanese world of mountain asceticism is distanced, in its emotional and philosophical contents, from the image of the Lord descending in fire upon Mount Sinai.

'The Lord descended in fire.' This symbol tells us that God cannot be domesticated by human spirit or hand. The fire will consume anyone who approaches it. In this religious and cultural world of Mount Sinai the language of crisis and discontinuity is spoken. The 'beyond' here refuses to be tamed by us. It is not a certain section of mountain to which we can ascend. Yet in careful reflection we see these passages of Exodus speak about God who 'descends upon Mount Sinai' even though 'in fire', and speaks to us in a voice even though in a thunderous situation. God, whom we cannot domesticate, is in communication with us from God's own side. 'Am I a God at hand, says the Lord, and not a God afar off?' (Jer. 23.23). God is both 'at hand' and 'afar off'. God descends 'in fire', yet comes to speak to us.

The Sinai tradition is, in essence, that tradition which is to do with this God who keeps communication with us from God's own side. God refuses to be frustrated by our faithlessness. God appears to people and gives them the Ten Commandments. Moses comes down from the mountain with the stone tablets upon which God has written the commandments. 'The tables were the work of God, and the writing was the writing of God, graven upon the tables' (Ex. 32. 16). Finding the people at the foot of the mountain, under the leadership of Aaron, engaged in a religious orgy of idolatry around a golden calf, Moses destroys those God-written tablets. He then returns to the mountain to intercede with the angry God, who listens to Moses and forgives the people. Once again the Commandments are given and once again Moses descends with them to the people. This is the great story contained in the Book of Exodus (19.1–40.38). The theological orientation and contents of this section is the 'Sinai tradition'. The fundamental theological message I see in it is God's forbearing forgiveness of a wayward and idolatrous people, and God's own recreation of history through faithfulness to the covenant relationship. This basic theological character is expressed in the first part of the Sinai tradition; 'You have seen what I did to the Egyptians, and how I bore you on eagles wings and brought you to myself' (19.4). This bringing the people, in spite of all their faithlessness, 'to myself' continues. This holy God, loving the unholy people over and over again, comes to them to bring them back to himself. The Sinai tradition clearly points to the central message of the Bible.

The scribes of the Pharisees, when they saw that he was eating with sinners and tax collectors, said to his disciples, 'Why does he eat with tax collectors and sinners'? (Mark 2.16)

Jesus embodies the mind of the holy God who comes to sinful people. This God is trustworthy. 'Thou art my rock and my fortress' (Ps. 31.3). This is the main theme of the Sinai tradition. In this tradition we find that God gives the commandments twice, once before (Ex. 19.1–20.17; 24.1–18) the idolatry of the golden calf (Ex. 32.1–35) and once after (Ex. 33.1–34; 35) this unfaithful incident. This willingness to endure profound disappointment and overcome personal frustration is the historical contents of God's faithfulness to the covenant. It is through the story of this painful way of God's dealing with us that the tradition of Mount Sinai exposes and heals human idolatry. This teaching of God's overcoming the frustration posed by human sinfulness represents the core of the biblical message. God is involved in our history. God does not give up our world. God comes back to our history and to our world again and again. This is the 'Wisdom that has gone Beyond', *Prajna-paramita,* in the sense that this wisdom of God is gone far *beyond* human imagination and expectation. But God's wisdom must not be understood in terms of 'beyond this world' and 'beyond entanglement with this world'. It is the wisdom involved in this world for the sake of salvation of the world. The *Prajna-paramita* of Mahayana Buddhism teaches us to become detached from this world and to go to 'the beyond' this world. Here God comes to the sinful people twice. God is agitated. History is agitated.

The theology of Mount Sinai, then, affirms the gracious manner in which God deals with us. The image of 'eagles wings' is central to this tradition. The laws given in this section must be interpreted through the grace expressed in the preamble of the Ten Commandments; 'I am the Lord your God, who brought you out of the land of Egypt, out of the house of bondage' (20.2). Mount Fuji on the other hand, speaks about the value of our 'spiritual heat' (*tapas,* Sanskrit word) generated by our own ascetic practices. Through the power of this *tapas* we may reach the realm of 'beyond'.

One way to see Mount Fuji and Mount Sinai in comparison is to see them from the perspective of Psalm 121.1.

Lift up my eyes to the hills
Where shall I find help?

Help comes from the Lord,
maker of heaven and earth (NEB).

In contrast the Fuji tradition would say that 'help comes from heaven and earth, the cosmos, the life-system of nature. The 'beyond' in the Mount Fuji tradition is a cosmologically defined 'beyond'. It is the 'beyond' which originates with nature'. In my mind this is the most basic difference symbolized by the two mountains. The implications of this distinction will be discussed in due course. In brief, the distinction is that Mount Fuji is cosmological, oriented toward nature, while Mount Sinai is eschatological, oriented toward history. The cosmological conceives 'help' to be from within the workings of the cosmos while the eschatological suggests the possibility of 'help' coming from *beyond* the cosmological.

You are wearied with your many counsels; Let them stand forth and save you, those who gaze at the stars, who at the new moons predict what shall befall you (Isa. 47.13).

There is no suggestion in the Bible that 'those who gaze at the stars' can help us.

The Japanese cultural outlook is characterized by confidence in the continuity of nature in spite of the pervasiveness of decay and death. A people fascinated by nature are continuity oriented. God and humanity are continuous. All living beings share the same life principle (*jiva*, Sanskrit). Continuity is experienced as more mysterious and creative than discontinuity. This observation is made not only of Japan, but fundamentally of the whole Asian cultural perception. Mount Sinai says that God and humanity are not continuous. Salvation is not a simple perpetuation of our life through generations. Asian spirituality appreciates discontinuity against the background of continuity. Here the subtle emphasis is that continuity gives meaning to discontinuity. In biblical spirituality, on the contrary, it is discontinuity that gives meaning to continuity.

What theological value or relevance does this symbolism of the two mountains have for us today? My view is that the present discussion can help to expose the idolatry, its subtle persuasion and structure, which is destroying humanity on this planet. Thousands of people were destroyed in an instant in Hiroshima. On that day, as groaning of agony filled the Japanese heaven, the idolatry of Japanese ultranationalism was judged. In sober reflection, however, we must say that all war is inter-idolatry conflict. No nation is free from idolatry. No historical time is free from the presence of false prophets, whether they are hidden or known. Though I think that history as we know it will always be idolatrous, I also believe Jesus' words;

'Behold, the kingdom of God is in the midst of you' (Luke 17.21). I shall attempt a biblical theological criticism of idolatry in the context of cosmological and eschatological tensions.

2. Let us go up to the mountain of the Lord

For the Japanese Isaiah's words; 'Let us go up to the mountain of the Lord, ... For out of Zion shall go forth the law and the word of the Lord from Jerusalem', involves a long and possibly perilous journey, spiritually and philosophically. Yet I must admit a fascination with this 'mountain of the Lord'. I was captivated by the biblical stories that opened up before my eyes a number of new scenes in which the world and human lives are described critically from the perspective of the law and the word of the Lord; the story of the creation of the world and human beings, Moses and the Exodus, David confronted by the prophet Nathan, Elijah and the prophets of Baal, Jesus' parable of the Good Samaritan.

These are the stories that intimate to us of 'history as God's experience'. The law (*torah*) and the word (*dabar*) of God reveal such experience of God. This is the secret of our fascination with the law and the word that come out of the theological experience of the people of Israel. Over the main counter in the Library of the National Diet in Tokyo (comparable to the Library of Congress in Washington, DC) are inscribed in Greek and in Japanese the words taken from the Gospel of John: 'The truth will make you free' (8.32). Are these words not inviting us to go to 'the mountain of the Lord'? I was moved to learn that Nishida Kitaro, perhaps the greatest philosopher Japan has ever produced, had consistently paid a great respect to the Bible. In his own way he, too, says, 'Let us go up to the mountain of the Lord'.

When we say, 'Let us go up to the mountain of the Lord', we may think that we will hear there only comforting words. But the *torah* and *dabar* are disturbing to us. In the call of Jeremiah we read this powerful proclamation:

> Then the Lord put forth his hand and touched my mouth; and the Lord said to me, 'Behold, I have put my words in your mouth. See, I have set you this day over nations and over kingdoms, to pluck up and to break down, to destroy and to overthrow, to build and to plant' (Jer. 1.9,10).

The word challenges the destiny of the empires, criticizing their internal and foreign policies. It will reorganize the world history by accomplishing what it intends (Isa. 55.11). Human morality and historical events are dealt with as one when the word comes to us. The God of the *torah* and *dabar* speaks against human sins in history.

> For if you truly amend your ways and your doings, if you truly execute justice one with another, if you do not oppress the alien, the fatherless or

the widow, or shed innocent blood in this place, and if you do not go after other gods to your own hurt, then I will let you dwell in this place, in the land that I gave of old to your fathers forever (Jer. 7.5–7).

These words of Jeremiah, a part of his Temple Sermon, demonstrate how serious and direct an impact human moral action has on historical events. The word of God, in sharp contrast to the relationship of the Japanese gods to the Japanese people, dares to criticize God's own people, calling them 'stiff-necked' (Ex. 32.9), 'stubborn' (Deut. 9.27), 'you who cast down righteousness to the earth'(Micah 5.7).

> Be appalled, O heavens, at this, be shocked, be utterly desolate, says the Lord, for my people have committed two evils; they have forsaken me, the fountain of living waters, and hewed out cisterns for themselves, broken cisterns that can hold no water (Jer. 2.12,13).

The word of God addressed to our human history awakens our resistance against it. It is too disturbing to our hearing. 'Come, let us smite him [Jeremiah] with the tongue and let us not heed any of his words' (Jer. 18.18). The word of God is not welcomed by the community. It is given a mocking response. 'For the word of the Lord has become for me a reproach and derision all day long', cries Jeremiah (20.18).

When such a critical word of the Lord comes from Mount Zion, why do we still say, 'Let us go up to the mountain of the Lord?' Why do we not go to other mountains, less serious and more pleasant? Why do we go to the world of the Bible, and not to the different worlds such as those of the Analects of Confucius, of the profound Buddhist *tripitaka*, of the Bodhisattva of Mahayana Buddhism, of the sublime philosophy of the *Upanisads*, of the soaring imagination of the *Ramayana* or of the faith closely knit with nature which Japanese shintoism presents?

Our fascination with the word of God comes from the sense that the word of God is full of God's dynamic inner feeling and emotion. 'For I the Lord your God am an impassioned God' (Ex. 20.5) (translation by The Jewish Publication Society of America). In Heschel's lucid language:

> There is no dichotomy of pathos and ethos, of motive and norm. ... It is because God is the source of justice that His pathos is ethical; and it is because God is absolutely personal – devoid of anything impersonal – that this ethos is full of pathos. Pathos, then, is not an attitude taken arbitrarily. Its inner law is the moral law; ethos is inherent in pathos. God is concerned about the world, and shares in its fate. Indeed, this is the essence of God's moral nature: His willingness to be intimately involved in the history of man.[8]

Human history, from the destiny of empires to social programmes for the alien, orphans and widows, must be examined in the light of this divine unity between ethos and pathos. Human history must embody this divine unity of spiritual spontaneity and social justice if it intends to be meaningful and healing to humanity. God's *torah* and *dabar* point to this remarkable unity of pathos and ethos, and this unity in turn points to the *torah* and *dabar* of God. 'Thy words were found, and I ate them, and thy words became to me a joy and the delight of my heart' (Jer. 15.16). These words were not pleasant, neutral words. They were critical words that challenge the empires. They were words in which passion and morality come together. 'Let us go up to the mountain of the Lord.'

I see yellow cabs on Broadway from my window at Union Theological Seminary. ... Many years ago, when I was only five years old, my father, a Christian and once a successful businessman, who lost his entire fortune in the disasterous earthquake of 1923, died from acute pneumonia in a Buddhist hospital run mainly by charity. He breathed his last in the name of Christ on a bed provided by the generosity of Japanese Buddhists. I am grateful for the help he received from this hospital. My mother wrapped the body in a blanket and brought him home in a taxi. For the driver it must have been inauspicious to carry a dead body which would pollute his cab. I am always grateful to this unknown taxi driver who helped the poor widow. My father died a Christian accepting the kindness of the Buddhists.

I see tall buildings in New York. ... Many years ago my maternal grandfather, at the height of his financial success, partly owned Tokyo's first skyscraper, a building of twelve storeys. It was called *Ryounkaku* or the building rising over the clouds. There is a picture of this skyscraper on page 284 of *Japan, A History of Art* by Bradley Smith. My grandfather understood the fascination of a vertical climb in the land of horizontal architecture. It amuses me to think of this enterprising spirit of doing business with verticality. He lived a peaceful life and died at a good old age, very much a man of Mount Fuji culture, yet, ... somehow he understood the excitement of verticality.

My paternal grandfather became a Christian after he listened, in Tokyo, to a certain British gentleman, Mr Herbert George Brand (1865–1942). Mr Brand, a layman, came to Japan in 1888, not sent by any mission body, and worked until 1921 in Japan and Korea. It was through this man, a graduate of Cambridge University in 1887, that the great tradition of Mount Sinai came into the Koyama clan and many others at about the turn of the century. The gospel of Christ which my grandfather heard was presented in broken Japanese with a heavy English accent. What a moment of inspiration to hear the gospel in a broken language! One of the few things I heard and I still remember from my grandfather about his conversion to

Christianity from Buddhism was that he was impressed by this man who was able to say that Jesus Christ is Lord without ever making derogatory comments upon Japanese culture or Buddhism. 'This made me to follow Christ!' he told me.

The Bodhisattva hospital, the unknown taxi driver, the twelve storey skyscraper and the Cambridge gentleman, ... all come to my mind as I conclude this introductory section. They are all in my mind when I participate in the ancient saying of the believing community: 'Let us go up to the mountain of the Lord.'

In the light of the words of Heschel that we in theology must try to see the mystery of history as experienced by God, I shall now to narrate the recent history of Japan under the sway of her own destructive parochial god.

2
Parochial god – Attractive yet Destructive

Ideology of parochial god destroyed Japan.

The Japanese government called it the Great East Asia War. It began on 8 December 1941 and ended on 15 August 1945. The imperialistic ideology of the Great East Asia Co-Prosperity Sphere was behind the naming of the war. The government was concerned, in fact, not with 'co-prosperity' but only with the prosperity of Japan. Postwar Japanese historians call it the 'Fifteen Year War'. Beginning in 1931, when Japan sent her troops into Manchuria and continuing until the defeat in 1945 the Japanese leaders perpetrated upon the Japanese people and other peoples in and beyond Asia a violence which reached demonic intensity. Japanese citizens who were critical of government policy were expelled from their positions or even assassinated. Rightist leaders held absolute power and the cult of the emperor worship was forced upon the people. 'The Glory of the Emperor that Reaches to the Four Corners of the World', a kind of pagan ecumenism, was the essence of the national ideology. The result was that all other spiritual and physical forces were devoured by the imperial force so that it could grow unchallenged. It was a pagan 'theology of glory'.

Dr Tatsukichi Minobe (1873–1948) was a member of the Imperial Academy, Professor emeritus of Tokyo University and a member of the House of Peers. He disagreed with the accepted interpretation of the 1889 Constitution that the sovereignty of the nation resides in the person of the emperor. He held that the emperor embodies the highest function of the state and that the sovereignty of the state resides with the people. In 1935 his book, *Kempo Teiyo* or *The Essentials of the Constitution*, (1932) was banned and the ministry of education issued a direction to the schools throughout the nation that the divine entity of the state must be taught. A ritual of worship was prescribed to be held before the photograph of the Emperor and the Empress every morning at all schools.

In 1937 The Ministry of Education published its book, *Kokutai No Hongi* or *Fundamental Doctrine of the National Entity*. A few lines from this book will illustrate its contents.

Our country is established with the Emperor, who is a descendant of Amaterasu Ohmikami [Heaven Illuminating Great Goddess], as her centre, and our ancestors as well as we ourselves constantly behold in the Emperor the fountainhead of her life and activities. For this reason, to serve the Emperor and to receive the Emperor's great August Will as one's own is the rationale of making our historical 'life' live in the present; and on this is based the morality of people.

Loyalty means to reverence the Emperor as (our) pivot and to follow him implicitly. By implicit obedience is meant casting ourselves aside and serving the Emperor intently. To walk this Way of Loyalty is the sole Way in which we subjects may 'live', and the fountainhead of all energy. Hence, offering our lives for the sake of the Emperor does not mean so-called self-sacrifice, but the casting aside of our little selves to live under this August Grace and the enhancing of the genuine life of the people of a State.[1]

Kokutai No Hongi was about forty pages in Japanese print. It was required to be taught in all high schools and colleges. Students were forced to commit its entire contents to memory. The philosophy of the crude glorification of Japan and the Japanese style of totalitarianism were 'solemnly' expressed in it. It was a concoction of Japanese mythology and ethnocentric pride. The emperor was characterized as divine, in the lineage of the Sun Goddess Amaterasu. His subjects were to be prepared to give their lives for him without reservation. This 'supreme doctrine' was said to 'transcend the teaching of Confucianism and Buddhism'.[2] That Japanese educators and scholars would consent to use a text of such inferior quality over a period of time is difficult, with hindsight, to believe.

In 1940 the government dealt a decisive blow to all honest scientific studies about Japan's history when it banned *Shindai Shi no Kenkyu* or *Studies on the Ancient (Divine) Period of Japan* by Sokichi Tsuda, one of the most conscientious scholars of the nation. The same year was declared to be the 2600th year of the Japanese nation. It is difficult to imagine what kind of calculation could produce this wonderful round number. According to the official propaganda, the first emperor Jimmu founded the nation exactly 2600 years ago! All schools were ordered to teach this calendar to the children. A 2600th Year Celebration was held throughout Japan. All religious bodies participated in this celebration including Christianity, the religion of the enemy as it was called at the time. On 17 October 1940, 20,000 Christians gathered in the compound of Aoyama Mission School in Tokyo. A choir of 1,500 voices provided music. The declaration issued on this occasion expresses the principle of co-operation with the military and fascist government.

Declaration

We Japanese people feel greatly privileged to know that our nation has continued for the last 2600 years without interruption since the rule of the first emperor Jimmu. This glorious history makes us proud, Christians in Japan humbly offer our homage to the emperor. The world situation today is very disruptive and we indeed must attend to it constantly. In the West we see wars, in the East we have the China Incident which has not been concluded peacefully. In such a world by the providence of heaven our rulers have been able to steer the destiny of the nation without making errors. We have no doubt that our national system of one emperor and subjects is incomparable throughout the world. We are now progressing towards the establishment of a new order within East Asia. We Christians respond positively to this national destiny. We are resolved to participate in this great work by uniting our denominations and leading the spiritual life of the people for the purpose of the realization of the national aim.

In accordance with this declaration we wish to make three public announcements;
1. We will propagate the gospel of Christ and save the soul of the nation.
2. We will unite ourselves into one body.
3. We will inspire the spiritual life and uplift the moral life of the people.
Declared: October 17th 1940
National Assembly of Christians on the Occasion of the Celebration of the 2600th Year of the Founding of the Nation.[3]

The Japanese Christian church, both Catholic and Protestant, was caught in a critical situation in which suddenly the words of Jesus became extremely relevant and important; 'Render to Caesar the things that are Caesar's and to God the things that are God's' (Mark 12.17). The name of Jesus Christ and that of the emperor had come into conflict. There was a sense of uneasiness in the minds of Christians with their own declaration. They sensed that in demanding absolute personal commitment to the emperor the state was usurping control over the things of God in the name of Caesar. When all belongs to the state (totalitarianism), the name of Jesus Christ is subordinated to the national ideology of the glory of the Japanese empire.

The issue of *Jinja Sanpai* (worshipping at the shinto shrine) sharpened the conflict, particularly in Korea which was a colony of Japan. The interpretation which was proposed by the Japanese government and accepted by some of the Protestant leaders was a rather simple one. It defined shintoism not as a religion but as national custom. To pay respect to the image of the emperor need not be seen as a religious act but a part of the national custom of the people. This solution would theoretically preclude the conflict caused by bowing before the image of the emperor and also worshipping Jesus Christ at the divine service of the church. The Moderator of the United Church of Christ in Japan at that time, Rev. Mitsuru Tomita, travelled extensively as far as Korea persuading the Christians that the government was not persecuting the church but simply asking Christians to practice what is a normal part of Japanese life, i.e. paying homage to the Imperial Household at the shinto shrines. This argument proved least persuasive in Korea. Christians there firmly insisted that the emperor worship and the Lordship of Jesus Christ were mutually incompatible. For this conviction the blood of martyrs flowed in Korea.[4]

It is important to note that a number of religious groups in Japan which were outside the Christian church stood against the imperial cult and suffered brutal persecution at the hands of the regime. In my mind this is a significant demonstration that the human community, without explicitly confessing the name of Jesus Christ, can find spiritual resources to resist tyranny. Following their own doctrines, they insisted that government does not have the authority to define what belongs to the gods and what belongs to the inner sanctuary of human faith.

In the critical year of 1941 there were four Imperial Conferences held on 'The Essentials for Carrying Out the Empire's Policies' vis-à-vis the attitudes of the United States, Great Britain, and the Netherlands. In each of these conferences, including the final one (1 December 1941) which ratified the decision to make war, the emperor consistently remained silent. The Prime Minister of the day, Tojo Hideki, was recorded to have concluded the Conference with the following remark:

> I would now like to make one final comment. At the moment our Empire stands at the threshold of glory or oblivion. We tremble with fear in the presence of His Majesty. We, subjects, are keenly aware of the great responsibility we must assume from this point on. Once His Majesty reaches a decision to commence hostilities, we will all strive to repay our obligation to him, to bring the government and the military ever closer together, to resolve that the nation united will go to victory, to make an all-out effort to achieve our war aims, and to set His Majesty's mind at ease. I now adjourn the meeting.[5]

During the day's conference, according to the record, 'His Majesty nodded in agreement with the statements being made and displayed no signs of uneasiness. He seemed to be in an excellent mood, and we were filled with awe!'[6]. They 'trembled with fear' and 'were filled with awe'! The divine emperor did not speak human language but silently nodded! Being divine, the emperor is beyond history. He nods, even though he has been informed that the petroleum reserve for the war operation would last ony eighteen months. He nods, knowing that with his decision to send the nation to war the lives of millions of Japanese and other people would be shattered by war. It is certain that many of those who attended this highest level conference 'trembled with fear', though not in awe at the divine qualities of the emperor but with the weightiness of the decision he had made. They should indeed have trembled with history and not with phantasy.

At this critical moment the leaders of the nation dispensed with the normal human sense of responsibility. Though they sat together to make this fateful decision, no one felt responsibility for it because one of them was 'beyond human'. The emperor, beyond human, beyond history, beyond human morality, made the decision. The leaders of the nation can refer to this super-historical person for their justification whenever necessary. They 'trembled' but they were freed from being answerable to their fellow humans. The people, forced to worship the emperor but unable to use him for their benefit, suffered. In the end the whole nation was ruined. I witnessed 'the rise and fall' of the cult of emperor worship.

On 8 December 1941 (Tokyo time) Japan declared war on the United States, Great Britain and the Netherlands. The declaration is a highly religious document.

> We, by the grace of Heaven, Emperor of Japan seated on the throne of a line unbroken for ages eternal, enjoin upon you, our loyal and brave subjects; ... the situation being as it is, our Empire for its existence and self-defence has no other recourse but to appeal to arms and to crush every obstacle in its path. Hallowed spirits of our imperial ancestors guarding us from above. .....[7]

Japan went to war with this powerful presentation of the 'three truths'; that the divine emperor possesses the grace of heaven; that the war is a war of self-defence; and that the nation is under the protection of the hallowed spirits of the imperial ancestors. The ideology of self-defence was neatly tucked between two reassuring religious ideas. It requires, almost always, some religious rhetoric in order to mobilize a nation to war. As a war-making document I think the Japanese declaration is a standard text-book sample in which we find the right mixture of religion, patriotism, sense of mission and indignation.

At the Battle of Midway in the Pacific (5 June 1942), only six months after the declaration of war, the major forces of the Japanese Navy went down to the bottom of the sea and the fortune of the entire war had been decided. The Japanese people were told that at Midway it was the enemy that suffered a decisive loss. How could Japan move towards some kind of truce when she had started the war with the three glorious truths unique to Japan? Under cover of a false optimism, people were mobilized to sacrifice their lives in a hopeless war effort. Air raids became frequent and then continuous. The official propaganda had assured us that Tokyo, in which is the palace of the divine emperor, would be inviolable. Yet the B29s flew in Tokyo's airspace without any apparent or significant resistance. They bombed it bit by bit until it was completely destroyed. I began to see the burned bodies of my compatriots in the streets.

On 7 April 1945 the Suzuki Cabinet was inaugurated. On that day the Supreme War Command declared that the nation would mobilize all its power and rescources for the final defence of Japan Proper. It was also on that day that the battleship, Yamato, the glory of the Japanese Navy, and believed to be unsinkable, went to the bottom of the sea off Kyushu under the repeated air attack of 386 enemy planes. It had become obvious to everyone that Japan had already been defeated. The massive air raid of 10 October 1944 upon Okinawa had signalled the beginning of the desperate struggle for control of that island. The Japanese military leaders already knew that by November 1945 the American army would land on the southern tip of Kyushu in Operation Olympic and that in the early part of 1946 it would approach the Kanto Plain in which Tokyo is located with the strength of 25 divisions in Operation Coronet. By then Japan would have been surrounded by 700 battleships, 90 of them aircraft carriers, 3000 landing boats, 15,000 airplanes, all poised to deal the final blow upon her.[8]

Yet the Supreme War Command kept pressing the people with slogans; 'Mobilization of All to the War Effort' and 'One Hundred Million Kamikaze'. The Command itself was in the process of moving, with the emperor, to the mountain regions of central Japan, abandoning the five million people of Tokyo to the enemy. They knew that there was no hope whatsoever of turning the tide of the war.

Bombs rained incessantly over Japan from the bellies of the American B29s. In the night of 10 March 1945, 88,000 people perished in Tokyo in two hours twenty-two minutes of bombings. From 13 to 15 April Tokyo was devastated by 4069 tons of fire bombs. The job of destruction was complete in May (23rd to 25th) when American planes dropped 6,908 tons of fire bombs on the already charred city. The night of the 25th May began with an ominous silence, but by midnight our section of Tokyo became a sea of fire as the fire-bombs rained upon it. The raids continued until early morning. I was alone, running from one shelter to another. I heard the screech of a bomb coming towards me. In a panic, I ran as fast as I could in what proved to be the wrong direction. Had I run a little faster my head would have been crushed by the impact of a hugh bomb which landed in front of me and by some chance did not explode. It disappeared into the ground, I jumped over it and ran towards another shelter where I hoped to find the other members of my family.[9]

When, in June 1945, Okinawa fell to the Allied Powers and Japan was completely encircled by the superior military might of the enemy the rulers of Japan decided to launch the *Ketsugo Hondo Sakusen* (The Final Mainland Operation). The people were instructed to defend the sacred shores of the Divine Land with bamboo spears in hand. According to the military doctrine of the 'Power of the Japanese Spirit' the bamboo spears are able to destroy any enemy, presumably even the most technologically advanced military forces the world had ever known. The Chief of Staff of the Army, General Umezu, now urged the people to have 'Faith in the Ultimate Victory'. The *Instruction to the Soldiers* provided by the War Minister, General Anami, spoke of the mysticism of the Divine Land. The military leaders told the people that they were confident that they could repel the first wave of the enemy attack on the shore, but no one talked of the second and third wave. At the same time the Command itself was preparing to flee to the mountains. At about that time the passage from the Gospel of John came to me with unusual force;

> He who is a hireling and not a shepherd, whose own the sheep are not, sees the wolf coming and leaves the sheep and flees, and the wolf snatches them and scatters them (John 10.12).

That was in June. In August the Japanese sky was violently disturbed. A nuclear bomb fell on Hiroshima on the sixth day and another on Nagasaki on the ninth. The Supreme War Command broadcast through the radio that the enemy had used a 'new bomb' and it gave instructions to the public in anticipation of further attacks. Such remedies as the application of ointment to burns and such defence as the wearing of white shirts demonstrate the complete helplessness of the nation in face of the terror. They were only the first in a line of similar senseless suggestions made by governments that pretend that the danger is less than it is. Yet, as calamitous as the experience of the bombing was, careful studies indicate that it was not the two nuclear bombs but the declaration of war by the Soviet Union that forced the Japanese rulers to accept the Potsdam Declaration of unconditional surrender of Japan.[10] Counting from the date of the Japanese victory over China in 1895, the Japanese Empire was annihilated exactly in her fiftieth year.

Parochialism is basically a geographical concept meaning that one's view of reality is limited to the confine of one's own parish. But its serious meaning emerges when it is understood in its spiritual and intellectual implications. A person who has travelled extensively has not necessarily transcended the parochial outlook. On the other hand, it is possible that a geographically confined person can have spiritual and intellectual imagination to free himself or herself from the grip of parochialism. Self-righteousness is the source of parochialism. All nations are self-righteous. All nations are, in this fundamental sense, parochial.

The concept of self-righteousness must not be confined to religious dimensions. Human behaviour in education, politics, economics, international relations and military preparation is shot through with self-righteousness, though we are remarkably clever at camouflaging it to appear otherwise. The inner emotion of self-righteousness expresses itself outwardly in the form of imperialism. Self-righteousness frees the nation's imperial propensities but it paralyses the nation's ability to make moral judgment, particularly in the area of her international relations. The Japanese gods told us, during the war, that the difference between Japan and China was that Japan told the truth and China told lies. It also declared repeatedly that evil emanates from the United States and good has its homeland in Japan. Our moral judgment crippled by self-righteousness, we were free to turn our energy to imperialism. It is a peculiar component of human tragedy that a paralysed morality can produce such enormous spiritual energy in the service of the demonic.

I have in my mind two images of God; one is called the parochial god; the other, the Universal God. Obviously, there is a tension between them and this tension has been one of my life struggles since the day of Hiroshima. The worship of the parochial god took the form of enforced devotion to the emperor; polytheistic Japan suddenly became monotheistic. People gradually began to feel that they, too, were divine. The whole national god-system placed Japan at the centre of the world. Whatever Japan did was thought to be the expression of the 'Mind of the Righteous Heaven'. Anyone who doubted this was a traitor. Japanese interest was focussed upon the glory of Japan. It had no regard for the welfare of the Chinese, Koreans, Americans, Italians. This god could not speak any language other than Japanese. It had no international experience. It was parochial. This parochialism appeared on the horizon of world history when the leaders of the nation identified the mind of Japan with the 'Mind of the Righteous Heaven'. Was not something essentially finite given infinite significance here?

This parochial god who never criticized its own people was attractive. But it proved to be most destructive to the people of Japan.

And Tokyo became wilderness ...

3
Wilderness Tokyo

The waste and void confronted me. Even the sun
momentarily became a stranger to me.

15 August 1945: a cloudless, blue summer day. Even now I remember the
strangeness of it. Exactly at noon we heard the Diamond Voice of the
emperor, the *akitsu mikami*, the god manifested in human form, through a
radio broadcast. This voice for some fifty years had been thought too
sacred for any mortal to hear. Now it spoke in a special imperial language,
far removed from the Japanese one hears in everyday life. It said:

> To our good and loyal subjects;
> After pondering deeply the general trends of the world
> and the actual conditions obtaining in our Empire today,
> we have decided to effect a settlement of the present
> situation by resorting to an extraordinary measure.
>
> We have ordered our Government to communicate to the Governments
> of the United States, Great Britain, China and the Soviet Union that our
> Empire accepts the provisions of their joint declaration.
>
> To strive for the common prosperity and happiness of all nations as well
> as the security and well-being of our subjects is the solemn obligation
> which had been handed down by Our Imperial Ancestors and we lay it
> close to the heart, ...[1]

The war was over. With five hundred other high school students who had
been mobilized to work in a military factory, I listened to the broadcast,
standing at attention in a badly bombed compound. I went home ... to a
small hovel in which our family had taken shelter after our house had been
destroyed. Physically and mentally exhausted from the lack of food and
sleep and from the fear of death by the constant air raids, I stood like a
ghost and once again saw Tokyo. As far as my eyes could survey Tokyo had

become a wilderness. Familiar landmarks were gone; rice shops, temples and shrines at which the people had prayed for victory ...even railway stations had disappeared. The inhabited world had become a desolate world. A threatening silence enveloped the place which had been called Tokyo, City of the East. The land, it seemed 'had vomited out its inhabitants' (Lev 18.25). I was dwelling in wilderness Tokyo. I slept, and in the morning I watched the sun rise over a horizon of utter destruction. The sun itself, I felt at that moment, had become a part of the cosmic 'waste and void' (Gen.1.2). Several years later the scene was brought back vividly when I heard these words of Jeremiah which touched me deeply:

> I looked on the earth, and lo, it was waste and void; and to the heavens, and they had no light. I looked on the mountains, and lo, they were quaking, and all the hills moved to and fro. I looked, and lo, there was no man, and all the birds of the air had fled. I looked, and lo, the fruitful land was a desert, and all its cities were laid in ruins before the Lord, before his fierce anger (Jer.4.23-26).

What I have felt is that the mythological 'waste and void' of which Genesis speaks, became concrete in human experience when thousands of B29s, made in Wichita, Kansas, rained down fire on Tokyo until it was completely devastated. In 1945 the mythological became historical for me fused by the American fire-bombing of Tokyo. I was struck by the truth that is contained in the myth, and later was able to appreciate the view of Mircea Eliade and others that myth does not mean 'false story' but it contains a 'true story' when it describes the crisis moments of human existence.

By their own standards the Japanese had created chaos in Asia. The ancient Japanese definition of sins (*tsumi*) is said to be breaking down the ridges (between rice paddies), covering the irrigation ditches, opening the sluices (causing flood), double planting (sowing other seeds between the rows of rice), setting up stakes (denoting false ownership), skinning alive, flaying (an animal) backwards, and defecation in the wrong place.[2] *Tsumi* disturbs social organization in an agricultural community. It brings chaos into ordered society. Japan broke down the ridges between the Southeast Asian nations for her own advantage, opened the sluices and damaged the welfare of other peoples, setting up stakes and occupying the territories of other nations, murdering Koreans and Chinese by skinning alive, defecating in the sacred places of other peoples. We did not know that what we were doing to other peoples would come home to us. Chaos did come to us, extensively and profoundly. I have become aware of the boomerang effect in history. I have seen 'waste and void' concretely and personally in history. It descended upon Tokyo.

On the same day that General MacArthur, the conqueror of Japan, arrived in Toyko, 30 August 1945, the Prime Minister, Prince Higashikuni gave his first press conference after the war. 'All one hundred million Japanese must repent' (*ichioku sō zange*), he said, in order to start a new national life. In the confusion and emptiness of wilderness Tokyo, I welcomed gladly the suggestion of national repentance. My Christian sentiment told me that the suggestion was right and timely. We had committed a crime against humanity, as the Americans had put it.

To my surprise I began to hear from my friends and others strong objections to the *ichioku sō zange*. They argued that the Japanese people were victims, not perpetrators, of the crimes committed by their military and fascist rulers. Our leaders must repent, but we were innocent. The brutal truth about human community, I learned, was that the majority of the people can be hostaged by a tiny section of the community. 'Japan did not go to war', I repeated to myself, 'Some Japanese leaders took the Japanese nation to war'. This was my first experience with the complexity of history. There is no destruction without manipulation. Historical 'waste and void' comes to us when one section of humanity manipulates others. The manipulators must indeed repent of their crime against humanity. Yet, I felt that the manipulated are not completely innocent. The leaders of Japan were able to act violently against her neighbours because the majority of the people allowed themselves to be manipulated by the few.

'Repent!' the Prince Prime Minister Higashikuni had shouted in wilderness Tokyo. News reporters asked him whether the government would immediately and clearly tell the entire nation the reasons why Japan lost the war. He answered:

We were defeated because of the rapid destruction of our military power. ... In addition to this, the appearance of the nuclear bomb of incredible annihilating capacity and the military advance by the Soviet Union caused the defeat. So many rules and laws had been issued almost indiscriminately during the war years, and they had incapacitated national life. This may be one of the major reasons for the defeat we suffered. Then I am afraid that the government itself, government bureaucrats and military persons led our nation unconsciously and unknowingly in this context, I mean that they thought they were struggling for the country while in truth during that time our country had fallen into the illness of arteriosclerosis, and the result was that the nation suffered a sudden death by stroke. I must also mention the miserably low quality of national morality to be one of the reasons for the defeat. That is to say, the military and government people openly and the people at large secretly had engaged in activities of black market. I of course understand that the bad policies of the government had driven people to black market, but I still maintain that the general low standard of national morality was one of the reasons for the defeat, Now I make a call to all Japanese people, including those in the military and government, that we must examine what we had done and repent. The first step for the reconstruction of our nation begins with the repentance by the hundred million Japanese people. This is, I believe, the first step to unite the nation.[3]

The Prime Minister reviews the war years and enumerates possible reasons for the defeat of the war. Japan was defeated primarily because of the inadequacy in military might. Then comes this mysterious yet very useful Japanese expression; 'unconsciously and unknowingly' which implies that the leaders were not really responsible for the war and its tragic end. They were sincere and dedicated to the war aims, but somewhere, where their knowledge could not reach, 'arteriosclerosis' was taking place. They were not directly responsible for this illness. One day, suddenly, came a stroke and the nation died. We encounter this 'sudden stroke' view of history in the Rescript of Ending War.

But now the war has lasted for nearly four years. Despite the best that has been done by everyone – the gallant fighting of the military and naval forces, the diligence and assiduity of our servants of the State and the devoted service of our one hundred million people – the war situation has developed not necessarily to Japan's advantage, while the general trends of the world have all turned against her interest.

In this paragraph and in the rest of the Rescript there was not one word or one line that calls for a critical examination of Japanese ideology and behaviour up to the end of the war. The Rescript says that all Japanese worked diligently to achieve the war aim, but 'the war situation has developed not necessarily to Japan's advantage'. Japan is, somehow, from the emperor to everyone on the streets, not really responsible for what had happened to her and to her neighbours. She was diligent. She suffered a stroke and died.

'Repent!' But to whom? To ourselves? To the emperor? To the Americans? To the Buddha? To the principle of humanity? The emperor 'repented' 'before the hallowed spirits of the imperial ancestors' as he indicated in the Rescript of Ending War. What did it mean to repent before the 'hallowed spirits of the imperial ancestors' under whose protection we began the war? They had not saved the nation. When fanatical state shintoists and military leaders committed suicide by *harakiri* to atone for their sin before the emperor I felt their act, though intensely patriotic, to be futile. There is something common between suffering a stroke and committing *harakiri* in the context of a historical crisis which poses questions regarding human responsibility. In both cases the persons involved escape, ultimately escape, the question of responsibility. And what does it mean to feel responsible to the departed spirits, even the spirits of the imperial ancestors? Should we not acknowledge our guilt to living persons? To the Koreans, Indonesians, Singaporeans and Burmese?

Would it be appropriate to repent before the spirits of the war dead, military and civilian, of our own poeple and of other nations, who lost their lives in a war which we started? When thought goes to the dead, the Japanese culture places more emphasis upon the 'pacification of departed spirits' (*irei*) than upon the repentance of the living. The tradition of *irei* is a deep stream in Japanese religiosity. Unpacified spirits (*onryo*) are greatly feared by the people for the havoc they can cause among the living. Yet I have never heard, at least from the official quarters, the suggestion that the defeat in 1945 was caused by the countless *onryo* the recent violent history of Japan had produced. Should we be consistent to our own ancient tradition about the vengeful acts of the *onryo*, then, we must honestly say that the defeat came because of the retaliation by the unpacified spirits.

In the ancient tradition no distinction had been made between the dead as to whether they had fought for the emperor or not. All spirits must be equally pacified. But this tradition has been changed since 1869 when the Japanese government established the Shrine of Pacification of the War Dead inviting 3,588 spirits that had been loyal to the emperor only to be enshrined. This partial arrangement, I would suppose, must have produced many *onryo*. This point, however, has been conveniently ignored since such discussion will effect anti-patriotic feeling about the state. The important point is that it is thought to be possible to engage in the efficacious act of the pacification of the spirits without going through spiritual repentance on the part of the living. That the living must receive decisive importance over the pacifiction of the dead, and that it is by not repeating war we may in truth pacify the spirits of the war dead goes against the 'sudden death by stroke' type of view of history. It asks with all seriousness the location of responsibility for the war. We are responsible to history. We must not becloud this clear sense of historical responsibility by rhetoric of 'the spirits of imperial ancestors'.

Should we repent before the victorious Americans? This was a good possibility. Many people apologized to the Americans for what we had done. But then we remembered the saturation bombings of population centres and the nuclear attack upon two cities which had taken place only a month earlier. If we had destroyed others, they had destroyed us. Was it necessary for American bombers to draw a circle of fire with the fire-bombs and then to crisscross within the circle so that no one could escape the fire? The important difference between Japan and the United States at that moment seemed to be that Japan was defeated and the United States was victorious. Somehow, we sensed, in history to be victorious is not necessarily to be righteous. When we thought of repenting to the Americans we were faced with the disturbing image of saturation bombing. In spite of the atrocities we ourselves had committed during war, how could we repent of our sin to a nation that had dropped nuclear bombs upon two fully inhabited cities? In the concrete historical situation of 1945 the question to whom should they repent was not an easy one for the Japanese.

It seemed to me that we should repent before the defenceless peoples upon whom we had inflicted injury; the Chinese, Filipinos, Koreans, Malaysians, Burmese, Indonesians and others. We had scarcely known these people. Japanese education had mentioned them only as 'inferior' and 'subordinate' peoples. We had not studied their cultures and languages. They were just people 'over there' without any human reality. How could we repent before people of whom we had no knowledge? In the frantic history of our self-righteousness we had ignored the peoples. Self-righteousness had destroyed our education and finally it deprived us of our mental ability to repent meaningfully.

Japan had perpetrated a great injury outside herself. Yet when the moment of repentance came she retreated into her own parochial mythology, to the 'hallowed spirits of the imperial ancestors'. We were not happy with this parochial retreat, but what could we do, finding ourselves so ill-equipped to repent? There was no way to communicate our sense of repentance to the neighbouring peoples through such 'hallowed spirits'. The call to repentance made by the first prime minister in the post-war period, which seemed so noble, was miscarried. I envied the simple straightforwardness of the son in the parable of Jesus who was able to say, 'Father, I have sinned against heaven and before you,...'(Luke 15.18); I was particularly impressed by the words 'against heaven and before you'. They indicate both universal and particular contexts in which his repentance took place. What he did was wrong in the eyes of universal humanity, or simply before 'God', and in particular it injured the person to whom he was in the most fundamental sense related. I know that no nation, as nation, would engage in an act of repentance, even though some of its members may do so. It is perhaps the lack of a sense of responsibility for historical events that made even personal repentance difficult for the Japanese people. How one understands history has a determinative effect upon the spiritual capacity for repentance.

Yet, by the grace of God, the moment of defeat was a time of purification. The demonically inflated ideology of the state was eliminated – it came violently and it went away violently – and we began to search after a universal perspective of human value from which we could look at ourselves. The historical experience of 'nearing to zero' was a strangely creative moment. I cannot read the story of the prodigal son without thinking of that time in 1945.

So he went and joined himself to one of the citizens of that country, who sent him into his fields to feed swine. And he would gladly have fed on the pods that the swine ate; and no one gave him anything. But when he came to himself... (Luke 15.15–17).

He became a spiritually awakened person when he was forced to feed the swine!

In wilderness Tokyo we were hungry. We were confused. The wilderness outside invaded our souls. There was, however, one attractive aspect of the desolation as I knew it now. Desolation is uncluttered. It has a stark simplicity. The wilderness threatens but it also issues an invitation to meditate upon the essentials. Desolation had purified our souls. With a certain sense of surprise I was able to appreciate a bit from Jeremiah; 'I remember the devotion of your youth, your love as a bride, how you followed me in the wilderness, in a land not sown' (2.2). In my Christian experience the image of baptism and that of wilderness became inexpressibly united. Baptism, the renewal of life, has meant to me, all these years, an experience of spiritual purification 'in the wilderness, in a land not sown'. In my mind an outer event, the destruction of proud, violent Japan, and an inner event, my baptismal death in the hope of new life in the risen Christ, coincided. What happened in 1945 to Japan has become a part of my Christian identity.

I understand that in the wilderness we also show our worst stubbornness and destructiveness. The uncluttered space contains the intersection of schemings and mutual oppressions and of spritual purification. Yet, basically my experience of wilderness Tokyo was expressed in the words of Jeremiah quoted above. It is a strange feeling to see the wilderness Tokyo in the light of the prophet who lived in such a distant time and place. I was looking at the Japan of 1945 not in the light of the 'hallowed spirits of the imperial ancestors' but in the words of the sixth century BC prophet, Jeremiah. This experience, which, with all its implications, was not clear to me then, has stayed with me ever since. In the post-war years I became the Jeremiah-theologian.

On 11 September 1945, from the Headquarters of General MacArthur, Supreme Commander of the Allied Powers, came the directive for the arrest of the war time leaders. As the International Military Tribunal for the Far East progressed the Japanese people came to know how irresponsible their war time leaders had been. They had enjoyed a 'sacred' system of irresponsibility built upon the divinity of the emperor.

On 27 September the emperor paid a visit to Douglas MacArthur. A photograph taken at the time of their meeting was published by the

Japanese press. Here we saw a small man, whom we had thought to be divine, standing with a tall Westerner. Whatever the intention of MacArthur may have been, the impact of that photograph upon the Japanese people was shocking. It was driven home to us that the Japanese people are not a special people, but a very ordinary people – even an inferior people – among other peoples of the world.

A few days later, on 4 October the Supreme Command of Allied Powers issued the Directive on the Removal of Restrictions on Political and Other Liberties which since then has been called 'The Japanese Bill of Rights'. It began in the following manner:

> In order to remove restrictions on political, civil and religious liberties and discriminations on grounds of race, nationality, creed or political opinion, the Imperial Japanese Government will: (a) Abrogate and immediately suspend the operation of all provisions of all laws, decrees, orders, ordinances and regulations which; (1) Establish or maintain restrictions on freedom of thought, of religion, of assembly and of speech, including the unrestricted discussion of the Emperor, the Imperial Institution and the imperial Japanese Government.[4]

'Unrestricted discussion of the Emperor'! This had been unthinkable for about eighty years. An invitation to free exercise of reason has been issued to the Japanese people. The Article 97 of the post war Constitution of Japan (1947) reads:

> The fundamental human rights by this Constitution guaranteed to the people of Japan are fruits of the age-old struggle of man to be free; they have survived the many exacting tests for durability and are conferred upon this and future generations in trust, to be held for all time inviolate.[5]

During the years when the discussion of the Emperor was strictly forbidden, deemed as treason, there was a small number of people who fought for fundamental human rights. They were brutally suppressed by the government. We must remember their costly sacrifices for their vision of human rights as we think of the great history of struggle unfolded in the nations of the West over many centuries. The fruits of that age-old struggle reached Japan in 1947. In the language of the fundamental law of the land now Japan has been grafted to the sacred heritage of Western humanity.

The victor treated us more generously than we deserved. In 1948 on the day when seven A-Class War Criminals were hanged in Tokyo, the president of Tokyo Union Theological Seminary read II Kings 25.6,7 in the morning worship service:

> Then they captured the king, and brought him up to the king of Babylon at Riblah, who passed sentence upon him. They slew the sons of

Zedekiah before his eyes, and put out the eyes of Zedekiah, and bound him in fetters and took him to Babylon.[6]

The members of the imperial family were not put to death in front of the emperor. The emperor did not lose his eyes. We were not taken into exile to slavery. Japan was not divided into West Japan and East Japan, or North Japan and South Japan. We were well treated by the Americans even to the degree that our Asian neighbours, the people who had suffered much under Japan during the war, felt that justice had not been done.

What had happened in 1945?

Tokyo, like many other Japanese cities, had become a wilderness. 'How lonely sits the city that was full of people! How like a widow has she become, she that was great among the nations!' (Lam.1.1). The glory of Tokyo was broken, discontinued. So complete a destruction of the great cities of the nation gave the people the despairing impression that the life of the nation was discontinued. But this is a philosophical description. There is no complete discontinuity in human history so long as there are survivors. The discontinuity was of another nature. What we felt was that the Japanese tribal gods – the legion of them – could not save the people from the hands of the Americans this time.

Japan has twice in her long history been engaged in war with mighty nations, first with the Mongols in the thirteenth century and now with the United States in the twentieth century. The former was a war within Asia, a culturally local war, while the latter was between two very different cultures, religions and civilizations. The military might of the Mongols was far superior to that of the Japanese when they invaded Japan in 1274 and 1281; but twice the invasion was frustrated by the sudden arrival of a strong typhoon, which from that time has been called the 'Divine Wind' (kamikaze) by the Japanese. Japan was narrowly spared from the Mongols by sheer accidents in nature. The end of the war against the United States came with a far greater violence. The bombs blasted over inhabited cities. When these two international wars occurred, some 660 years apart, the government asked the people to pray at the shinto shrines and Buddhist temples for the 'surrender of the enemy and victory of the Divine Land'. In the thirteenth century it seemed that the nationwide prayer was answered. There was, as a matter of fact, a strong feeling of jealousy after the war on the part of the warriors against the gods and buddhas. The warriors felt that their sacrifice was not properly appreciated when the nation became so enthusiastically thankful to the Divine Wind. I think every war situation would produce this kind of tension between 'warriors' and 'gods'. The nationwide prayer did not succeed in the case of war with the United States. The kamikaze did not blow. The spirits of the imperial ancestors were unable to protect the nation and the nation was destroyed. For the first time, in a serious manner, the Japanese people's faith in their own tribal gods was shaken.

What does this mean? It means that the national politics based on the ideological mythology of the solar goddess did not work. This was the message to the Japanese. But not to all the Japanese people. The great majority of the people never have believed in the imperial religion of ultranationalism. The imperial religion was a state ideology forced upon all the people without their willing consent. They were not surprised by the fact that the spirits of the imperial ancestors did not save Japan from the United States. They were, on the contrary, relieved from the spiritual and mental strain of their subordination to the power of the mythical state ideology. It had taken a great deal of national psychological energy to keep alive the impossible mythical ideology! The defeat of war showed the people that their gods were powerless and irrelevant to the challenges human-kind faces in the twentieth century. Humour had disappeared from the nation. People became incapacitated to laugh about themselves. When idolatry intensified humanity progressively disappeared. An old man came to me one day when I was a young boy and whispered to me that if Japan did win the war against the United States, she would lose it all the same since there is no way for Japan to govern the vast land and people of the United States beyond the great Pacific Ocean! Besides that they speak a different language than Japanese and there will be thousands of snipers aimed at the 'Japanese Occupational Force'! He continued and said that, of course, if Japan loses the war, it loses it! In both cases Japan is lost. Then he laughed heartily. This was my only humourous moment in the war time of idolatrous dead-seriousness.

The nation was paralysed under the tyranny of the divine mythology. When the best of Japanese scholars were banned, the exercise of reason was condemned and the people were fed with unreasoned slogans which proclaimed that Japan was the righteous nation and her enemy was devilish. The world seemed divided into two camps; that of good people and that of the bad. The Japanese were good and the United States was the focus of all evil. Any attempt to reason about the validity of such a sweeping and unreasonable position was dealt with quickly by the mythology committed government as coming from unpatriotic and dangerous elements of society. The identification of one's own country as a righteous nation is idolatry. The words of the apostle Paul sound sharply against national as well as personal self-righteousness.

I have already charged that all men, both Jews and Greeks, are under the power of sin, as it is written: 'None is righteous, no, not one, no one understands, no one seeks for God. All have turned aside, together they have gone wrong; no one does good, not even one' (Rom. 3.9–12).

The devastating effect of the edging out of reason by political mythology is that soon ethics will be ousted. Ethics arise from a human concern with understanding human conduct, individual as well as collective. To reflect critically on human conduct requires that the neighbour be taken seriously. Any ethics or human morality which ignores the presence of the other is a self-centred system which works against the common good of humanity. Human ethics must aim to achieve the broad, common good of humanity. The mythological ethics of Japan aimed only at the good of the Japanese nation, perhaps, in the final showdown, at the good of her leaders. This spelled the moral downfall of Japan. A self-centred ethics, if it can be called ethics, is idolatrous.

With reason and ethics out of the way the stage was set for the worst kind of social manipulation. Political propaganda about the cult of the divine emperor made it possible for the leaders to take away from the people their right, even their ability, to protest. They were led as sheep to the slaughter. Families surrendered their young men to be sacrificed on beachheads, in the air and on the sea. Food, freedom and security were sacrificed on the altar of the imperial cult. Yet there were probably few, even among the leaders, who believed that the emperor was divine. After the war government leaders, including the emperor himself, openly said that the idea of the divinity of the emperor was illusory.

The manipulation of the people receives its inspiration at the altar of idols. What, then, is idolatry?

But before we move on to the discussion of idolatry, we must make one more observation of the experience of Japanese people. The imperial cult did not save the nation from the attack by the United States. They prayed to their gods; the gods did not respond to their prayers. The classic image of the non-response of the idols is given in the story of Elijah as he battles against the prophets of Baal.

> 'O Baal, answer us!' But there was no voice and no one answered. ... And they cried aloud, and cut themselves after their custom with swords and lances, until the blood gushed out upon them. And as midday passed, they raved on until the time of the offering of the oblation, but there was no voice; no one answered, no one heeded (I Kings 18.26,28,29).

The God of Elijah, however, answered Elijah's prayer. The people cried out; 'the Lord, he is God; the Lord, he is God' (v. 39). The Elijah episode of Mount Carmel gives us a powerful paradigm for our theology of false gods and true God. The true God responds while the false gods do not and cannot. It may be said, however, that this is not necessarily what faith in God experiences all the time. It is possible that the true God does not respond to our prayer, and the false gods respond to the prayers of their believers. Perhaps the most agonizing of sayings in the whole Bible is the cry of Jesus on the cross: 'My God, my God, why hast thou forsaken me?' (Mark 15.34), which points to the first possibility. The Japanese gods and buddhas respondings to the prayer of Japanese people at the time of the Mongol invasion may illustrate the second possibility.

The religious experiences of humanity are extremely complex. We must take up the Elijah paradigm with our utmost theological perception so that we may hear from it its fundamental message. As we do so the concept of the holy comes into the background of our thought. If God is the holy One then God is someone we cannot place under our control. Hence, the following chapter is titled 'The Holy God repudiates idolatry'. The chapter will begin with the question; 'what is idolatry?'

4

The Holy God Repudiates Idolatry

Idolatry defrauds God, denying him his proper
honours and conferring them upon others. It adds
insult to injury.
(Tertullian, *On Idolatry*)[1]

The word 'idolatry' (Greek, *eidolon* – idol, image; *latreia* – service,
worship) raises the mental picture of 'heathen' peoples worshipping
grotesque images at their temples in 'non-Christian' lands. We see Indians
venerating images, half elephant and half man, of *Ganesha;* of an
emaciated woman devouring the intestines of a child, *Kali*; of Vishnu
sleeping on the huge coils of a serpent floating on the cosmic ocean, and so
on. Christians are thought to be free from idolatry.

Isaiah, in a remarkably picturesque way, speaks about the origin of idols
and idolatry:

He [carpenter] cuts down cedars; or he chooses a holm tree or an oak
and lets it grow strong among the trees of the forest; he plants a cedar
and the rain nourishes it. Then it becomes fuel for a man; he takes a part
of it and warms himself, he kindles a fire and bakes bread; also he makes
a god and worships it, he makes it a graven image and falls down before
it. Half of it he burns in the fire; over the half he eats flesh, he roasts
meat and is satisfied; also he warms himself and says, 'Aha, I am warm,
I have seen the fire!' And the rest of it he makes into a god, his idol; and
falls down to it and worships it; he prays to it and says 'Deliver me, for
thou art my god!' (Isa. 44.14–17).

Idols come into being neither mysteriously nor ambiguously. Their material
origin can be easily traced to a tree in the forest. Out of one piece of wood
are made fire wood and a graven image. We pray to the image made out of
wood saying 'Deliver me, for thou art my god!' The story about idols is
straightforward.

Idolatry is defined as fetishism according to Yehezkel Kaufmann.[2] The Bible criticizes it as the worship of 'wood and stone' in more direct and simple language. Jeremiah amply sets forth his conception of pagan religion: It is the worship of wood and stone (2.27). The 'other gods' are the handiwork of men (1.16), 'stone and wood' (3.9), 'graven images and strange vanities' (8.19), 'no gods' (2.11;5.7). On the day when the nations repent of the sin of idolatry they will say:

> Our fathers have inherited nought but lies, worthless things in which there is no profit. Can man make for himself gods? Such are no gods! (16.19,20)

When people stop worshipping 'no-gods', then idolatry shall come to an end. Deuteronomy has these words:

> You know how we dwelt in the land of Egypt, and how we came through the midst of the nations through which you passed; and you have seen their detestable things, their idols of wood and stone, of silver and gold, which were among them (29.16.17).

The idols made of 'wood and stone, silver and gold' cannot be God simply because they are made of these things. Idolatry as fetishism is, according to Yehezkel Kaufmann, the primary observation the Bible makes about idolatry. The word 'fetish' comes from the Portuguese *feitico* meaning 'skillfully made'. Fetishism is a magical religious attitude which holds that certain natural or artificial objects are endowed with supernatural value, and are to be the object of devotion. We may think that such biblical characterization of idols and idolatry is too simplistic or static to describe the complicated social and political phenomena of idolatry in our complex world. Perhaps Tillich's definition of idolatry gives us a clearer conceptual image of the subject. As we have seen idolatry, according to Tillich, comes into being when 'something essentially conditioned is taken as unconditional, something essentially partial is boosted into universality and something essentially finite is given infinite significance'. Human culture, for instance, is conditioned, but when a particular culture is taken to be unconditional, idolatry emerges. Thus Japanese culture, for instance, will begin to behave like 'god'. Technology is partial. It cannot, no matter how sophisticated and extensive its influence, cover the total meaning of human life. But when an obsession with technology begins to represent the universal meaning of human existence, then idolatry will take place. Our human mental capacity is finite. To reject its limitation and give it infinite significance is idolatry.

I do not think that the biblical view of fetishism as idolatry and Tillich's 'boosting partial to universality' are different. There is a subtle psychological connection between the two. When a certain object, natural or artificial, is thought to possess supernatural virtue, there is a 'boosting' in it. The feeling of psychological expansion concomitant with this boosting from object to supernatural gives us a sense of satisfaction and pleasure, though it is usually short lived. This boosting of the finite into the infinite is spoken of in Jesus' parable of the Rich Farmer (Luke 12.16–21).

> I will pull down my barns, and build larger ones; and there I will store all my grain and my goods. And I will say to my soul, 'Soul, you have ample goods laid up for many years; take your ease, eat, drink, be merry'.

Here the larger barns carry fetish significance for the successful farmer. The barns standing before him – though they may be large barns – are conditioned, partial and finite. Theologically what this means is that 'wood and stone, silver and gold' cannot be God. No matter how precious they may be they are 'conditioned, partial and finite' in their meaning for human life. Our fetish emotion, that is our uncontrollable desire to boost finite into infinite, however, paralyses our thinking and makes us to believe that the object of our interest is unconditional, universal and infinite. When he gives 'infinite significance' to these barns, he becomes idolatrous. Upon this fetishism of the rich farmer comes the judgment of God: 'Fool! this night your soul is required of you; and the things you have prepared, whose will they be?

Nuclear weapons, skilfully made, are humanity's most impressive fetish in the world today. Before the image of the weapons we fall down and worship. We know where this fetish has come from. It comes from Uranium hidden in the mountains. But this fetish contains an element which differentiates itself from all other fetishes. Worshipping 'stone and wood' is indeed destructive to human welfare, but 'stone and wood' do not have explosive power of nuclear bombs. 'Stone and wood' cannot annihilate humanity upon this planet, but nuclear bombs can! In the most concrete sense the fetish object has reached the point of absolute destructiveness. Psychologically speaking, however, the same mind-set is at work with the nuclear fetishism and a dried tail of elephant which the natives believe to have supernatural virtues.

The words of the Psalm speak of the inner effect of idolatry upon human beings.

> Their idols are silver and gold, the work of men's hands. They have mouths but do not speak; eyes, but do not see. They have ears, but do not hear, noses, but do not smell. They have hands, but do not feel, feet, but do not walk; and they do not make a sound in their throat. Those who make them are like them; so are all who trust in them.

When we trust in idols, then boosting will take place and the idols begin to 'speak, see, hear, smell, feel and walk' for us. When this happens we will become 'like them', that is, dumb. A vicious exchange takes place in idol worship. When the idols become eloquent (boosted) then the human become dumb (squelched). The idolatrous situation is one of the most 'dynamic' situations that the human mind can produce, but its product is paralysis and destruction, not creativity.

When I hear the word 'idolatry' I think of a man impeccably dressed in military uniform and mounted on a magnificent white horse named White Snow (*Shirayuki*). It is the image of the 124th emperor of Japan, who was born on 29 April 1901. This picture of the 'divine' emperor was circulated during the war. The image is a pleasing one. There is nothing grotesque about it, as with the Hindu image. He is not unreal, not 'wood and stone'. He is not a piece of fetish but a natural person, a human being. But the idolatrous boosting took place about his person. He was elevated to the status of god, 'beyond human'. This boosting resulted in the squelching of people's aspirations. As the emperor began to speak divine language the language of the people became less and less rational. All of us, including the emperor himself, were impaired.

What makes the idols 'speak' is the elusive secret of idolatry. That we should feel secure when idols become eloquent and we become dumb is a demonstration of the demonic power of idolatry. It was the insight of Martin Luther that 'the confidence and faith of the heart' will make both idols and the true God. Here are his famous, yet not readily understandable words;

> A god is that to which we look for all good and where we resort for help in every time of need. To have a god is simply to trust and believe in one with our whole heart. The confidence and faith of the heart make both God and an idol. If your faith and confidence are right, then likewise your God is the true God. On the other hand if your confidence is false, then you have not the true God. [3]

If our confidence and faith were placed in the image of Abraham Lincoln in the Lincoln Memorial, we would be worshipping him as god. If we put our confidence and faith in a piece of wood, that piece of wood would be our god. Without our confidence and faith neither idolatry nor any other kind of religion is possible. The question of God and idol are very much related to our faith and confidence. It happens at the depth of our soul. 'If your faith and confidence are right then likewise your God is the true God.'

But how do we know that our faith and confidence are right? By what standard can we judge that our faith and confidence are right? To this difficult question Tillich's definition of idolatry may throw some helpful light. If Your 'faith and confidence' engage in 'boosting of conditional to the unconditional', then your faith and confidence are wrong. Then consequently you will have an idol, the false god. Can we say that if we do not engage in the boosting of the partial to the universal, then our faith and confidence are right and thus have the true God? Can we thus expand and apply what Tillich said about idolatry to the discussion of the true God? Luther seems to respond affirmatively.

The Indian image of the elephant-headed god and of the god with many hands strike me as monstrous. I prefer to see a body with a human head and with no more nor less than two hands. Indian iconographic imagination is too strong for the Japanese mind. Indian iconographies are, of course, expressing philosophical observations which Indian people have made about nature and human life. The gruesome image of *Kali* devouring human intestines depicts the fundamental truth about human existence, that life feeds on life. *Kali*'s unusually fecund breasts indicate that the one who destroys is also the one who produces the milk of life. All life continues in a cyclical motion. This is a philosophical observation. In contrast, the Japanese are primarily fascinated by this passing phenomenal world, in what they see and touch. It is beyond the Japanese unsophisticated mind to produce images such as the Indian *Kali*.

Buddhism introduced the Indian inconography of sublime philosophy into Japan. Since the eighth century there have appeared Buddhist images made by Japanese artists imitating the original. As a result- Japan has accumulated a wealth of great religious images (*Zo*) throughout the long centuries. It is only natural that the tolerant Japanese would show veneration to and 'worship' these images, even though emotionally they may not feel quite at home with them. How do we understand the human need for visual symbols and image in worship? Gandhi understood this problem and addressed it in support of Hindu imagery.

> I am a reformer through and through. But my zeal never takes me to the rejection of any of the essential things of Hinduism. I have said I do not disbelieve in idol worship. An idol does not excite any feeling of veneration in me. But I think that idol worship is part of human nature. We hanker after symbolism. Why should one be more composed in a church than elsewhere? Images are an aid to worship. No Hindu considers an image to be God. I do not consider idol worship a sin.[4]

Gandhi is speaking of something subtly different from the fetishism which the biblical prophets condemn. The images made of 'wood and stone, silver and gold' are simply 'an aid to worship'. They may become 'detestable' if we take these images to be God. 'No Hindu considers an image to be God.' They are symbols, and 'we hanker after symbolism'. We do not place our faith and confidence in the images. Our devotion goes beyond these images which are symbols, to the Eternal One who they represent. In this sense Gandhi says that he does not disbelieve in idol worship.

It seems to me that the magical element in fetishism arises when we do not see the fetish objects as symbols. In general magic infers immediate efficacy rather than symbolic significance. Gandhi insists on the symbolic quality of images and on the need of people to have such symbols. The important point here is that for Gandhi images are symbols, and not that symbols are images. He places value on the symbolic function of the images. In this sense, then, I may say somewhat awkwardly that for Gandhi the symbol is primary and the image secondary.

A similar line of thought is found in the tradition of the Orthodox Church. Discussions relating to the meaning and use of visual symbols occupied the Orthodox Church for some one hundred and twenty years in the eighth and ninth centuries. The Iconoclast controversy was a dispute between the icon-smashers (iconoclasts) and icon-venerators (iconodules) about the use of the icons in religious liturgy. Against the iconoclasts Leontius of Neapolis (d. *c.* 650) said:

> We do not make obeisance to the nature of wood, but we revere and do obeisance to Him who was crucified on the Cross. ... When the two beams of the Cross are joined together I adore the figure because of Christ who on the Cross was crucified, but if the beams are separated, I throw them away and burn them.[5]

The beams themselves have no sacred quality. When they are arranged in a certain way and are given meaning they become a symbol. A symbol cannot be isolated from its meaning. There must have been at some time, a verbal explanation given. So the beams arranged in a certain way symbolize 'the cross on which the prince of glory died' under the Roman procurator Pontius Pilate. But we must know that if the beams are separated they can be used to bake bread. Christians place two beams together in a cross to symbolize Christ. As soon as some sense of 'boosting symbol to the unconditional itself' takes place a subtle process begins which leads to idolatry. When the symbol is invested with power of its own, it becomes a fetish. It produces idolatry.

This means that even our most valuable symbols can become idols. Fetishism exercises a powerful attraction among us. The human ability to create symbols corresponds to our ability to create idols. So long as we are a symbol creating animal, we will not be free from the temptation of making idols for ourselves. Something of this was in Luther's mind when he said that both the true God and the false gods come from our 'faith and confidence of the heart'. Gandhi makes the same point when he says; 'I think that idol worship is part of human nature'. If we want to free ourselves from idolatry, we will have to relinquish our ability to make symbols. This would leave us in a world devoid of meaning. It seems that we cannot avoid the responsibility to hold our symbols in reverence while we remember their limitation. A well functioning symbol will share the nature of the person of John the Baptist; 'He must increase, but I must decrease'. (John 3.30). Only the broken symbol, paradoxically, can have meaning to us without enslaving us. The broken symbol is neither fetish nor ideological.

Gandhi and Leontius were travelling the same road though Gandhi speaks about images and Leontius about symbols. Can we treat symbols and images in the same way? The Hindu images, for example, are far more anthropomorphic than the Hindu symbol of the sacred Primordial Sound, *OM*, written in the Sanskrit letter. Similarly there are many pictures and images of Jesus and of Mary as over against the symbol of the cross in the Christian religion. What is the relationship between these anthropomorphic images and the non-anthropomorphic symbols?

Both forms point to a reality beyond them. They are aids to worship. The Hebrew-Christian tradition has been, however, uneasy with imagery. Tertullian, the theologian of the second and third century, expressed it strongly,

> God forbids the making of idols no less than the worshipping of them. Just as any object of worship must first be made, so what must not be worshipped must not be made. That is the prior obligation. For this reason, in order to root out the materials of idolatry, God's law proclaims; 'Thou shalt not make an idol'. [6]

This was Tertullian's appreciation of the Commandment which is the most direct expression of the prohibition of images.

> You shall not make for yourself a graven image, or any likeness of anything that is in heaven above, or that is in the earth beneath, or that is in the water under the earth (Ex. 20.4).

The Hebrew word for 'graven image' is *pesel*, which comes from a root meaning 'to carve' and suggests a sculptured object. The word 'likeness' is translated from *t*e*munah* which signifies the outward shape or form of an object. Did Moses institute an aniconic (without a likeness) cult? Scholars are not in agreement on this point and I am not competent to join their debate. I do feel sympathetic to the view of Tertullian that 'what must not be worshipped must not be made', but I find some difficulty when I try to apply this view to the creation of all things by God.

> And God saw everything that he had made, and behold it was very good (Gen. 1.31).

Good things are not here to be worshipped according to the biblical faith. But any good thing can become the object of human worship since it fascinates and inspires us. We may worship the creature instead of the creator, but that did not stop God from creating all things. There are innumerable enchanting shapes and forms in the world of nature. The whole creation is full of images. The same creation which may be an aid for our worship of the creator may become an idol blinding our vision of God the creator. In spite of the likelihood that we would worship the creature instead of the creator, God created all things. The doctrine of creation involves the idea of a God who takes this risk. 'I am the Lord, that is my name; my glory I give to no other, nor my praise to graven images' (Isa. 42.8). The risk of the Creator God that we will use or misuse the creature, takes place in our mind, as Luther indicated. 'The confidence and faith of the heart make both God and an idol.' Deep inside of our mind we have freedom to frustrate the divine intention. John Philips writes:

> At no time was it possible to prove that idolatry was taking place, since the worship of a created thing in place of God occurs in the mind of the worshipper rather than in the image addressed. [7]

The unique and awesome truth about human history is that it can become creative or destructive, healing or damaging because at its basis there is a mysterious freedom of human confidence and faith of the heart which can make both God and an idol. This is the risk that the creator God took. Both image and symbol work with human confidence and faith of the heart. Both are then not operating neutrally. As they point to a reality beyond them, both can be the occasion for idolatry. When image and symbol point to the idol, then the criticism of such idolatry must come from image and symbol which point to the true God. The image of Stalin must be criticized by the image of the crucified Christ. If I expand the concept of image a bit I may say that the image of sexual commercialism flourishing in New York City (around 42nd street) must be criticized by the image of Mother Teresa taking care of the poorest of the poor in the city of Calcutta. The symbol of the cross must confront the symbol of the swastika. What do I mean by such criticism? What is the historical and theological understanding of such inter-symbol conflict? I shall discuss them in due course. The fact that I remain a believer of the biblical God means that I believe that such criticism, by the grace of God, is possible in this idolatrous world today.

A question whether image more than symbol tempts us to worship it, that is, whether the more anthropomorphic the visual representation is the more tempted we are to worship it, would be difficult to give a simple answer. Cultural factors may play a significant role here. In Japan one frequently sees people 'worshipping' the image of *bodhisattva,* the merciful Buddha who vowed not to enter salvation until all beings had been saved. The *bodhisattva* image has many hands (40 hands besides two main hands; since each of 40 hands signified the salvation of 25 worlds, the number 40 means 1000, hence the image is called the *bodhisattva* of 1000 hands) and it is believed that through these many hands this Buddha saves people of all possible situations and characters. The worshippers of this image are touched by the infinite mercy of the Buddha to broken humanity. This is what we observe at some of the old Buddhist temples in Kyoto, Japan, such as Sanju-San-Gen-Do which houses 1000 images of the *bodhisattva* of 1000 hands. It is easier, in general, to assume worshipping attitude before these 'concrete' images than before the symbol of, for instance, the Wheel of *Dharma*.

These images of bodhisattva are, in character, different from the image of Abraham Lincoln in the Lincoln Memorial in Washington, DC. The image of Abraham Lincoln, looking very much like himself, sits looking out over the reflecting pond, has no supernatural characteristics. He does not have 42 hands. He lived from 1809 to 1865. He is not a mythological figure that lives in the world of religious ideas. On the walls around him are inscribed words of his speeches, given at definite points in American history. His image points to something other than himself, to the history in which he participated to preserve the national integrity as he, the President, understood it. His image does not represent eternal principles but human struggle within certain definite historical realities. It is not worshipped. It is studied.

At the Lincoln Memorial we study the words of the Gettysburg Address and the Second Inaugural Address. What we 'remember' has meaning for our life today. The past becomes present through our act of remembering, and remembering will not take place without studying. Thus this image occasions studying instead of worshipping. It is not even an aid to worship. It is an invitation to study human history. The Lincoln Memorial represents historical events set in the context of other events as the Memorial itself is a memorial among memorials. That Lincoln himself saw these events in the perspective of the Judaeo-Christian tradition (memory) is attested to in the words of the Second Inaugural Address which are inscribed at the Memorial.

> Yet, if God wills that it continue until all the wealth piled by the bondsman's two hundred and fifty years of unrequited toil shall be sunk, and until every drop of blood drawn with the lash shall be paid by another drawn with the sword, as was said three thousand years ago, so still it must be said, 'The judgments of the Lord are true and righteous altogether'. [8]

When Lincoln studied the situation of American slavery in the nineteenth century he went back to a three thousand year old memory. It must have been because the tradition was so oriented to history that Lincoln found it so relevant. That 'the judgments of the Lord are true and righteous altogether' is a confession of the people of Israel in a concrete historical situation. It is a historical truth which was applicable to the nineteenth century crisis in the United States in the judgment of Lincoln. This bridging of the old memory to the present situation is suggested in an impassioned way in the following words of Jeremiah:

> The priest did not say. 'Where is the Lord?' Those who handle the law did not know me; the rulers transgressed against me; the prophets prophesied by Baal, and went after things that do not profit. Therefore I still contend with you, says the Lord, and with your children's children I will contend (Jer. 8.9).

In the Bible God's complaint is clear and a controversy is initiated which God does not give up easily. '...with your children's children I will contend'. History as God's experience expresses itself in the words of God's complaints and controversy with us. The three thousand years mentioned in Lincoln's Second Inaugural is indeed a congested time of many events. But theologically speaking it has been the time of 'God's controversy with your children's children'. History is shot through with the controversy initiated by God. The history of Israel and the church is a history of God's controversy with them for the sake of the salvation of all people. God's words are historical and controversial.

This passion of God – 'with your children's children I will contend' – makes biblical monotheism meaningful to us. There are not many gods, with varied functions and characteristics, who engage us in controversy. There is one God, one history-concerned God with a good intention of unfathomable depth, engaged in controversy with us. This God says, 'My glory I will not give to another'. The controversy that engulfed Lincoln was a part of this God's controversy. And in the context of controversy Lincoln expresses his ultimate trust in God by quoting the old biblical confession; 'The judgments of the Lord are true and righteous altogether'.

Thus the image of Abraham Lincoln at Lincoln Memorial and that of the bodhisattva in Kyoto are very different in their religious and cultural aspects. The former is historical and it demands to be studied. It comes to world history with a case of strong complaint and an equally serious concomitant controversy. It introduces a God who is passionately involved in history. Through the controversy continuing for three thousand years the image of Abraham Lincoln invites people to God.

The 'history' of bodhisattva is, on the other hand, mythological. With one thousand hands and eleven different faces, the bodhisattva confronts the world with the religious principle of the value of infinite mercy. It is not that this image has no connection or relevance to the history in which we live at all. It can speak to our history in its own inspiring way, as has been demonstrated by some Buddhist movements in Japan as a symbol for anti-nuclear disarmament and world peace. In this way it could be said that it is participating in the tradition of the Lord's controversy. But the bodhisattva is a mythological, not a historical, figure. It is a product of speculation and philosophy, no matter how sublime it may be. It's relationship to history is different from that of Abraham Lincoln who lived more than a century ago in history just as we do today.

Our relationship with the images of bodhisattva and Abraham Lincoln should not involve the fetishism or the 'boosting' that Tillich warns us of. We will come to appreciate what they mean for our historical moment if we see how these two particular images are related to that controversy of the Lord which is continuing down through the ages, to 'children's children', even to our own generation. Both of them point to the value (the Lord's controversy) beyond them. They become in this sense symbols. I can happily make such positive assessment with these two images, one in Washington, the other in Kyoto, for they both signify the positive ethical value. It is this ethical quality that plays the decisive role in our thinking about idolatry. I am tempted to paraphrase Luther and say that 'if your ethical value is right you have the right God, and if your ethical orientation is wrong, then you have an idol'. I believe that the swastika symbolism of National Socialism or the 'theological and moral principles' supporting *apartheid* race policy in South Africa has the false gods, since their ethical orientation is wrong.

If our ethical value is right we are able to resist fetishism and the boosting that Tillich discusses. The right ethical perception takes a critical attitude towards magic (fetishism) and self-aggrandisement ('boosting'). Both ethical and anti-ethical values can express themselves through symbols and images. The former are sustained by the sense of the holy while the latter deny the presence of the holy in history. It is the sense of the presence of the holy in history that can give us the ground on which we stand against the temptation of fetish self-enlargement, idolatry.

Fetishism is primitive. It is magical. It locates supernatural virtue in things we may be able to hold in our hands. The holy is, as it were, captivated in various natural and artificial objects of veneration. Mount Sinai would become a fetish mountain if God were captivated in it. But, in the biblical tradition, God is completely free from the confine of this mountain. God 'descends upon it in fire'. The biblical God rejects all possible fetish understanding of God.

> Behold, heaven and the highest heaven cannot contain thee; how much less this house which I have built! (I Kings 8.27)

These are the anit-fetish words of King Solomon's prayer at the dedication of the great temple in Jerusalem. The greatness of God cannot be a meaningful concept if it is not related to and nourished by the holiness of God. It is not simply that God is so great that 'heaven and the highest heaven cannot contain' God. It is because God's greatness and holiness are one that 'the highest heaven cannot contain' him. In the biblical tradition there is a strong and profound conviction that the holy God cannot be arranged, controlled and manipulated by us. This is the reason why there has been always some sense of uneasiness attached to the term 'Systematic Theology'.

We either avoid or ignore this holy God. The ancient Psalmist says, 'They exchanged the glory of God for the image of an ox that eats grass' (106.20). By this art of 'exchanging' we have avoided the holy God. The holy God (the glory of God) is transformed into 'an ox that eats grass', and now we feel that we can deal with this transformed God. Here we have a tamed God who is no longer dangerous. This God does not come down on the top of Mount Sinai 'in fire' and does not speak to us 'in thunder'. 'Exchanging' is an important sociological and political word. There must be many meaningful acts of exchange in our human history. But when these exchanges are inspired by this particular exchange that the Psalmist talks about our civilization will become dishonest, distorted and idolatrous. It is the mission of Christian theology to say this as clearly and concretely as possible. Tertullian says that 'idolatry defrauds God, denying him his proper honours and conferring them upon others. It adds insult to injury'. Exchanging of 'the glory of God for the image of an ox that eats grass' does precisely what Tertullian describes as the essence of idolatry.

If such taming of God by the art of exchanging is one phenomenon of idolatry, then the other is found in our ignoring of God. A painful complaint of God comes to us through the prophet Hosea:

> They made kings, but not through me. They set up princes, but without my knowledge (Hos. 8.4).

'They' are the people of Israel, 'the house of the Lord' (v.1) The line expresses Hosea's evaluation of Israel's monarchy. James L. Mays writes:

> The succession of royal governments in Israel were the independent work of men thinking of kingship as an institution whose management was their prerogative. By deceit and murder one king had displaced another without any appeal to Yahweh (7.1-3). Sovereignty over Israel belonged to him in the older charismatic conception of kingship. The king was Yahweh's elect and regent.[9]

The politics of Israel had become independent of God. The kings, in fact, rejected their most essential self-identity of being God's elect and regent as they willingly colluded with the political power game unmindful of the God who is the real King. Hosea's message through the painful experience of history of Israel to humanity is that governments and those who exercise political, economic and military authorities are answerable to 'God'. They must not have the ultimate authority. They are subjected to the Higher Authority. In the very process of making kings and setting up princes the whole community must know that politics independent of God will lead eventually to the destructive influence of idolatry.

We rashly build all our political systems and power structures 'not through me'. We elaborate and expand our technological, economic and religious life heedlessly 'without my knowledge'. In this, our going ahead on our own, we are not concerned about the holy God who would have a different view in making kings and setting up princes. Ignoring this God, we schedule events and timetable history. In ignoring this God willfully the civilization will become idolatrous. Hosea 'puts idol and king on the same level of guilt – both are made by Israel, the work of their rebellion against Yahweh'.[10]

I take the position that though Japan does not have the theological understanding to recognize the structure of idolatry in the way of 'exchanging' or 'ignoring', what happened in Japan during the war years substantiates what Hosea said in the eighth century BC. We might compare this to the digestive system, which, though we may not understand how it works, will punish us if we disobey one of its laws by eating too much or unwisely. Whether we have a Christian, Buddhist or Marxist understanding of history of human value, idolatry is harmful to human welfare.

I have lived with a difficult theological sentence which reads: 'Japan made the divine emperor, but not through me'. This is a difficult thought because if through God, Japan would not have made the divine emperor at all. 'Through God' is the principle of the critique of idols. The holy God refuses to tolerate the divine emperor for the sake of his holiness. This is the way God experiences history. This line of thought, however, is quite foreign to Japanese cultural heritage. Japan made the divine emperor quite openly without 'guilt feeling'.

The imperial cult of Japan reached its denouement when the Imperial Rescript of the Emperor's Disavowal of His Divinity was issued on 1 January 1946. It contains this paragraph:

> We stand by the people and we wish always to share with them in their moment of joy and sorrow. The ties between us and our people have always stood upon mutual trust and affection. They do not depend upon mere legends and myth. They are not predicated on the false conception that the Emperor is divine and that the Japanese people are superior to other races and fated to rule the world.[11]

I welcomed the Rescript. It seemed a good way to begin a new year and a new era. This particular paragraph, however, disturbed me. We had been forced to accept that the emperor was divine and that the Japanese people were to rule the world. Japan was, in the official propaganda, the righteous empire supervising the morality of humanity. And the emperor was the ultimate moral principle in the world. People who had resisted this state ideology had been brutally destroyed. Now the Rescript says simply that this was a misconception of a myth. The Rescript indeed moves in the direction of science and honesty, abruptly taking a critical attitude towards myth in the name of the historical 'mutual trust'. There had been such a mutual trust before the imperial cult was introduced, but the imperial ideology had demolished all that. A great deal of fear and mistrust had been infused 'between us and our people'.

The imperial ideology that created fear and mistrust among people was established 'not through me' and 'without my knowledge'. This stupendous self-aggrandisement is rectified by the 'universal principle of humanity' of the post war Constitution of Japan. Japan is beginning to speak a universal language. The 1889 Constitution of the Empire of Japan opens with this impressive yet parochial phrase:

> Having, by virtue of the glories of Our Ancestors, ascended the Throne of the lineal succession unbroken for ages eternal, ...

The emperor's 'eternity' is by succession. 'Eternity' in the Japanese understanding means a long continuous time. It is not 'timelessness'. Like the Greek word *aeon* it has a touch of concreteness. *Aeon* originally refers to 'vital force' or 'life time'. It is not unrelated to human biological time. In the context of human life, time is experienced as vital force. Thus the Greeks understood *aeon* as 'the relative time allotted to a being'. [12] This concept is similar to the Japanese understanding of 'eternity'. For the Japanese 'eternity' suggests long, continuous time in which vitality is unbroken. This Japanese philosophy has been solemnly expressed in the Constitution with the words 'succession unbroken for ages eternal'.

What could have been an innocuous statement of Japanese eternity became harmful to the people when it was combined with the concept of imperial ancestral spirits which gave the emperor a unique source of holiness. In the religious history of Japan there is a connection between the spirits of the imperial ancestors and the spirit of the cereal god. One of the most sacred imperial ceremonies is the occasion of the new emperor to 'commune' with the spirit of the cereal god during the season of his enthronement. The agricultural cereal god that represents the vitality of the Japanese people quickly lost its innocence when the Japanese vitality was equated with the concept of the holy nation under the imperial holiness. When vitality is identified with holiness, the critical nature of holiness is lost and it can no longer judge the misorientation and misbehaviour of vitality. Thus in this identification both vitality and holiness deteriorate in their quality. When this happens vitality becomes irresponsible. Vitality is deified ('boosted') and idolatry appears. The German National Socialism of Hitler combined the vitality of German nation with the transcendent concept of holiness. The God of Hosea rejects such equation between vitality and holiness.

The bankruptcy of the Japanese combination of vitality and holiness was symbolized by two events. First, it was symbolized by the recantation of the emperor's divinity declared in the Rescript. When the emperor is restored to the level of normal humanity, the idea that 'the Japanese people are superior to other races and fated to rule the world' lost its political basis. The disavowal of the divinity meant the separation of vitality from holiness, the first step towards spiritual emancipation.

Secondly, the bankruptcy of the combination of vitality and holiness in the Japanese history is symbolized by the discontinuance of the use of the Rescript of Education. The Rescript of Education issued 30 October 1890, decreed,

> ...The way here set forth is indeed the teaching bequeathed by our Imperial Ancestors, to be observed alike by Their Descendants and the subjects, infallible for all ages and true in all places.[13]

The Japanese Diet passed a resolution for the discontinuance of this Rescript in October 1946. The Way 'infallible for all ages' died after fifty-six years of convulsive life. The infallible teaching was guided by the spirit of the union of vitality and holiness. The holiness politics rooted in the imperial ancestors was idolatrous. The post-war Japanese Diet rejected the Infallible Teaching because it realized the harm it had done to the life of the people.

The God who descends upon Mount Sinai in fire is the Holy God. In the words of the Sinai Tradition this God is an impassioned God,

> for I the Lord your God am an impassioned God, visiting the guilt of the fathers upon the children, upon the third and upon the fourth generations of those who reject Me, but showing kindness to the thousandth generation of those who love Me and keep My commandments (Ex. 20.5,6).[14]

God is impassioned because God intends to be with the people 'showing kindness to the thousandth generation'. The impassioned God is a God who is deeply involved in our history. Yet this involved God is the holy God. These two words, 'holy' and 'impassioned' indicate in the fundamental way how God is related to us. God is deeply involved in history, but God does not allow himself to be domesticated by us. Only in this way is salvation in the name of God possible. All idols must be examined in the light of this 'holy and impassioned' God. Our human drive towards fetishism, the boosting of the conditioned to unconditional, fetish approach to symbols and images, magical appreciation of historical events, our inner ability to create false gods through our confidence and faith, our fascination in 'exchanging' and 'ignoring' the true God, our tendency to declare something to be 'infallible for all ages and true in all places', and our *ad hoc* creation of the combination between vitality and holiness – these must be carefully examined in the light of this 'holy and impassioned' God.

Idols are not holy. They are not impassioned. The prophets of Baal staged an impassioned orgiastic religious ritual and called upon the name of Baal. Baal remains to be not impassioned. When they appear hopeless, Elijah takes over the centre stage. He orders. 'Fill four jars with water, and pour it on the burnt offering and on the wood' (I Kings 18.33). Three times he drenches the altar of the impassioned God. He himself does not get impassioned in the manner of the prophets of Baal. He does not cut himself with swords and lances. Here we see a symbolic and psychological contrast between the passionless Baal and his impassioned prophets, on the one hand, and the impassioned God and the cool Elijah. Elijah firmly believes in the impassioned God who would 'consume the burnt offering, and the wood, and the stones, and the dust and lick up the water that was in the trench' (18.38). Here is suggested, in a dramatic way, the confidence of the servant of the living God as he pours water over the altar.

The rule of the contest, however, remains problematic. It is possible that the living God, holy and impassioned, may not abide by the rule of the prophet. It is possible that God may choose to stay silent not being an idol! This rule which intends to decide which god is the true God must be subject to the holy and impassioned God.

5

Before the Fierce Anger of God

Is Japan destroyed by the Lord or by the Americans?

The prophet Jeremiah saw in a vision the impending destruction of Judah; '...all its cities were laid in ruins before the Lord, before his fierce anger' (Jer.4.26). He saw that it was not the Babylonians but the 'fierce anger' of the Lord that would bring about the destruction of his country.

Is there any way that I can apply the truth derived from Jeremiah's vision to twentieth-century Japan? Was Japan detroyed before the fierce anger of the Lord? If I believe this I have a theological secret which is kept from my own people. In general they understand that Japan was destroyed 'before the fierce anger' of the Americans. They would also say that Judah was destroyed by the Babylonians. Military victory is decided by sheer military might! Still more, it might have been the Americans who were destroyed 'before the fierce anger' of the Japanese had that fateful weapon been in their hands. Was it before the Americans, before the Lord or, indeed, before someone else that Japan was destroyed? The problem of the 'befores' confuses me and impresses upon me the complexity of history.

Is there any reason that we should take up a *vision* of Jeremiah with such seriousness? On the vision of cosmic destruction (4.23–26), Bernhard Anderson writes:

> It seems to have been composed toward the end of Jeremiah's career, around the fateful turn from the seventh to the sixth centuries BC, when the nation Judah stood on the eve of destruction. In a terrifying vision the prophet portrays the results of a devastating invasion from the North. His poetic eye sees, however, not just the coming of the Foe from the North, but the invasion of chaos itself, as though the earth were returned to its primeval condition of 'waste and void' – *tohu wa-bohu* that prevailed before the creation, according to the Priestly account (Gen.1.2).[1]

People, beasts, vegetables, plants, the dry land and the heavens are created.

But in this vision all things are, as it were, 'uncreated' and primeval chaos
returns. The earth becomes waste and void. The heavens give no light. The
mountains quake. There is no man. The birds of the air have fled. Fruitful
land becomes a desert! As Anderson points out Jeremiah saw more than the
destruction of Judah. He saw the return of the primeval chaos which was
before the creation.

How frightfully and forebodingly relevant these words of his vision are to
us who live today before the constant threat of cosmic catastrophy by the
50,000 nuclear bombs which we ourselves have made in order to keep peace!

Nuclear weapons are unique in that they attack the support systems of
life at every level. And these systems, of course, are not isolated from
each other but are parts of a single whole: ecological collapse, if it goes
far enough, will bring about social collapse, and social collapse will bring
about individual deaths. Furthermore, the destructive consequences of a
nuclear attack are immeasurably compounded by the likelihood that all
or most of the bombs will be detonated within the space of a few hours,
in a single huge concussion. ... a nuclear holocaust would devastate the
'outside' areas as well, leaving the victims to fend for themselves in a
shattered society and natural environment. And what is true for each city
is also true for the earth as a whole; a devastated earth can hardly expect
'outside' help. The earth is the largest of the support systems for life, and
the impairment of the earth is the largest of the perils posed by nuclear
weapon.[2]

Frightful possibility!

The heaven does not give us light because of the thick smog. There is 'no
man' because the twentieth century is first of all a century of genocides of
incredible proportion. The birds of the air have been decimated by the
pollution of the air and the land. And the fruitful land is devastated by
dioxin, the most toxic of all chemicals. It did not take 50,000 nuclear
bombs, poised to strike at any moment day and night, for Jeremiah to see
the coming of the primeval waste and void. He saw this in the sixth century
BC as he looked towards the North, the direction from which the
Babylonians would come. He did not say, however, Judah would be
destroyed by the Babylonians. It was from God but through the
Babylonians that the cities would be laid in ruins.

Jeremiah's observation of the critical international situation is related to
his theological conviction that God is impassioned. A God who is
impassioned shows anger. Let me quote lucid words of Heschel:

He [God] is also moved and affected by what happens in the world, and
reacts accordingly. Events and human actions arouse in Him joy or
sorrow, pleasure or wrath. ... Quite obviously in the biblical view, man's

deeds may move Him, affect Him, grieve Him or, on the other hand, gladden and please Him. This notion that God can be intimately affected, that He possesses not merely intelligence and will, but also pathos, basically defines the prophetic consciousness of God.[3]

The central theological assertion is that 'God can be intimately affected'. That is why God may become angry. The wrath of God is not his essence. God is provoked to anger (Jer. 7.17,18). Even in the moment of anger God desires that the anger should be annulled by people's repentance. 'For his anger is but for a moment, and his favour is for a lifetime' (Ps. 30.5). Yet, – no, because of it, – the wrath of God is terrifying. It must not be taken lightly since it is a righteous indignation. It is the moment of true and upright judgment. 'Before his fierce anger' Judah will be demolished because of her unfaithfulness to God. Jerusalem is full of wickedness and violence. 'Be warned, O Jerusalem, lest I be alienated from you; lest I make you a desolation, an uninhabited land' (Jer. 6.8).

Should I then say that the judgment of God came to Japan through the Americans? 'Be warned, O Tokyo, lest I be alienated from you...' The problem I feel is that I cannot 'prove' to my people that Japan was destroyed 'before the fierce anger of the Lord'. It is clear enough that American B29s came in thousands and dropped bombs on our cities. Everyone saw it. But 'the Lord' we did not see. The American planes were visible. The Lord was not.

Our awareness of value in culture and religion is inescapably involved in things visible and invisible. Strangely, humans cannot live meaningfully with that which is visible only, nor with that which is invisible alone. There is something deep within us that responds to the famous passage in the Book of Samuel;

The Lord sees not as man sees; man looks on the outward appearance, but the Lord looks on the heart (I Sam.16.7).

Or to the words of the prophet Joel:

Rend your hearts and not your garments (2.13).

The whole concept of 'the Lord looking on the heart' is invisible to us. When we rend garments everyone will see it immediately, but when we rend our hearts it constitutes an invisible event. Human culture and religion need both 'hearts' and 'garments' in order to construct a sound perspective through which we can examine our life. Do not look only at the 'outward appearance', that is, 'garments'. Look at the 'heart' also. And it is the assertion of the Bible that 'your hearts' should have priority over 'your garments'. It was the Japanese heart that started that destructive war. War originates in the invisible sphere of the mind. A violent mind produces violent history. Therefore, 'rend your hearts and not your garments'.

The relationship between the visible and the invisible characterizes an ambiguity in human culture which no one can escape. We sense that culture is both creative and destructive. It can humanize but it can also dehumanize persons, as does our technological culture. If we could choose to live simply in the visible or the invisible that ambiguity would not exist. Therefore history also is ambiguous. And theology is ambiguous since the most 'problematic' of all that is invisible is 'God'. The biblical affirmation that 'God is Spirit' (John 4.24) decides the character of theology and the way theology looks at history in a fundamental way. No history or theology are free from this painful ambiguity. It is not, however, a blind ambiguity. We are even more aware of the complexity of history when we look at it through our faith in the holy and impassioned God. Apart from this faith we would not be saying with Jeremiah; 'Why does the way of the wicked prosper? Why do all who are treacherous thrive?' (12.1).

In the light of the holy and impassioned God of the Bible, in whom I, as a member of the believing community, trust, I cannot say that it was by the American military might alone that Japan was destroyed. At the same time if Americans were to claim that the United States had acted on behalf of God to execute justice upon earth by destroying Japan, I would feel the name of God had been taken in vain. Japan destroyed herself primarily by her own idolatry. This is my understanding of the situation and this, I find, is congruent with the spirit of the words of Jeremiah; 'before the fierce anger of the Lord'.

In my view it is a positive message that the destruction of Japan had not just military reason but a 'theological' cause. This will give us a mind that is sensitive to the evil of idolatry, and which will resist the paralysing enslavement to idolatry. Idolatry begins in our hearts. It is therefore said by the prophet; 'Rend your hearts and not your garments'. How can I speak about these words of the prophet to my own people who are distanced culturally and religiously from the heritage of the holy and impassioned God? This question takes us to the theme of Part II.

PART II

My Help Comes from the Lord Who Made Heaven and Earth

(Psalm 121.2)

6
Reed-Shoot Culture

Botanical mind is challenged by historical crisis.

'Idolatry' is a simple English word. But what does this word mean to the people of Asia, or in particular, of Japan? The question demands a study of Japanese culture. In what way may the very concept and the critical issues relating to idolatry be presented to the people of Japan today? And in what way has this question a relevance beyond the cultural world of Japan?

A classic image which expresses the spirit of Japanese culture is that of the 'sprouting reed-shoot' (*ashi kabi*). This image is found in the opening section of the *Kojiki* or Records of Ancient Matters, compiled in AD 712.

> Next, when the land was young, resembling floating oil and drifting like a jelly fish, there sprouted forth something like reed-shoots (*ashi kabi*). From these came into existence (from these 'became' deities) Excellent Reed-Shoots Male Deity (*umashi ashi kabi hiko ji no kami*), next, Heavenly Eternal Standing Deity (*ameno tokotachino kami*). These two deities also came into existence as single deities. They have hidden their bodies.[1]

From this beginning the *Kojiki* recites the names of the next seven generations of gods, concluding with the pair of male and female procreative deities; Male-Who-Invites (*Izanagi*) and Female-Who-Invites (*Izanami*).

The land, which was 'young, resembling floating oil and drifting like a jelly fish', was Japan. The mysterious vitality of nature is expressed in the fascinating image of the sprouting reed-shoot. Whether this image was native to Japan or was imported from China, it proved to be meaningful for the Japanese who lived in the mushy 'floating' land. All Japanese gods are basically the *musubi* gods (*musu* – production, procreation, increase; *bi* – spirit) or 'productive spirits'.[2] The reed-shoot is a living image of the productive spirits. Life appears from the mushy land and continues.

Maruyama Masao says that 'Excellent Reed-Shoot Male Deity' summarizes
the basic character of Japanese religion, culture and philosophy of life. The
Japanese world is 'one of constantly becoming. The original image of this
"becoming" is given in the excellent scene of sprouting up of the *ashi kabi*
of *umashi ashi kabi hiko ji* (Excellent Reed-Shoot Male Deity)'.[3]

The cultural spirit that is expressed through the *musubi* gods is that of
'continuity'. According to Maruyama's article there are three words which
are crucial for the Japanese understanding of history. The first is *naru* 'to
appear' and *to become*. History is an expression of the *naru* force. The
second important word is *tsugi* or *tsugi-tsugi* ('next' or 'next-next'). The
Kojiki abounds with the *tsugi-tsugi*. History is made up of 'next-next'
continuity. The concept of *naru* naturally integrates well with the image
tsugi-tsugi. *Tsugi* can mean 'heir' or 'succession'. The imperial family is
said to be co-eternal with the universe by the *tsugi-tsugi* succession. The
preamble of the Constitution of the Empire of Japan begins in this way as
we have noted before:

> Having, by virtue of the glories of Our Ancestors, ascended the Throne
> of a lineal succession unbroken for ages eternal. ...

The third word which is important in Japanese history awareness is *ikioi*.
This word means spiritual force. It implies the influence of happiness,
authority, sovereignty and momentum which together constitute the
spiritual force. The emperor is the *ikioi* person. His personality is replete
with authority and force. Because he embodies the momentum of history
within himself he is sovereign. *Ikioi* contributes to the force that already is
in *naru*. It is the force which propels the *tsugi-tsugi* process. It is the basic
principle of Japanese optimism.

Thus the basic attitude towards history can be expressed, according to
Maruyama, in (1) the *naru* orientation; at the basis of history is the principle
that what exists appears by itself, (2) the *tsugi-tsugi* orientation: that which
appeared will continue by 'next-next', and (3) the *ikioi* orientation: that
which continues will gather momentum from unseen spiritual forces. Thus
Maruyama summarizes the fundamental history awareness of the Japanese
people in the following phrase: *tsugi-tsugi-ni-nari-yuku-ikioi* or 'next-next-
continuously-becoming-by-momentum'. This ancient layer of Japanese
history awareness was, in my view, at work when, in 1941, Japan decided to
go to war against the world powers. It was emotionally and philosophically
hard to believe that the Western powers could disrupt this amazing flow of
historical power described as 'next-next-continuously-becoming-by-
momentum'. Japan is the *ikioi* nation and she will continue.

Motoori Norinaga, the eighteenth-century Japanese scholar, expressed
the *ashi kabi* interpretation of history in his presentation of the ancient layer
of Shinto Thought (*Ko Shinto*, Ancient Way of Gods). According to him

there are two cosmic principles in history; *kichi* (good; the Chinese character used portrays the image of a mouth full of food) and *kyo* (evil; the Chinese character presents a pictorial image of a mouth empty of food). Corresponding to the two cosmic principles are *kichi* gods and the *kyo* gods. Ancient Shinto is confident of the ultimate superiority of the *kichi* gods over the *kyo* gods, of good harvest over famine. The energetic image of the sprouting reed is always hopeful. In fact, the *kyo* exists only as an agent to produce a higher *kichi*, the *kichi* using the *kyo* to enhance itself. This dialectical outlook of optimism is obvious in the *Kojiki* mythology. The primeval deities, Izanagi and Izanami, procreate the universe. This is the positive work of the *kichi*. But this *kichi* process of procreation suddenly, at its height, changes into *kyo*. Izanami gives birth to the fire-god, is burned to death and must go to the underground world. Izanagi, out of his affection for her, follows her to the underground world but in doing this he pollutes himself. This is the height of *kyo*. When he comes out of the underground world he washes himself in the clear stream and becomes clean again. Clean he becomes *kichi*. As he washes his left eye the sun goddess *Amaterasu* (Heaven Illuminating Deity) comes into being. This is the height of a *kichi* period. But the Heaven Illuminating Deity is annoyed by the rude behaviour of her brother god who was born when Izanagi washed his nose. She hides herself in a rock cave and the world is enveloped in utter darkness. This is *kyo*. When *Amaterasu* steps out of the rock cave the light returns to the world again. This is *kichi*. The philosophy behind this process is that the *kyo* is not final. The *kichi* will in the end prevail. History is *kichi* oriented in spite of the *kyo* events.[4]

The ancient Shinto prayer used at the time of the harvest festival reads:

Even with heaven and earth/ Together with the sun and moon/ The people assemble in joy!/ Food and drink is abundant,/ For all generations without end./ Day by day ever more flourishing,/ Until myriads of years hence/ The pleasure will not cease.[5]

These are Japanese words of benediction. When the cosmos (heaven and earth, sun and moon) is friendly, the people will enjoy the abundance of nature's produce, and 'until myriads of years hence, the pleasure will not cease'. Here is a suggestion that abundance is the essence of *kichi* as Chinese character indicates. There is a significant episode in the *Kojiki* in which abundance is salvation. Izanagi travels down to the underworld to see his consort Izanami who died by giving birth to the fire-god. Izanami asks Izanagi not to look at her. When he breaks the ban and looks at her, she curses him and sends her Ugly-Female-of-Underworld to chase him. At the border line between the Land of the Dead and the Land of the Living, Izanami swears that she will destroy a thousand lives every day, to which Izanagi responds with the thought of abundance: 'If you do this, I will in one day set up a thousand and five hundred parturition-houses'.[6]

The Hiroshima experience of 1945 can be seen as the height of the *kyo* which suddenly came to Japan after a long period of what appeared to be continuous *kichi*; victory over China (1895), over Russia (1905), the extensive colonization of Korea (1910–45) and of Formosa (1896–1945). Soon after the defeat Japan was able to pursue a course of miraculous economic recovery that culminated in the festival of Expo 70. This again is *kichi*. The *kyo* may interrupt history; in the end, however, *kichi* will prevail. Can we say, then, that even the experience of Hisoshima and Nagasaki could not change this fundamentally optimistic Japanese faith in the benevolent continuity of history? Has the reed-shoot culture survived the nuclear bombs?

The reed-shoot orientation must be seen in relation to similar basic outlooks of China and India. In pre-Confucian ancient Chinese philosophy, communication between heaven, where the ancestors are, and earth, where we are, was of fundamental philosophical concern. To be human, to use a modern expression, meant to be related to the ancestor-heaven called *dih*. Probably the first cineform for dih was ▽ or ▼ which is the image of the fruit from the tree. The fruit of the tree falls to the ground (downward movement) then begins to grow towards heaven by the life hidden in the fruit (upward movement). The symbolism for the ancestor-heaven contains this dynamism of upward and downward movements.[7] It is imaginatively expressed in a botanical image which makes upward and downward movement between heaven and earth, between the ancestors and the living. Through it all the cosmos continues. There is a strong communication tie between heaven and humanity since heaven is identified as the ancestor.

In the Indian tradition we also find the expression of basic upward and downward movement but the image is that of smoke, which rises, and rain, which comes down. Into this observation of nature the doctrine of rebirths was incorporated. The soul of a person will rise to heaven on the cremation smoke and come down in rain to enter a woman's womb to be born again.[8] Here the doctrine of *karman*, that human action creates invisible energy, is at work in a setting of nature's upward and downward movement. Both in China and India life (fruits, soul) is presented as something that will continue through the unending repetition of upward and downward movement. It is basically a crisis-free continuity which is congruent emotionally and philosophically with the continuity symbolized by the image of the circle. The circle assures continuity.

In Thailand the Buddhist monks talk about the doctrine of *pen eng* (*pen*, to be, *eng*, by itself) which means that all things come to be spontaneously. In the inspiring cosmogonic hymns of the Hindu *Rig Veda* we find the motif of spontaneity expressed in mysterious language:

Neither death nor immortality was there then,
No sign of night or day.
That One breathed, windless, by its own energy
Nought else existed then.[9]

Spontaneity is a sign of full health and happy intention. It signifies an auspicious moment of primordial vitality in the image of upward and downward movement which is basic to botanical life. There is something in the image of the botanical reed-shoot to inspire the Japanese. It must be the sense of vitality and spontaneity. Where there is soil, moisture and warmth there will be botanical life. The most ancient philosophy of China on the spontaneity and continuity expressed in the image of the fruits from trees, and the Vedic hymns of India that sing about water, earth and warmth impress the Japanese as being of basically the same mind as their own.

In the context of spontaneity and continuity of life, the Japanese botanical mind prefers to speak about 'decay' rather than 'the end' or 'destruction'. Reed-shoots come out of the soil, preparing it for the new life to come. The inevitability of decay is acceptable. The botanical mind accepts that spontaneity comes with inevitability, and continuity with decay. Yet all being will continue to be because the cyclical mode of existence is not external to all things, but internal. I must understand myself, for instance, through the image of the sprouting reed-shoot. I go up (upward) and eventually come down (downward) because inevitably I shall decay. But in decaying I prepare the next (*tsugi*) life to go up (upward). I must not contend against this profound truth about myself. This is the emotional and philosophical content of the awareness of history of the Japanese botanical mind: 'Next-next-continuously-becoming-by-momentum'. I call this mind 'botanical' mainly because of its doctrine of the beginning (soil, moisture, warmth) and of the end (going back to soil through decaying). In it the beginning is 'pen eng' spontaneity, and the end is decay-inevitability.

The *ashi kabi* view sees both the meaning and the mystery of history in continuity. Continuity is the fundamental cosmic context in which 'discontinuity' can take place. In fact, the 'tsugi-tsugi' view of history cautions us, whenever we use the 'nervous' word 'discontinuity', to be at least sure what we mean by that. For instance, in what sense can we ever speak about discontinuity at all? Are not all things, whatever they are, interrelated in this world in which we find ourselves? When we want to speak about discontinuity, we should, perhaps, speak of 'discontinuous continuity'. The Christian theologians often emphasize the discontinuity between God and humanity. The *ashi kabi* view of history would suggest that God and humanity are discontinuously continuous, if we cannot say simply continuous. In this context the biblical passage such as Genesis 2.7 becomes extremely intriguing.

> Then the Lord God formed man of dust from the ground, and breathed into his nostrils the breath of life; and man became a living being.

Since the material for the creation of man comes 'from the ground', in terms of 'material' it is clear that God and humanity are discontinuous. We are different in this fundamental sense. We are not an extension of God. But then we are told that we have the breath of life which comes from God, and made us to be authentically human beings. There is a suggestion that 'spiritually' (breath meaning 'wind' and 'spirit') there is some continuity between God and us. The breath of God is within us. The *ashi kabi* culture would at least pose a question here whether we can really speak about a complete discontinuity between God and humanity. Even the very fact that all things are created by God suggests that there may be *some kind of* continuity, though it is not easy to define between the creator and the creature in the context of creation.

The word 'continuity' is an unwelcome word in Judaeo-Christian-Islamic theological tradition. This tradition suggests that continuity-theology is highly dangerous since it can become, at any moment, idolatrous. It warns, in fact, that the idea that God and humanity are continuous is exactly the basic formulation of idolatry. Instead of the concept of continuity we must speak of the presence or deeds of God in history. The God who descends upon Mount Sinai 'in fire' cannot be a God who is continuous with humans. The *ashi kabi* view of history challenges Christian theology when it says that all things are continuous, or at least discontinuously continuous. The *ashi kabi* culture is a cosmological culture. It is nature oriented. Representing, as it does, the primordial emotion of humanity, this outlook cannot be taken lightly.

I would like to make three brief observations about the continuiuty-centred *ashi kabi* mentality. First, a sense of resignation characterizes the *ashi kabi* mentality. There is a difference between the decay of life and the violent destruction of life. Yet the Japanese condemned war criminals who faced execution after the war expressed the botanical sentiment in their statements just before execution. Their testimony shows a remarkable sense of resignation in the face of death. Sakuta Keiichi says of 674 prisoners, that only 68 were unable to find any satisfactory rationalization for their fate.[10] That is to say, about ten percent of the prisoners were not 'reconciled' with death while the rest 'accepted and understood' it. Frequently, even such a sentiment as 'with a smile I shall go!' was expressed. I shall quote here two paragraphs only.

At 10.30 this morning I am going to join the beautiful company of those who have died in the war....Someone must accept the fate and I take it upon myself. I accept death. I have been thinking of the countless war-captives who died and the suffering of the families related to these people. ... (to his daughter) ... Let a dragonfly go as soon as you catch it. Live peacefully respecting the gods and the buddhas.
(a medical lieutenant, aged 41)

Here is one written by a navy lieutenant, executed at age 29.

I have no intention to retaliate or blame anyone. The human being is after all a frail and ephemeral being. ...After several hundred years we will all become like a lump of soil. Then why do we make a great turmoil over trivials? The heaven must be laughing about us. I am grateful that I have had a chance to be born as a son of the Buddhas.

The sentiments expressed in these two paragraphs are representative of the testaments collected. Sakuta classifies four major attitudes which he found in the testaments; (1) death as paying for one's guilt, (2) death as the moment of joining the company of the war-fallen, (3) death as vicarious suffering, and (4) death viewed under the light of eternity. I am not prepared to say at all that these testaments betray a superficial understanding of life and death. What I wish to drive home is that these documents present a different attitude and philosophy from those of Western culture. In the *ashi kabi* culture we hear of guilt, vicarious suffering and eternity, but they are discussed within the tradition and spirit of the *ashi kabi* orientation, just as these themes have been discussed in the West in the light of monotheistic spirituality. Just before their execution they speak about 'freeing a dragonfly' and 'becoming a lump of soil'. There is a subtle suggestion in these images that they are themselves going back to that primeval upward and downward movement.

That which is at the beginning is beyond dispute. The continuity in the image of upward and downward movement is primordial. It is the image of continuity. We should return to this primordial continuity without argument. Without argument? Yes. When we do this it takes the form of resignation. But the contents of it is submersion in the great cosmic continuity. I die, but I live in the cosmic continuity! The cosmos has *ikioi* and it is essentially *kichi*.

Secondly, the continuity oriented *ashi kabi* mentality is not directly involved with the question of true god and false god, and true prophet and false prophet. There is a certain distance between the two. Sprouting reed shoots point to the presence and activity of life. In the *ashi kabi* culture the presence of life is more fundamental and primordial than the discussion about truth and falsehood. The question posed by Martin Luther that 'if our confidence and faith are right, we have right god' is not an immediate problem for the people who live in the *ashi kabi* culture. This culture of continuity does not have a concept of 'the unconditional', the word that appears in Tillich's definition of idolatry. The people who live in this continuity culture find Tillich's warning against 'boosting' intellectually and psychologically difficult to appreciate. The line between the concepts of 'boosting' and 'growing' is confused. If all things are in the upward and downward movement – a cyclical movement – where do we locate the unconditional? If the soil, moisture and warmth point to the mystery of life where do we find the unconditional which can even challenge the mystery of life?

Is it a right god or a right prophet if this god or that prophet maintains and fosters the continuity of life? Should truth be judged in the light of continuity? What is the relationship between ethics and the vitality expressed in the sprouting reed shoots? At this point, what are the dangers involved in the *ashi kabi* cultural outlook? In the time of the emperor cult the continuity of the imperial throne dictated all ethical values. Studies on possible nuclear holocaust tell us that it is completely possible that we can put the final 'discontinuity' to life on this planet by exploding the thousands of nuclear bombs we have in our own hands. Shall we do this in order to uphold the 'right god', 'right ideology', 'right religion' and 'right political system'? Are any of these worth massive destruction to protect? Shall we destroy the half of humanity or even all of humanity – including American humanity – in order to defend American democracy? Is not continuity of life more important than any particular ethical or political value? Yes? No? Both 'continuity' and 'right god and ideology' can become tyranny over humanity. How is it possible to avoid these two types of idolatries which are in truth one?

Thirdly, for the continuity oriented *ashi kabi* mentality the discussion about the beginning and the end is secondary. The beginning and the end must receive their meaning from continuous time, the time in which continuity is maintained, which is located between the beginning and the end. In the image of cyclical history the beginning is the end, and the end the beginning. Therefore, in fact, there is only 'continuity' and no moments of crisis as beginning and end discussions would suggest. At the height of the *kyo*, appears the *kichi*, and also at the height of the *kichi* comes the *kyo*. This arrangement assures continuity and in this scheme crises are controlled by the momentum of continuity.

Sprouting reed shoots give us a botanical image of vitality. It also can suggest a political image of vitality. In the *Kojiki,* and in the subsequent ideological history of Japan, this botanical image has been a hidden political ideological image, and it came back openly during the time of the imperial absolutism in the recent history up to 1945. Japan is uniquely a nation of full vitality, and *consequently*, of full righteousness.

Charged with meaning, myths and symbols are particularly open to misuse. A certain image, such as sprouting reed shoots, can take on ideological significance and become an ideological symbol. Even the image of the Son of God crucified on the cross for the sake of humanity can be misused as an ideological symbol of self-righteousness. This is seen in the traditional attitude of Christians towards the people of other great religious traditions, especially towards the Jewish people. Self-righteousness is a fundamental ingredient of idolatry.

How does the sprouting reed shoots culture deal with what Eliade calls the 'misfortune' and 'terror' of history.[11] Until calamity hits, whether natural or man-made, people may remain happy with the message of the continuity of vitality that the *ashi kabi* image supplies, but what happens to them when misfortune, tragedy and terror come to them? Can the *ashi kabi* view of life and history survive Hiroshima in 1945?

We are moving toward this question. It is now necessary first to explore the cosmological character of Japanese culture.

7

To Dust You Shall Return

Does salvation come to us when we are embraced by
Cosmic Totality?

The Japanese culture assumes the mystery of continuity to be primary over that of discontinuity, *chronos* (gradual time) over *kairos* (critical time), space over time, cosmology (totality image of cosmos) over eschatology (crisis moments in history), curved line over straight line, embrace over confrontation, and to use biblical expressions, 'the house of the Lord' over 'the day of the Lord'. For in the Japanese way of thinking, continuity contains discontinuity; the *kairos* is a hiccup within *chronos,* time is but a servant to space; cosmology is more fundamental than eschatology; curved line is more meaningful than straight line; embrace embraces confrontation; and 'the house of the Lord' is more life-giving than 'the day of the Lord' for the welfare of the people.

Entering Union Theological Seminary, we find ourselves in the rotunda, a space cosmologically designed. There is a feeling of heaven and earth, male and female, and, to use the expression of the people of the Ngaju Dayak of South Borneo, the realm of the hornbill and the watersnake. The spirally ascending staircases are in the image of vines or of the serpent around the cosmic tree. There is a sense of stepping into the womb, into a primordial totality. Union Theological Seminary first embraces its visitors cosmologically, then invites them to square classrooms to discuss God who speaks to us through the thunderous atmosphere. My intuitive reaction to this arrangement is that I would prefer to study the 'God who comes in fire' (Ex. 3.2;19.18) in the cosmological rotunda.

Reed shoots grow in the marshy land. By the time they become old and decay new ones are sprouting with vigour. Their cycle is an eloquent demonstration of the cosmic power of life. Life comes from nature. When we need help, that help will come from 'heaven and earth', from the total vitality of nature. The message of the cosmological rotunda is that salvation comes to us from heaven and earth. It seems to be a simpler and more straightforward position than saying that salvation comes from the Lord who made heaven and earth. Both *kichi* and *kyo* come from 'heaven and earth'. 'The Throne of a lineal succession unbroken for ages eternal' also comes from 'heaven and earth.'

The word 'cosmos' comes from the Greek word *kosmos* which in its original sense expresses the idea of building or establishing. More specifically, it means, 'that which is well assembled or constructed from individual constituents'. There is a strong sense of 'orderliness', 'ordered whole' and 'the order whereby the sum of individual things is gathered into a totality'. The *kosmos* is by nature *kalos* (beautiful, noble, praiseworthy, contributing to salvation). It is *kalos* because it integrates individual things into an ordered totality. This ordered whole is, according to Anaximander, like a perfect *polis* (city, city-state). The orderliness of the cosmos is like the proportions between numbers (Pythagoras), and it corresponds to the character of the *logos*, 'the supreme norm of the thinking and conduct of men' (Heraclitus).

> The mathematical and aesthetic view of the world, which is peculiar to the Greeks, perceives in the *kosmos* the epitome of all order and beauty. In its spherical form and circular movement it is the most perfect and therefore the most beautiful *soma* /body. To contemplate this beauty is bliss. This is expressed e.g., by Euripides when he calls the student blessed who contemplates the never-changing cosmic order of immortal nature.[1]

The cosmos is *kalos*. The ancient Chinese also felt that the cosmos contributes to human salvation. For them what the Greeks meant by cosmos was represented by 'heaven'. It is well to remember that in the Greek tradition also *kosmos* and *ouranos* (heaven) were sometimes interchangeably used. According to Kano, a Japanese scholar on Chinese philosophy, the ancient Chinese has four focal points; ancestors; spiritual beings other than ancestors; the sun, moon, mountain, river and other natural phenomena; and heaven. The concept of heaven is replete with meaning. It represents far more than the physical phenomenon of the vast expanse of sky above us. Heaven is personified as the one who judges what is happening on earth. The fact that sacrifices were offered to heaven supports this observation. The personified heaven is called *dih*. As we have noted before heaven is also the primordial ancestor of all beings, the One through whom all things came into being. 'In the beginning was the heaven. All things were made through it.'! The principle of human morality is embodied in the concept of heaven. The authority to rule over the people is bestowed to rulers by heaven, which itself is the primary deity over all other gods. According to Kano the ideal relationship between subject and ruler, child and parent, wife and husband is also called 'heaven', and food is the 'heaven' of the people without it they cannot live, so it rules with authority over them.

In the documents of the ancient Chou period of Chinese history there appears mention of a religious ceremony directed to the earth. This development must have had a relativising effect on the cult of heaven. Kano thinks that there were at least two reasons for the emergence of earth worship alongside the worship of heaven in the religious documents; first, there appeared in the meantime a philosophical outlook that if heaven was the original principle of human life, the earth must be the concrete manifestation of it; and secondly, there was influence from the current thought which explained all things in terms of the interaction of the female principle (*ying*) and the male principle (*yang*).[2]

The natural world – the totality of nature – is *kalos* whether it comes to us by way of the ordered whole or by way of the image of the benevolent ancestors. The Greek cosmos or the Chinese 'heaven and earth' (*tiandih*) give welfare and peace to the people. 'From whence does my help come?' asks the Psalmist. The aesthetic Greek would respond that the help (blessing) comes from 'contemplating the never-changing cosmic order of immortal nature', and the Chinese would say that it will come from 'heaven and earth', the embodiment of the benevolent ancestor. If 'contemplation' is an important word for the Greeks, then to the practical Chinese 'eating' is certainly one of the central words. 'Heaven and earth' is the space and time that provide food for us. 'My help', then, in the very fundamental sense comes from heaven and earth. Thus understandably 'heaven and earth' is a ritual reality for the Chinese. Worshipfully we are to look at the beauty and productivity of the totality of nature. Such ancient thoughts on heaven and earth have exercised immense influence throughout the centuries upon the Chinese mind.

The philosophical understanding of 'heaven and earth' which originated and developed in China deeply influenced Japanese culture from the seventh century on. 'Heaven and earth' (*ame tsuchi* in Japanese) is both benevolent and resourceful towards humanity. The help we need comes from *ame tsuchi*. It is the image of salvation in which the Japanese mind sees the power that heals and renews decaying reality. While the spiritual world of Mount Sinai says:

> The steadfast love of the Lord never ceases, his mercies never come to an end; they are new every morning; great is thy faithfulness (Lam.3.22, 23).

The world of Mount Fuji expresses its spirituality by changing these lines into the language of heaven and earth.

Ame Tsuchi never ceases, It's mercies never come to an end; It is new every morning, great is its faithfulness.

Nature or natural world (*shizen, Jinen* in Japanese) means, first of all, 'things by themselves', 'as things are from their origin without having had any artificial tampering'. There is a sense of excluding the human touch in order to maintain nature as nature. It is, in this sense, an opposite to the concept of culture. In the ancient usage of the Japanese language it is *shizen* (natural) that a person dies, because when death comes it will exclude all human effort to prolong life. Prolongation of life by means of medical and technological devices is not 'natural', it is 'cultural'.

The infusion of the higher civilization of the Asian continent gave Japan a new perspective for the appreciation of the world of nature beyond that of the old animistic approach. Countless poems in *Manyoshu* (a collection of more than four thousand poems from seventh- and eighth-century Japan) that sing of the beauty of nature indicate a freedom of spirit that has burst through the confines of animism. Their authors saw beauty, purity and noble spiritual qualities in nature. The sight of nature never tired their eyes. Here is a poem by Kakinomoto Hitomaro 'on an imperial visit to the Pleasure-palace of Yoshino'.

> Though, in the Land where rules our Sovereign
> The provinces are many,
> She loves, in Yoshino, the field of Akitsu,
> Encircled by clear streams and towering mountains,
> Where cherry-flowers fall,
> And there she has reared herself
> A mighty-pillared palace.
> Here the courtiers row their barges
> Side by side across the morning waters,
> And race upon the evening stream.
> Endless as this river flows,
> Lofty as these mountains,
> Will it stand for aye,
> And never tire my eyes,
> This palace by the stream.[3]

'Clear streams and towering mountains' will 'never tire my eyes'. With these simple words the *Manyoshu* expressed the fundamental Japanese attitude towards the nature, according to Ienaga Saburo.[4] From this tradition of the appreciation of nature in *Manyoshu* developed, according to Ienaga, the sentiment that nature can heal our mental and spiritual ills. This ancient appreciation of nature by Japanese people, further inspired by the similar Chinese conviction that the beauty of rivers and mountains has healing effects, has continued throughout Japanese history. 'This world is a not easy place to enjoy our life,' says Natsume Soseki, one of the greatest recent writers of Japan, 'and therefore we must try to make pleasant, and that is the mission of arts. But in order to do so we must take distance from the world of people and submerge into the world of nature which is the only place able to heal human suffering'.[5] Cosmos is *kalos* indeed. The rotunda has more healing effect than square shaped classroom.

The Buddhist monk Saigyo (1118-90) stands out as a prominent figure in the history of the Japanese appreciation of salvation in nature. Ienaga suggests that Saigyo found his salvation not in the discipline of Buddhist life, but in deepening his appreciation of the beauty and healing presence of nature. 'For him nature has acquired the same prestige and power as gods and buddhas, and yearning after nature has assumed religious character'.[6] When people renounce 'this world of suffering' where do they go? They go to the mountain and there they build a small simple hut for themselves, and stay there in the bosom of mother nature. Thus not a small number of people escaped this world and stayed in 'mountain huts', Saigyo did exactly this. According to Ienaga, this idea of escaping to a solitary mountain hut as an act of seeking one's own salvation is influenced by Chinese and Buddhist thoughts.

Chinese people certainly had a spiritual capacity to appreciate the beauty of nature and found solace in it. But in their delight of nature they remained practical, never allowing themselves to submerge into the depth of nature with religious devotion as the Japanese did. They indicated their gratitude to nature for giving them the rational principles by which they can live a better life. In China nature was 'used' in the practice of living and even of politics. The basic Chinese idea of making a contrast between the world of nature and the world of people, and giving the priority to the former over the latter, has influenced the Japanese tradition in general. The subtle but decisive difference between the Japanese and Chinese appreciation of nature is that the former is that of utter devotion, while the latter looks at nature from the practical needs of life.

Buddhist thought also has exercised influence upon the Japanese spirituality about seeking salvation in life in a mountain hut. From the beginning Buddhism taught of the great spiritual value of leaving 'this world' behind and going into a life of renunciation. This usually took the monk to isolated places, such as mountains or forests. To seek one's own salvation in isolation is actually against the spirit of Mahayana Buddhism, which purports to be a great (*maha*) vehicle (*yana*) to carry many to salvation. Yet, the great Japanese Buddhist monks such as Saicho (767–822) and Kukai (774–835) have left a strong impression upon subsequent Buddhist spirituality of the positive value of having spiritual and intellectual discipline in mountains. In the course of time, then, in the Japanese Buddhist mind there was created a kind of union between the way of the

Buddha and the way of the beauty of nature. They are unified in the level of inspiration, and the monks have come to accept that the inspiration they receive from the beauty of nature will expedite their achievement of *nirvana*, the salvation of Complete Detachment. Saigyo was a man intoxicated by the beauty of nature. His 'rationalization' would have been that the beauty of nature in the mountain is conducive to reaching the *nirvana*. There was no tension between the two inspirations; one from the Buddha, the other from nature.

Can the solitary life in the mountain, though replete with the abundance of nature's beauty satisfy the deep need one feels in the depth of one's soul? Ienaga suggests that even Saigyo was not able to find complete peace in his soul. He could not deny that his soul was missing his loved one who was still 'in the world'. Then what should one do? Stay in mountain? It would be too lonely. Go back to the world? No. That is the place that one has just renounced. Where should one go? According to Ienaga the Japanese mind solved this problem by simply accepting this dilemma. Life with nature is lonely but because of its loneliness, it has exerted a special fascination. This fascination has given pleasure and religious satisfaction. The aesthetic appreciation of nature was a kind of salvation for the people. Ienaga suggests that Saigyo is representative of this tradition.

According to Ienaga the tradition of the mountain hut was developed further in the tea ceremony room as Japan began to receive the influence of Zen Buddhism. The tea ceremony room was designed and built to look as if it is deep in the mountains. A remarkable wealth of creative art in painting nature was produced by the Zen tea ceremony tradition. The renowned Japanese *haiku* poet Matsuo Basho (1644–94) comes from this aesthetic Zen tradition of the tea ceremony room.

One of the well known *kaiku* of Basho reads:

Old pond/ Frog plunge/ Water sound.

A quiet pond in the compound of an old temple somewhere in the mountain side. A soft breeze gently moves the aged pine trees. By the pond the rocks of all sizes are covered with ancient moss. Tranquillity. A frog squats motionless by the pond. Suddenly, of its own accord the frog makes a solitary jump into the pond, ...plop! ... a small sound in the briefest moment enhances the quietude of the surroundings. All is again quickly invaded by peace and tranquillity. The frog has disappeared into the water. It is now embraced by the cosmic sea of the bosom of heaven and earth, silently and without words. It is a symbol full of wisdom for the human search for salvation in the undisturbed totality of mother nature. Totality does not speak. It does not argue, nor does it seek to prove. Rather it is ready to embrace us. Basho speaks with Saigyo and further back with

Saicho, Kukai and the poets of the *Manyōshū* that when we see the warm embrace of nature our eyes never tired.

'Heaven and earth' is not a totality created by One who is beyond it. The gods and buddhas are within heaven and earth. This position is neither atheistic nor humanistic. It does not define itself in philosophical terms. It is quite free from such arguments. It simply states the feeling of salvation we have when we are embraced by the totality of nature, 'heaven and earth'. This feeling is not concerned with scientific preciseness. It is poetic rather than propositional. It does not seek to understand the social existence of humanity in terms of social analysis and criticism. In the perspective of this 'plop spirituality' sociological and theological debates disappear as we ourselves disappear into the bosom of the cosmic embrace. 'My help comes from nature.'

The word 'totality' is used here in a symbolic, not a scientific sense. The symbol of totality has a healing effect upon the human soul. It can give us our needed self-identity, showing us where we are between creation and destruction, life and death, and good and evil. The words 'heaven and earth' carry a therapeutic message because it will give us an image of 'all things'. Nature surrounds us. We come from nature and we go back to nature. The well-known Dancing Shiva (*Nataraja*) of India is another expression of the philosophy of totality as salvation. Shiva has four arms. The upper right hand carries a drum. This 'connotes Sound, the vehicle of speech, the conveyer of revelation, tradition, incantation, magic and divine truth'.[7] It is a symbol of the activity of life. The upper left hand holds a flame which signifies destruction. Thus in the pair of upper hands we see creation (drum) and destruction (fire). The second right hand shows the 'fear not' gesture (*abhayamudra*) and the second left hand points to the foot which signifies release. Shiva engages in the cosmic dance of creation, maintenance and destruction.

> The cyclic rhythm, flowing on and on in the unstayable, irreversible round of the Mahayugas, or Great Eons, is marked by the beating and stamping of the Master's heels. But the face remains, meanwhile, in sovereign calm. Steeped in quietude, the enigmatic mask resides above the whirl of the four resilient arms, cares nothing for the superb legs as they beat out the tempo of the world ages. Aloof, in sovereign silence, the mask of the god's eternal essence remains unaffected by the tremendous display of his own energy, the world and its progress, the flow and the changes of time.[8]

In his cosmic dance the dancing god embodies the opposites, thus assuring us that the world will never come to an end. Death cannot stop this dance since death itself is being danced together with life. This is the secret of the mysterious 'sovereign calm' – corresponding to the plop sound made by a frog – on the face of the dancing Shiva. The symbol of totality maintains a sovereign calm. This symbol fascinates our souls. As we contemplate the drama of the duality of life and death, creation and destruction, and acceptance and rejection from the position of 'sovereign calm' we achieve the salvation of our souls. This sovereignty is not with 'the Lord who made heaven and earth' but inside of the dance of nature's totality. As the frog disappeared into the water of the pond, our souls make a transition from the realm of the affected to the unaffected.

There is a striking Hindu image called *Harihara*. *Hari* is a popular name for Vishnu. *Hara* represents 'he who takes away', Shiva. In this image half of the body expresses Vishnu (creation) and the other half Shiva (destruction). It symbolizes 'mutually antagonistic principles whose perennial conflict is perennial harmony'.[9] Only cosmos, with its own magnanimity can produce a situation in which 'perennial conflict is perennial harmony'. In the 'old pond' the perennial conflict is perennial harmony, the 'sovereign calm' which, with differing cultural accents, the Indians, Chinese and Japanese and other nature-oriented Asians have found to be 'contributing to salvation'.

Hans Schärer tells us that the Ngajus, South Borneo uplanders, have a profound cosmological and psychological understanding of their living environment as meaningful totality. The Ngajus divide the world into two realms; the upperworld of the hornbill and the underworld of the watersnake. Primeval mountain, sun, west, upstream, good spirit and life belong to the upperworld of the hornbill. Primeval waters, moon, east, downstream, evil spirit and death belong to the underworld of the watersnake. 'Hornbill' and 'watersnake' together constitute the totality of the cosmological and psychological life of the Ngajus. Yet they are free to look at the hornbill and watersnake as separate principles of their total experience. Together they make a totality and each, by itself can also make a totality.[10] Here it seems that perennial conflict is perennial harmony. This freedom to appreciate the possibility of both or the single as totality is a 'calm' psychological principle. The totality symbol of nature is abundantly embracing. The people of Borneo and the people of the poet Basho share the sense of finding salvation in the totality of nature.

We search for our self-identity. The image of the Dancing Shiva may give this needed self-identity to us. The World Period is moving on from one stage to another as he dances with cosmic beat. We are somewhere in the period between creation and destruction. The Great Cycle goes on. The master of the universe is unaffected. The vision of the face of sovereign calm is the ultimate mystical identity we may possibly attain if our soul is attuned to such symbolic presentation of the cosmic life and cosmic totality. It is only natural that we humans establish our identity within the framework of the nature that surrounds us and embraces us. Saigyo found that more than Buddhist *dharma* (doctrine, teaching), the fascinating beauty of nature has given him inner peace. Since we live within the natural environment of the ordered cosmos we feel 'at rest' somewhere in the depth of our being when we are embraced by the symbol of the totality of heaven and earth. Heaven and earth, as I have noted before, can only embrace us intuitively, poetically and symbolically. One of the inspiring spiritual traditions of this symbolical embrace is given to the Asians in the image of the face of sovereign calm which means, in philosophical language, 'perennial conflict is perennial harmony'.

The words that appear in the opening section of Augustine's *Confessions* '...because you made us for yourself and our hearts find no peace until they rest in you'. [11] are a sharp contrast to the teaching that we can find peace for our hearts in nature. To seek rest in a Creator God is a theological orientation. This seems an unnecessarily complicated arrangement to people of the 'plop outlook'. The words of Augustine stand in the tradition of Psalm 121.2, 'My help comes from the Lord who made heaven and earth'. I believe that this one line from the ancient Psalms expresses one great spiritual pilgrimage and history of humanity. At the same time, however, I acknowledge that the tradition that says 'my help comes from heaven and earth' has a significant spiritual pilgrimage and history throughout centuries of human civilization. And both of them have been used and misused, creative and destructive depending upon our own 'faith and confidence'. Those who said that 'my help comes from the Lord who made heaven and earth' have fallen to idolatry as often perhaps as those who have said that 'my help comes from heaven and earth'. We shall take up this discussion later.

Psalm 121 speaks confidently about the Lord of heaven and earth. The symbol of totality of heaven and earth cannot claim finality for itself. There is, as it were, one 'Higher Being' than heaven and earth. This disturbing element – to the people of the embrace of nature – is the Creator God. This God has sovereignty over the whole world of nature. This God utters the words that would change human relationship with the world of nature:

> ...cursed is the ground because of you; in toil you shall eat of it all the days of your life; thorns and thistles it shall bring forth to you; and you shall eat the plants of the field. In the sweat of your face you shall eat bread till you return to the ground for out of it you were taken; you are dust, and to dust you shall return (Gen. 3.17–19).

Because of human sin 'a cleft, a mutual recalcitrance' now comes between man and earth. [12]

> Man was taken from the earth and so was directed to it; she was the material basis of his existence; a solidarity of creation existed between

man and the ground. But a break occurred in this affectionate relationship, an alienation that expresses itself in a silent, dogged struggle between man and soil.[13]

'In the sweat of your face you shall eat bread'. This is a universal predicament of humanity. The history of Japanese agricultural harvests would, no doubt, substantiate these words of Genesis. Therefore, there have been many agriculture related gods (*kami*) in Japan, as in other countries, and people have sought protection and abundance of harvest from them. But Japan has lived many centuries without these 'theological' words about the 'break occurred in this affectionate relationship'. In ancient China and, from its influence, in Japan, people have believed that if anything goes against agricultural welfare, such as flood or drought, it must be caused by the personal failure of the emperor in his moral and liturgical life. The emperor's 'sin' can cause alienation between man and soil. This is said and thought, however, within the thought world of the totality of the cosmos. The Chinese cultural and religious context is different from those of the Bible that can speak strong 'theological' words. The Chinese emperor was a liturgical person who stood at the centre of the cosmos, who, by conducting a certain solemn cosmological liturgy, assured the regular and benevolent movement of the universe for the welfare of his people. He was a cosmological symbol within the cosmological totality. In this sense he stood in the tradition of 'my help comes from heaven and earth'.

The people of the cosmological culture find it difficult to accept that the ground can be cursed because of people. The ground (heaven and earth) can be offended by violent and immoral acts of people, but it can always be cured by the performance of liturgy in the names of cosmological gods. The Japanese gods will not curse the ground of which they are a part as they are of nature. To suggest that the ground is cursed because of human evil is too anthropocentric an idea for the people of the cosmic totality.

> For a memento of my existence
> What shall I leave (I need not leave anything)
> Flowers in the spring, cuckoos in the summer
> and maple leaves in the autumn.[14]

The monk Ryokan (1758–1831) composed this poem on his deathbed. In a moving way these lines indicate a far less anthropocentric sentiment about human life. As he lay dying he expressed his deep feeling for the beauty of nature that had enriched his life. Even though he goes, these inspiring touches of nature will stay. 'Flowers in the spring, cuckoos in the summer, and maple leaves in the autumn.' Out of such beautiful nature we come and we shall return to the same nature that will receive us again. As long as nature is there, we will never become, live or dead, 'homeless'. In the view of the nature oriented people an anthropocentric view of nature is a 'nervous' one and may threaten us with the danger of becoming homeless.

In the biblical tradition humans become centrally important because the word of God comes to them. The centrality of the word of God gives centrality to humans. The words; 'you are dust, and to dust you shall return' are acceptable and comforting for the people who say 'my help comes from heaven and earth'. The only disturbing things about it is that it is said not by nature but by God the creator of heaven and earth. In the context of salvation by heaven and earth we can come to say these words too. But the fact that it is said by Some One who is 'greater' than nature is an essential part of the biblical message. As long as these words of God come to us, though we are dust and destined to go back to dust, we are centrally important. We are somehow different from nature in the depth of our being. In fact, if there were no difference at all, how could we humans come to a special appreciation of nature at all? Yet the sentiment expressed by the monk Ryokan remains to be meaningful even today among the Japanese people. The anthropocentric view of nature is not preferred throughout the history of mountain hut to tea ceremony room or to the Japanese poetic imagination and expressions in recent times.

Have Japanese people, in truth, found salvation in heaven and earth? This is a critical question to pose not only to the Japanese but to all peoples who, more or less, live with 'faith in nature'. Have they experienced salvation in nature? When they heard nature saying to them 'You are dust, and to dust you shall return', was this a part of their salvation? Did it really make them feel that they are not abandoned or threatened or homeless? 'My help comes from heaven and earth'. Can this truly meet the spiritual need of the Japanese people?

Ienaga asks this question as he concludes his article from which I have already quoted. He writes:

> Indeed nature has meant healing to the spiritual yearning and suffering of the Japanese people. Was this salvation, however, a perfect salvation? Was the life in the spiritual culture of mountain hut able to eliminate all human spiritual darkness? Here we must acknowledge that this unique Japanese religious life has a decisive limitation.[15]

Ienaga sees, in his extensive and erudite study of the subject, that in the depth of Japanese soul, there is a realization that there is something in and about being human that nature cannot satisfy. One may take abode deep in the mountain, but still the question of human darkness (*avidya*, Sanskrit) and death will be with them. There is no way whatsoever to escape from it. The human problem follows the person as a shadow follows it's body. Even with Saigyo, Ienaga suggests, it may be doubted whether he found complete salvation in the retreat into the mountains. Out of the tradition represented by Saigyo, however, has come a religious attitude that takes up the problems of human existence in a straightfoward and intensive fashion. This is the movement that has understood the noble aspiration and also the limitation of the way of Saigyo, the movement of Honen and Shinran of which I shall deal later. The religious awareness of limitation in obtaining salvation from the aesthetic approach to nature is a precious cultural experience in the spiritual history of Japanese people. It is wrong then to say that Japanese culture has never experienced moments of negation.

I find the experience of moments of negation to be important for defining the character of culture, therefore I present here, in a brief summary form, the classic discussion on the subject produced by Ienaga. Ancient Japanese thought lacked the concept of negation. (This observation can be confirmed by Maruyama's remarkable phraseology; 'next-next-continuously-becoming-by-momentum', or Motoori's *kichi* centred view of history as we have seen.) The concept of negation came to Japan with Buddhism, through the person of Prince Shotoku when he said *Seken Koke, Yui Butsu Zeshin*, or 'This World is Illusory. Only the Buddha is Real'. This was a completely new idea for the Japanese people. This world must be negated in order to reach the real world. The affirmation of the Buddha must be reached through the negation of this world. By going through the gate of negation one reaches the absolute world of religious truth. The negation that Prince Shotoku expressed carries of course, a notion of 'discontinuity' which is both new and disruptive to the fundamentally optimistic Japanese mind. When this world is perceived as illusory and the Buddha is held to be real and trustworthy, then there is a 'discontinuity' between the two. In the thirteenth century the religious movement of Honen and Shinran emphasized human depravity and Buddha's mercy. Through their preaching people were again brought to face the moment of negation, though the aristocrats of the time were busy in building a model of pure land in their own gardens and thus 'ensure' while they were alive the entry to the Buddha's land. Such an attitude in the ruling class evades facing up to the negation.

Ienaga singles out the decline of the powerful Heike Clan in the end of the twelfth century as an event that impressed upon people the transitoriness of the glory of the rulers. It occasioned a reflective moment among the people which saw beyond sociological and military events to the issue of fundamental human anxiety and transitoriness. In brief, the people experienced historically what Prince Shotoku had confessed six centuries earlier.

The monk Genshin of the earlier century had left a strong impression with his book *Ojō Yo Shū* (The Essentials of Salvation) written in 985, describing most graphically the gruesome torment and torturing scenes of

hell. There people agonize and convulse with the most extreme and
excruciating pains. Genshin's aim in this book was to arouse in the minds of
the readers a loathing of this world. Ienaga observes that such frightful
description of hell was impossible had there not been a psychological
preparation, a way of looking at human existence from the angle of
negation. An awareness of the ugly or depraved side of human life. He
points out that Genshin's work presents the first radical antithesis to the
traditional Japanese way of looking at the world through beauty, health
and benediction; 'until myriads of years hence, the pleasure will not cease'.
Ienaga's articles are illuminating for our subject. He points out from his
scrupulous historical studies, the limitation of 'nature salvation'.[16]

The subject of 'negation' will be dealt with further in chapter 13 under
the title of 'The Coming of Universal Civilizations' as they express their
messages through persons like Prince Shotoku, Honen and Shinran. Both
Honen and Shinran preached that the moment we realize our own depravity
is the very moment in which the Buddha will embrace us with his infinite
mercy. This insight of the 'simultaneity' of penitence and grace points to a
new and unusual depth of Japanese religious experience.

Thus ancient Japanese thought did not know the concept of 'negation'. It
comes into Japan through Buddhism. The history of Japanese religion,
however, shows how persistent is the power of *ashi kabi* mentality over
against the Buddhist suggestion of the negation of this world. In general,
one may say that medieval Japan acquainted herself with 'negation'
through historical events of war and destruction and through religious
teaching. During the long Edo period of about two hundred and sixty years
up to the middle of the nineteenth century the philosophy and religious
understanding of 'negation' was neglected until the coming of Western
thought in a massive way during the last hundred years. Ienaga questions,
however, whether the thought on negation that came to Japan from the
West in recent years has been able to criticize the ills that modernization has
brought to Japan and to the world.[17]

I concur with Ienaga about his reservation on the thought of negation
that came from the West. This theme, of course, begs innumerable
questions because of a great historical complexity of the time. I may
highlight, however, a tension that exists today between Japan as an
advanced technological industrial nation and Japan as a lover of nature.
There is a strong view that disregards ecological integrity of nature for the
sake of the nation's economic thrust. What does Christianity – through its
message of negation – say to the Japan that lives in a serious contradiction
today? What kind of dialogue is possible between negation taught by
Buddhism and by Christianity if such dialogue take place in today's Japan?
What would it say to the important themes of modernization, economic
pursuit, human value and world peace?

...you return to the ground for out of it you were taken; you are dust, and to dust you shall return (Gen. 3.19).

We will all go back to dust. Indeed *Seken Koke*, 'this world is illusory', in the words of Prince Shotoku. But it is not 'dust' telling us that we will go back to dust. It is God who is telling us so. God is not *koke*, unreal and empty. Prince Shotoku did not say that all is *koke*. The teaching of the Buddha is not *koke*. Generations may pass away, but the words of the Buddha will stay meaningful to humanity. Prince Shotoku did not preach nihilism. There is a magnificent dialectic in his saying: 'this world is unreal, but the Buddha is real'. The first part must be understood in the light of the second part. There is some similarity in form then between this biblical saying and Prince Shotoku's dictim. We are to understand our going back to dust in the light of the Real Being, the Creator God. Then our going back to dust does not become a piece of nihilistic philosophy.

The Creator God affirms us and this world. But this affirmation is not a simple affirmation but one that goes through the moment of judgment, of negation. The affirmation of God contains negation. The love of God involves judgment. This points to the way of God's experience of history as suggested by the theology of Abraham Heschel. That God's affirmation involves negation is expressed in the words of the Psalm we have quoted; 'Help comes from the Lord who made heaven and earth.' This Lord affirms heaven and earth, but not without judgment (negation). That help comes from this God is not an easy-going affirmation. It is a critical affirmation. This critical affirmation is the help we need for our personal, community, national, international and civilizational life. The philosophy or religion of easy going affirmation invites self-righteousness which is the essence of idolatry.

Those who live according to the culture of 'my help comes from heaven and earth' also encounter their style of 'negation'. There remains doubt in their minds if indeed heaven and earth can give them a satisfactory salvation or not. But this negation is different in kind from the negation expressed in the biblical theology. There is no way to 'prove' that the negation the nature oriented people encounter is a 'false' one. It is meaningful for them.

The Bible refuses to say that this world is *koke*, since it is this world that God loves. When it says, however, that the world is not *koke* it is not saying so endorsing the *ashi kabi* view of continuity and the *kichi* optimism. Rather, the world is not *koke* because it is the object of the love of the impassioned God.

'To dust you shall return.' Though this saying has a comforting message to the *ashi kabi* people, it is a theological, not a cosmological saying. It makes the same affirmation as the words of the Psalm which says: 'my help comes from the Lord who made heaven and earth'.

When we say that 'my help comes from heaven and earth' we necessarily form symbolism of the centre of salvation within nature. Interpretation of centre symbolism in relation to cosmologically defined salvation is an urgent task. From the concept of the totality of nature we move on to a centre symbolism of nature. This is the theme of the next chapter.

8

Centre - Cosmological and Ideological

Idolatry as a misuse of Centre Symbolism

Mountains have always held religious significance for people. Towering, mysterious, dangerous, overwhelming, some parts always appearing bright and visible while others are shrouded in perpetual shadow, they are thought to be the abode of the spirits, demons and gods. Often the mountain itself is identified as a god, as was Mount Miwa in Nara Prefecture in Japan. In mythical systems of thought the mountain is thought to be the connection between earth and heaven, the centre of the world, *axis mundi*. Particular mountains have been endowed with the character of representing the entire universe, the cosmic mountain. 'In China the capital of the perfect sovereign stood at the exact centre of the universe, that is, at the summit of the cosmic mountain.'[1] The religious significance the Himalayas played in Hindu religious thought is substantial. The image of the mountain as *axis mundi* has inspired some of the most refined and impressive religious buildings of humankind, such as the hill temple of Borobodur in Java and the famous Angor Wat in Cambodia. They are cosmic mountains elaborated by religious symbolism.

In Japan since ancient times people have believed that the spirits of the departed reside on the mountains overlooking the villages, watching over their welfare. Eventually those spirits will become gods of the mountain, staying in the mountain during the winter months and coming out to the village from spring to autumn to help the villagers work in the rice paddy field. At a time of drought prayer is offered to the mountain. Graveyards are naturally located on the mountain. One name for a funeral procession is *yamayuki*, 'going to the mountain'. A certain part of the mountain, always dark, is understood to be the location of 'hell' and another part, which appears brighter and happier, is the place of 'heaven'. Thus the mountain itself suggests the totalities of light and darkness, life and death, salvation and damnation. The mountain must always be approached carefully and with awe.

Japanese veneration of the mountain goes back as far as the ancient Jomon period. This veneration of mountain as god or as the abode of spirits was amalgamated with the Chinese Way of Ying and Yang and also with esoteric Buddhism. The legendary founder of *Shugendo*, the Japanese way of reaching salvation by practising spiritual exercise in the mountain, was called En no Ozunu who lived in the seventh century. In the Heian period (tenth to twelfth century) mountain veneration prospered increasing the number of the practitioners of the *Shugendo*. The practitioners of the *Shugendo* were called *yamabushi* because they practised a ritual in which they are to receive the spiritual force of the mountain (*yama*) contacting it through lying (*bushi*) on the ground. With the spiritual force of the mountain, and the ability to perform some esoteric religious rituals, they were thought to be able to perform superhuman magic. People thought their prayers to be especially meritorious and flocked to them whenever they toured through the villages and population centres. At the core of *Shugendo* was a religious fascination for the mountain as god or as the abode of the spirits. When Chinese cosmological speculation and a complicated ritual of esoteric Buddhism are added to this mountain reverence it has become by itself a complex religious phenomenon. The *Shugendo's* main motivation of going into the mountain was to acquire supernatural magical power by engaging in special spiritual and physical exercises. *Shugendo* must be seen as a different phenomenon from the retreat into the mountain to seek personal salvation in the beauty of nature which was discussed in the previous chapter.

A number of mountains in Japan have become centres of *Shugendo* during the long centuries since the tenth century. One of these is the mountain cult centred about Mount Fuji. The name of Hasegawa Kakugyo (1541–1646) is associated with Mount Fuji as the one who opened up the mountain for religious purposes. Kakugyo was the founder and organizer of Fuji-Ko, the Mount Fuji Devotional Association. He taught that the god of Mount Fuji called *Sengen Dainichi*, is the creator of all things, and that those who believe in this god will live a long and happy life. In the middle of the Edo period the outstanding leader of Fuji-Ko was Jikigyo Miroku (1671–1773). He became a devotee to the god of Mount Fuji when he was seventeen years old, from that time climbing the mountain once a year to deepen his devotion to the god of Mount Fuji. In 1771 he became the head of the Fuji-Ko movement. He published his own 'Theology of Mount Fuji God' in 1729 in which he said that the god of Mount Fuji is the giver of all good things, including the rice harvest. His message to the people who were not engaged in agriculture was also positive. Faith in this god of Mount Fuji would make people honest and diligent, he said, and consequently they would become happy and rich, and live a long life.[2] What he said bears a strange similarity to the view expressed by the social scientist Max Weber about Protestant ethics and capitalism.

Fuji-Ko and Shugendo share the basic psychology of mountain veneration, but *Shugendo* is a way for specialists (*yamabushi*) while Fuji-Ko and many other such mountain devotional associations are people's movements. For them mountains have become their objects of religious devotion. The Fuji-Ko movement became a very popular cult in the Edo period. The name 'Miroku' of the leader of Fuji-Ko, Jikigyo Miroku, is Japanese transliteration of the Sanskrit word *Maitreya*, the name given to the future saviour Buddha who is to come from his present abode in the highest heaven to save all who failed to reach salvation through the work of Gotama Buddha. This Miroku future buddha will come, according to the doctrine, 5,670 million years after the demise of the historical Buddha. Jikigyo proclaimed the coming of the Miroku era by naming himself Miroku in 1731. Disappointed that the rulers of the time were not listening to his message of the new era of salvation, he climbed Mount Fuji in 1733, went into a month long fast and died. During his time of fasting he gave oral instruction about Fuji-Ko and the Miroku era to his followers. These words were compiled and called 'Words During the Last 31 Days'. Fuji-Ko prospered rapidly after his death. People in thousands began climbing Mount Fuji. From the middle of the eighteenth century the Tokugawa Shogunate began to be uneasy about the social popularity of Fuji-Ko movement. Their concern was that Fuji-Ko's 'theology' was not quite like the familiar Shinto, Confucianism and Buddhism. They feared that this new doctrine, which they could not quite place under any of these three traditional religions, might trigger social unrest. The political power of the day thus began to suppress the Miroku movement of the people.

According to Jikigyo Miroku, world history is divided into three sections:

> First 6000 years is under the rule of Precious Parents, next 12000 is god's period, and the last 30000 is the Miroku period.[3]

Human history is then in all 48000 years long. According to Jikigyo Precious Parents are male and female productive gods who appeared from the womb of Mount Fuji when the whole world was still an ocean of mud. The Parents gave birth to the god of Mount Fuji, *Sengen Dainichi* and therefore they possess supreme authority. They produced human beings and rice from their own body. The direct rule by the Parents continued for the first 6000 years.

In the period of the gods the Parents delegated authority to *Amaterasu*, Heaven Illuminating Deity. At this moment Japan became a 'divine' nation. There is some indication that Jikigyo did not attribute much prestige to *Amaterasu*. The Deity was only a servant to the Parents. All kinds of gods and buddhas came into being in the era of the gods, but they were only products of the human mind. Jikigyo suggests that the alienation between humankind and the Parents took place because people increased their devotion to the gods and buddhas which their minds had produced. In the Miroku period, however, *Sengen Dainichi* himself will rule the world. This period will be as excellent as the time under the rule of the Parents. In this period people will not believe in gods and buddhas out of the motivation of getting benefits for themselves. In contrast, Jikigyo said, in the Miroku period one person will help another person. For him this was the supreme task of the political system. Elaborating this new social ethics of neighbourly help, Jikigyo implied his criticism of the Tokugawa Shogunate.

We do not find a cyclical view of history in the thought of Jikigyo and his followers. The period of gods is placed between two excellent periods; that of the Parents and that of the Miroku. The period of the Parents is not identical with the period of Miroku. The Miroku period involves human decision and dedication to a social ethics based on the practice of neighbourly mutual help. Jikigyo's group was concerned about social betterment. Out of the general veneration of the mountain – the mountain cult – came this system of social ethics. What a combination between the Precious Parents born of the womb of Mount Fuji and an ethics of mutual help! This is one of the remarkable cases of the appearance of a 'liberation theology' in the religious history of Japan. In my view, it was the ethical emphasis which prevented this group from seeing history in terms of cyclical movement. Mount Fuji has its own right 'theology' which said something important to the people at that time.

Miyata Noboru, the Japanese scholar in popular religions of Japan, points out the fertility cult character of Fuji-Ko.[4] Jikigyo and his followers placed emphasis upon the importance of harmony of man and woman, male principle and female principle in the cosmos. In 1832, at the time that Fuji-Ko was in ascendancy, a book appeared by a certain man, Miyao Sadao, called *Onyo Shinseki Zu* or Diagram of the Ying-Yang Divine Stone, in which he described in detail the customs and beliefs observed by the rural people of his time. It was looked upon as the first scholarly work on the subject of religious faith and sexual fertility in Japan. It speaks of the veneration of sexual organs as an important part of the mountain cult. The view maintained is that perfect sexual harmony and productivity symbolize the era of the Miroku.

Finally Shibata Hanamori (1809–80) of Fuji-Ko combined the teaching of mountain veneration with the nationalistic emperor–cult. According to Hanamori, Mount Fuji is the foundation of the security of the nation and the brain of the whole earth. His nationalistic veneration of Mount Fuji has exercised a strong influence upon the emperor cult which had just begun towards the end of his life. Mount Fuji was seen as the primeval womb and the brain of the whole earth. Through this cult the new era of salvation of humankind, 'Era of Sunrise and the Pine Tree', in the words of Ito

Rokurobei (1829–94), a leader of Fuji-Ko, would come.[5]

Mount Fuji is a mountain of complex religious and psychological elements extending from simple mountain veneration to a view of history and from social ethics to a fertility cult and to political ideology. In this mountain the Japanese people found a chance to express, among other possibilities, their religious originality.

The religious history of Mount Fuji demonstrates the differences between the world of Mount Fuji and that of Mount Sinai. Mount Fuji is said to be the womb of the primal pair-gods, the brain of the world, the sacred place of the harmony of sexes, and the symbol of the new Miroku era. Mount Fuji is *axis mundi*. There is no such 'veneration' attached to Mount Sinai itself. No one speaks about the 'great spirit' the 'womb' or the 'brain' of Mount Sinai. It is a mountain with no intrinsic religious value of its own. Mount Sinai is the mountain on which the theophany of God took place. God 'descends upon it in fire'. What a contrast to the view that Parent Gods were born out of the womb of the mountain! The nature of the theophany makes it impossible to establish a 'Sinai-Ko' in the fashion of the Fuji-Ko.

The prestige of *axis mundi* is found in the idea that that which is at the centre of the universe is at the same time the very point at which the communication between heaven and earth takes place. This communication is understood to be salvation. This arrangement works nicely until the thought that 'my help comes from the Lord who made heaven and earth' comes to us. To be standing then at the point of *axis mundi* does not necessarily mean salvation. *Axis mundi* is challenged by the concept of the transcendental God. Salvation does not come from being in communication with heaven and earth. At this moment the cosmological is profoundly disturbed by the theological. This disturbance may mean a number of important things for the welfare of humanity today.

1. The prestige of axis mundi and the challenge of the mobile God

Mount Sinai is basically a theological mountain. It does not represent a cosmological *axis mundi*. The reason for this is theological. The biblical God, the God of Mount Sinai, is not a stationary, cosmologically fixed God. Put psychologically, God is an impassioned God. God's 'psychological' life is dynamic, vivid and active. God is not fastened to this mountain. The image of a mobile God threatens the cosmological concept of a God placed at *axis mundi*. The God who meets the people at Mount Sinai will meet them again in other places and in many critical events of history. Mount Sinai, the mountain of theophany, which the Hebrews encountered on the journey between the land of Egypt and the promised land, cannot become the symbol of a stationary centre. Here we encounter a new concept of the centre, that of a centre in mobility.

> And the Lord went before them by day in a pillar of cloud to lead them along the way, and by night in a pillar of fire to give them light, that they might travel by day and by night (Ex. 13.12).

God symbolizes the centre of salvation. This centre symbolism travels with the people. The concept of centre here is defined not cosmologically but theologically. The journey is accompanied by the two symbols; a pillar of cloud and a pillar of fire. These are not ordinary pillars. They indicate 'the help that comes from the Lord who made heaven and earth'. God travels purposefully leading the people to salvation. Wherever this God is, that place is the centre of salvation. The presence of God neutralizes our ordinary concept of centre. Not to be at the centre but to be with God is salvational.

In the gospel we read the story of 'a man with an unclean spirit who lived among the tombs'.

> ... and no one could bind him any more, even with a chain; ... Night and day among the tombs and on the mountains he was always crying out, and bruising himself with stones. And when he saw Jesus from afar, he ran and worshipped him; ... (see Mark 5.1–20).

This man's life style is not cosmologically acceptable. He violates the fundamental scheme of nature, confusing the zone for the living and the zone for the dead, heedless even of day and night. Instead of engaging himself in spiritual exercise as suggested by Shugendo, he, on the mountain, cries out and bruises himself with stones. Jesus heals him. He is not healed by the spiritual energy of the mountain, but by the words of Jesus, not by cosmological forces but by theological presence. Jesus is the mobile presence of the dynamic centre symbolism, God. Hence, 'the man who had been possessed with demons begged him that he might be with him' (v.18).

We are reminded of the famous words of the Psalm:

> Whither shall I go from thy Spirit? Or whither shall I flee from thy presence? If I ascend to heaven, thou art there! If I make my bed in Sheol, thou art there! (139.7,8)

No one can escape from the presence of God, not because the essence of God pervades the universe but because God the creator knows where we are because of love for us. The image of a stationary God and an impassioned God are incongruous. In the biblical tradition the symbolism of centre must be critically examined by the symbolism of love. 'Thou art there'! This points primarily to the God of love, not to God who is at the centre of all things. 'Thou art there' even to the man who is possessed by demons.

A passage from the Gospel of Luke makes the similar theological thrust with the words of the Psalm just quoted.

> As they were going along the road, a man said to him, 'I will follow you wherever you go'. And Jesus said to him, 'Foxes have holes, and birds of the air have nests; but the Son of man has nowhere to lay his head' (Luke 9.57,58).

This man declares his faith in Jesus, saying that he will follow him wherever he goes. He expresses his readiness to be mobile with Jesus who moves constantly from one human situation to another. Jesus responds by giving him two nature examples, one from earth and another from heaven, then by describing the depth of his passion – representing the impassioned God – that he 'has nowhere to lay his head'. The impassioned God cannot behave according to the way of nature, as illustrated by the life of foxes and birds. For these animals, holes and nests are 'cosmological' centres that will give them rest and security. In contrast, Jesus gives up his rest and security. He wanders about among people as he represents the love of God towards history. The God who is represented by this Jesus who 'has nowhere to lay his head' is the God from whom no one can flee. 'If I take the wings of the morning and dwell in the uttermost parts of the sea, even there thy hand shall lead me, and thy right hand shall hold me' (Ps.139.9,10).

According to Christian theology Jesus Christ is the very centre of all creation. The centrality of Christ, like that of the God of the theophany at Mount Sinai, is far too paradoxical to be domesticated into the cosmological image of the *axis mundi*. In the tradition of the Bible the temple is the most evident expression of the *axis mundi*. This is because the temple can be seen as a copy of the celestial temple. Yet the Bible says that 'heaven and the highest heaven cannot contain God' (I Kings 8.27) and the simple yet profound words; 'the Son of man has nowhere to lay his head'.

Centre symbolism is open to misuse. It can be exploited, for instance, by a destructive ideology. During the time of Hitler's Third Reich the ideology of the superiority of the Aryan race was placed at the centre, while all other races were defined as peripheral, destined to be subjected to the Aryan race, and some ethnic groups were relegated to destruction. In this demonic use of centre symbolism people at the centre acted destructively with evil intent towards those who were not at the centre. The misuse of centre symbolism is idolatry. The centre may be an individual person, community, ethnic group, nation or empire. When any of these units fail to acknowledge their limitation (sin, pride, arrogance, egocentric complex) and claim infallibility they misuse symbolism of centre.

So Shibata Hanamori dangerously misused the centre symbolism of *axis mundi* when he combined this cosmological symbolism with the emperor worship cult. Jikigyo Miroku, in contrast to Hanamori, moved from the mountain cult to social ethics advocating justice in the human community.

It is important to note that Jikigyo Miroku reached this position of social ethics not directly from Mount Fuji where the Parents dwell, but from his view of history, though influenced by the *axis mundi* cosmology.

The biblical concept of centre symbolism is dialectical. It is a centre always in motion. It is because God is passionately 'in search of man' (Abraham Heschel). This is the fundamental theological insight that challenges the cosmological prestige of the concept of *axis mundi*, and in particular, that exposes and condemns the demonic misuse of all centre symbolism. I am not suggesting, however, we cannot misuse this dialectical centre symbolism of the Bible. Tragically, we can. We can misuse the one who said that he has nowhere to lay his head when we use him in order to put ourselves at the centre. The corruption of the centre symbolism of *axis mundi* is less harmful to human existence than the distortion of the biblical symbolism of the centre of God who is in search of us.

2. Centre symbolism and 'before the mountains were brought forth ...'

Eternity, in the way of thinking of Mount Fuji, is a property of heaven and earth. The Chinese characters for the Japanese words *tenjo* (heaven and earth) and *mukyu* (eternal and unlimited) appear in the opening chapter of *Nihon Shoki* or Chronicles of Japan in the eighth century.

> Then she commanded her August Grandchild, saying:—This Reed-Plain-1500-Autumns-Fair-Rice-Ear Land is the region which my descendants shall be lords of. Do thou, my August Grandchild, proceed thither and govern it. Go! and my prosperity attend thy dynasty, and may it, like Heaven and Earth, endure for ever.[6]

These words which are obviously political refer to 'heaven and earth' as a symbol of eternity. The biblical tradition, on the other hand, places God's time above the eternity of heaven and earth, and therefore our human political time is judged by the time of God.

> Before the mountains were brought forth, or ever thou hadst formed the earth and the world, from everlasting to everlasting thou art God (Ps.90.2).

Here time is not measured against heaven and earth, but from God who was 'before heaven and earth'. We are to see our life not in terms of the 'eternity' of heaven and earth, but in terms of the 'eternal presence' of God with us ('from everlasting to everlasting thou art God').

For the totality of nature religions, time is characterized by repetition with successive circles of four great cosmic dramas; creation, maintenance, dissolution and slumber. This view is expressed in Indian speculation in this fashion; the universe makes one circle in 4,320,000 years by going through four world ages; *krita, treta, dvapara* and *kali*. In the *krita* period the world enjoys perfect moral order. In the *treta* period morality is at seventy-five percent of perfection. In the *dvapara* period fifty percent and in the *kali* period the world lives with the diminishing twenty-five percent of the moral order running towards the zero point. This one cycle is called *mahayuga*, the great aeon. One thousand *mahayugas* or 4,320,000,000 years constitute a single day of Brahma. At the end of one century of Brahma comes the state of total dissolution of all things for another Brahma century. After that the entire cycle of 311,040,000,000,000 human years begins anew.[7] These fantastic figures are the product of Indian speculation. The basic idea that the world will run a cyclical course is important.

Does it, perhaps, have another message? Is the Indian speculation telling us that history is deteriorating, not getting better? We can at this moment ignore at what speed history is deteriorating. The message is that it is deteriorating. There is a telling case in which this message of the deterioration of history produced a 'creative' moment in the religious life of people. Based on a similar idea but with a different time frame it was believed by the people of medieval Japan that the world had gone into the last period of its moral depravity in the year 1052, or, in Japanese chronology, the seventh year of the Emperor Goreizei. The reckoning was made on the Buddhist view of history developed in the sixth century in China according to which the 1000 years immediately after the death of the Buddha was to be the period of the full presence of his teaching (*sho-hō*), during the next 1000 years 'something resembling his teaching'(*zo-hō*) would be present, and finally there would be a long period of 10,000 years during which his teaching will gradually disappear among people, (*mappō*). They dated the death of Buddha in 949 BC, hence the year 1052 became the critical transition year to the last phase of history. History was running towards darkness. The religious leaders were confused. The violence of the monk-soldiers and uprisings of the warrior class added to the social unrest. People sought a way of salvation from the *mappo* world. They became existential, full of anxiety.

Against this background of people's awareness of the last phase of history, the monk Honen appeared to the Japanese people as John the Baptist appeared to the people of Judah. As we shall see later (in chapter 13) Honen urged people to trust in the infinite mercy of the Buddha. Perhaps this is one of the most remarkable examples in the history of religions in which a profound religious spirituality arose in the context of a time-table historical orientation. Would it have been possible for Honen to attract the minds of the people of his time if they had not known the meaning of 'the seventh year of the emperor Goreizei'? The awareness of this particular year triggered the moment of crisis. It produced an eschatological mentality. The worst time had arrived! There is, in the perception of history of religions, an intriguing similarity between Honen's call to repentance in the setting of 1052 and the call of Christ; 'The time is fulfilled, and the kingdom of God is at hand; repent, and believe in the gospel' (Mark 1.15). Both preached their respective gospels being fully aware of the critical quality of the historical moment, *kairos*.

What is the meaning of the view that history is deteriorating? Are we to welcome the deterioration of morality since after it will come the new age with the fullness of righteousness and morality as promised in the cyclical movement? Is this the doctrine of hope in the cyclical view of history? How is this cyclical time related to the time of 'heaven and earth', and to the time of God the Creator of heaven and earth? Does the cyclical view of history have its own centre symbolism? How do we appreciate this centre symbolism in the light of the biblical concept of the centrality of God? Does the cyclical view of history misuse the centre symbolism of God? These are inescapable questions to those who engage in theological study in an intercultural context.

The view that history is deteriorating cannot be proved in scientific terms. It belongs to the area of value judgment which is not free from the limitation of subjectivity. Myths and religions often have expressed such a view through imaginative images and impressive words. In general, they have told us that the condition of human life or human morality will deteriorate to the uttermost point, before the new period of righteousness will appear. There must be, in the depth of human mind, some primordial emotion that agrees with such a view of history. Perhaps, yearly transition from the lifeless winter to the life generating spring might have impressed itself upon human mind. This impression of nature's seasonal change suggests to human mind that nature is fundamentally cyclical. Our perception of nature's cyclical behaviour is transferred to our under-standing of history. Nature circles and so history circles too. There will be a serious psychological contradiction if we perceive that nature circles while history does not.

But still, how do we know that history is progressively deteriorating as Indian myths and Buddhist *mappo* doctrine indicate? Who are we to say that? Are we saying this after we have completely understood the behaviour of both nature and history? This is certainly a disturbing thought for us all. How can we make ourselves such a confident centre of judgment upon nature and history?

'Before the mountains were brought forth...' This is not a cosmological, but an eschatological statement. The eschatological (that which is to do with the last things) comes to us from 'beyond' and 'before' our thought and imagination. It surprises us. It shakes us. It does not tell us that we should plan our life in terms of the presence of twenty-five percent less morality in the world. It does not intimate to us how *kichi* and *kyo* work upon each other for the enhancement of *kichi*. The God who was 'before the mountains were brought forth' cannot be programmed or be made to fit into our understanding of history. God cannot be fitted into *our* eschatological scheme! God shakes the foundation we lay for our theological construction, including eschatology (Isa. 24.17–23). Amos speaks about this terrifying reality of God's own eschatology:

> Woe to you who desire the day of the Lord! Why would you have the day of the Lord? It is darkness and not light (Amos 5.18).

While the cyclical view of history emphasizes repetition and experience, Amos warns us with the message of the presence of God in history in terms of 'darkness and not light'. This God cannot be scheduled by us. The day of the Lord is darkness and not light! Amos challenges this scheduling of God. Is not this the centre symbolism of the cyclical view of history which the biblical concept of God exposes? In scheduling God are we not placing ourselves more at the centre than God himself? There must be a sharp line of distinction between the biblical eschatology and the scheduling of God.

In the context of mountain veneration Jikigyo Miroku talked about the three periods of human history. I have noted that his view of history is not cyclical. It runs towards the Miroku era of salvation. For him world history is about 48,000 years long compared to the Indian one cosmic cycle of 311,040,000,000,000 years. The doctrine says that the future Buddha of Miroku will come 5,670 million years after the death of the historical Buddha. But Jikigyo said that it had come in 1731. He was devoted to the god of Mount Fuji in whose womb he finally expired by self-imposed starvation. But he began to speak about 'history' within his speeches about Mount Fuji. This remarkable development in the spirit of this man is impressive. His social ethics of neighbourly mutuality did not come from Mount Fuji as such. It came from his questioning how the god of Mount Fuji is related to our historical existence. Cosmological centre symbolism – such as mountain as *axis mundi* – cannot directly produce social ethics unless it goes through the perspective of history. In an awkward way, Jikigyo did exactly this. And it is also significant that when he realized the importance of social ethics, he was no longer talking about the cyclical view of history. Such movement towards ethics delicately implies a movement away from the psychology of scheduling 'God'. It means a move from the domestication of God to experience God as God experiences history.

What happened to Honen, in its methodological character, is much like what happened to Jikigyo. Jikigyo went beyond the confine of mountain veneration to a kind of 'liberation theology'. Honen gave a refreshing and profound answer to the meaning of the 'seventh year of emperor Goreizei', even though his particular year was identified by arithmetic. He went beyond the world of predictability into that of religious decision. Choose!, he said, the mercy of the Buddha and live. He existentialized the cosmological year counting.

In the light of biblical theology, the scheduling God according to our understanding of human destiny is idolatrous. One of the most prevalent and enduring ways of doing this is by fitting God into a cosmological scheme of circularity. The time of God is measured against the time of mountains instead of the other way around. And the concept of mountain as *axis mundi* is tranferred to God who is the centre of the universe. Amos challenges this because this order is idolatrous. The eternity of mountain must be examined in the light of God who is 'from everlasting to everlasting' God. Both Honen and Jikigyo did not settle down in the security of cosmological arrangement. They moved towards Buddha's mercy and social justice. It is also possible to do exactly this in a negative and destructive direction. If anyone other than God claims a position 'before the mountains were brought forth..' the centre symbolism of God is misused. This will constitute idolatry.

3. Centre symbolism and social ethics

One of the ways by which we can protect ourselves from falling into idolatry is, as has been intimated, to bring centre symbols and social ethical concerns together. This is to say that the centre exists for the sake of the periphery. The centre does not exist for the sake of its own glory, but has a mission to benefit the periphery. This orientation is expressed in classical biblical form in the words that God addressed to Abraham; '...by you all the families of the earth shall be blessed' (Gen. 12.3). Abraham will become a centre person for the history of salvation. But Abraham at the centre is there for the sake of all the families of the earth. The centrality given to Abraham must not be privatized. It is, as it were, social property. he must remain a 'social' person.

Many noble spirited Japanese went into the mountain to seek salvation. The beauty of nature in the mountain had a healing effect upon their souls. Aesthetic salvation! But as we have seen, the limitation of this approach to salvation is located exactly in its lack of social dimension. They were embraced by the beauty of nature, but this experience remained a private experience which was not shared with others. It was this lack of social dimension that spelled the failure of this tradition of aesthetic salvation. Aesthetic emotion can be strongly egocentric.

One of the most significant religious phenomena relating to this distinction is the difference between Theravada Buddhism and Mahayana Buddhism within the Buddhist tradition. Theravada Buddhism is a monastic Buddhism in which the individual expends his effort to achieve *nirvana.* Theravada (Elders) Buddhism is concerned about private salvation. In contrast, Mahayana (Great Vehicle Buddhism) aims to save many. The central figure in this tradition is the *bodhisattva* (awakened being) who takes a vow to postpone salvation until all living beings have achieved salvation. Mahayana is sometimes called *Bodhisattva-yana.* Here is a strong contrast between private religion and social religion. The Mayayana teaches that the moment one achieves enlightenment is the moment one starts saving others by enlightening them. The bodhisattva is a being for others somewhat in the manner of Jesus Christ.

The prophetic tradition of the Bible condemns any centre symbolism as idolatrous if it loses the mission of benefiting the periphery. Indeed the temple is a strong centre symbolism, but the meaning of the temple is in its social implication.

> The word came to Jeremiah from the Lord; 'Stand in the gate of the Lord's house, and proclaim there this word,... Amend your ways and your doings, and I will let you dwell in this place. Do not trust in these deceptive words; "This is the temple of the Lord, the temple of the Lord, the temple of the Lord." For if you truly amend your ways and your doings, if you truly execute justice one with another, if you do not oppress the alien, the fatherless or the widow, or shed innocent blood in this place, and if you do not go after other gods to your own hurt, then I will let you dwell in this place, in the land that I gave of old to your fathers for ever (Jer.7.1–7).

In the view of Jeremiah the recitation of the centrality of the temple of Jerusalem is empty, indeed, it is 'deceptive' if the people of Judah want national security. It is the establishment of social justice that will give the nation security. The people must practise the meaning of what the temple stands for, the execution of justice one with another. The centre symbolism calls for kindness and concern to the alien, the fatherless and the widow and the weaker member of the community, that is those who are at the periphery. The centre will even become 'deceptive' if it does not show concern for the periphery! It is acts of social justice that will let the people have a place to live in, not the recitation of the 'sacred' centre symbolism.

Precisely because the temple is sacred it can be deceptive. Deception that is produced by deception is easily recognized and we are able to expose it. The real deception is that which comes from the distortion of the sacred. Here Jeremiah points out the possibility of the sacred becoming a deception. This tragedy takes place when the centre symbolism is divorced from the concern of social justice, precisely the point at which deception takes place. This deception results in idolatry. The recitation of the sacred – the temple of the Lord – without the effort to establish social justice is idolatry.

Cosmological phenomena – such as the sunrise in the east, foxes have holes, birds of the air have nests, the inspiring beauty of nature in the mountain, and the existence of heaven and earth – are not immediately ethical. The birds of the air or the lilies in the field do not engage in ethical discussion. But their vulnerability to human exploitation and misuse involves us in ethical discussion about the cosmos. Ethics is a fundamental concern of theology. Theological thought which does not involve ethical concern is an empty theology. That would be a theology of the mere recitation of the sacred against which Jeremiah spoke. Thus the cosmological and the theological are meeting at the ethical. 'The temple of the Lord' will become meaningful only when we 'execute justice one with another'. When the ethical is ignored the cosmological will suffer and the theological becomes meaningless. If we insist that it has not become meaningless, we are deceived. We are worshipping idols.

The centre symbolism – the temple of the Lord – must be protected from becoming an occasion for deceptive idolatry by our commitment to social justice and our effort to realize it in this world.

4. *Paradoxical centre symbolism*

In the discussion on 'totality of heaven and earth' I have noted that the word 'totality' in this context must not be understood literally but symbolically. It is clear that no one can have, as it were, the totality of heaven and earth in their hands. Totality is beyond our direct grasp. We can speak of it only imaginatively. The concept of perfection is like that of totality. In our aesthetic, ethical, and religious life, we cannot experience perfection. Perfection is something for which we aspire, and we speak about it only symbolically. I do not see this as a negative observation as though it were a human limitation. On the contrary, I find it to be a blessing of profound magnitude that we cannot directly grasp totality or perfection, and that we must resort to our imagination and symbols. This arrangement keeps us humble and wise. To grasp totality or perfection is an act of idolatry.

The concept of 'the centre of the universe' (*axis mundi*) is again like those of totality and perfection. A certain mountain cannot be claimed to be the centre of the world. Similar claims are made for other mountains. A particular tree cannot bear the prestige of standing at the centre of the world for the same reason. Nor can one country make a claim to be the 'Middle Kingdom' to which all other nations are peripheral. *Axis mundi* is a poetical and symbolic concept. It is not to be taken in a literal sense. To say, then, that 'I stand at the centre of all things' is identical with saying that 'I have in my hand totality and perfection'. When something is 'in my hand' it ceases to be the object of poem, imagination or symbol. It is a violent situation of controlling, manipulating, and devouring others for the sake of the increase of one's glory. The danger of literalism, in particular in the field of religion and politics, is that it produces the 'in my hand' situation. When I say that 'I have totality or perfection in my hand and I stand at the centre of all things', in effect I am saying that 'I have "God" under my control', that is, 'I am god'. Simply this is idolatrous. Luther would say that this is false faith and confidence inside me.

When I am fascinated by the idea of 'God in my hand' I must have forgotten my most valuable treasure 'human limitation'. Then Christian theology says that I have become ugly, destructive and demonic. My 'human limitation' reminds me that I am not standing at the centre of all things. Christian theology tells me that this awareness of limitation is a blessing that emancipates me from the unfreedom of self-aggrandisement.

Japanese Shingon (True Mantra) Buddhism treasures a pair of great mandalas; the Diamond Mandala and the Womb Mandala. In the former the emphasis is placed upon the process through which the truth of salvation expresses itself and reaches us, and in the latter it is placed upon the inner image of salvation itself. The former is extroverted and centrifugal, the latter introverted and centripetal. The truth must have these two aspects at once. Both mandalas are pictorial representations of the cosmological map of the religious pilgrimage to the point of ultimate salvation. At the centre of the mandala is salvation. Studying the mandala we discover where we are cosmologically and religiously. This is possible because the mandala combines the cosmological and the religious. No religious arts are possible apart from the participation of the cosmological. The centre is the point at which the cosmological and the religious meet in a dramatic fashion. As a result the space is charged with religious meaning. Studying this cosmograph of religious salvation we can find spiritual security. That is, we come to know where we are vis-à-vis the centre. We are invited to meditate upon the centre where salvation is. We can 'see' on the mandala where the centre is, but we are not allowed to grasp it in our hands. We are inspired and urged to begin a journey towards the centre. This inspiration is the 'mystery' of the mandala.

There is, however, an important difference between the spirituality of the Buddhist mandala and that of the Mount Sinai tradition. Exodus 33.18–23 reads:

Moses said, 'I pray thee, show me thy glory'. And he said, 'I will make all my goodness pass before you, and will proclaim before you my name "The Lord". and I will be gracious to whom I will be gracious, and will show mercy on whom I will show mercy.' But, he said, 'you cannot see my face; for man shall not see me and live.' And the Lord said, 'Behold, there is a place by me where you shall stand upon the rock; and while my glory passes by I will put you in a cleft of the rock, and I will cover you with my hand until I have passed by; then I will take away my hand, and you shall see my back; but my face shall not be seen'.

The holy God is a dangerous God. Yet it is in this dangerous God that humanity finds salvation. How can we know God if we are told that we shall not see God and live? Here God arranges the 'impossible possibility'. This God, beyond human control, who says, 'I will be gracious to whom I will be gracious', arranges a special space of grace. 'I will put you in the cleft of the rock, and I will cover you with my hand until I have passed by.' This is not an ordinary space. It is an extraordinary space in which a person 'sees' God and yet lives. ...but not the face of God, only the back of God!

> Even to be allowed to catch a glimpse of his passing from the rear is so awesome to the man Moses that God himself – note the strange paradox – must shield him with his own hand.[8]

That special space of grace is produced by 'the strange paradox'. It is created by the hand of God. This is the opposite of 'having God in our hands'. Shielded by the hand of God and seeing the back of God – we experience grace of God, resurrection of life, and hope in a new horizon of history. This space – in which we are freed from our inner drive to 'schedule God' – symbolizes the creative centre; at the centre we do not see the face of God, but the back of God. The centre symbolism is theologically restrained. At Mount Sinai we glimpse the back of the passing God.

In the Indian *Bhagavadgita* there is a chapter called 'Arjuna wishes to see the Universal Form of God' (Chapter XI). The human Arjuna desires to see the divine glory of Krishna. Krishna grants this wish and says to Arjuna:

> But thou canst not behold Me with this human eye of yours; I will bestow on thee the supernatural eye. Behold My divine power.[9]

Arjuna sees the divine glory Krishna with the supernatural eye.

> If the light of a thousand suns were a blaze forth all at once in the sky, that might resemble the splendour of that exalted Being.[10]

In the *Bhagavadgita* we do not see that 'strange paradox'. The story is rather straightforward. Krishna gives Arjuna the supernatural eye and through it he sees the divine splendour. In the Book of Exodus Moses sees God with his human eyes which are protected by the 'strange paradox' of the protective God. In general Asian religious traditions speak about the attainment of the 'supernatural eye' rather than the paradoxical arrangement by which humans achieve salvation.

The following words from the Book of Jeremiah (14.8,9) show the theology that sees God through the strange paradox.

O thou hope of Israel, its saviour in time of trouble, why shouldst thou
be like a stranger in the land, like a wayfarer who turns aside to tarry for
a night? Why shouldst thou be like a man confused, like a mighty man
who cannot save? Yet thou, O Lord, art in the midst of us, and we are
called by thy name; leave us not.

This is indeed a strange image of God. This God is not at the centre of
community, firm and unmoving, sustaining the direction of life and history.
Like a stranger, an overnight wayfarer, one who is mighty but confused and
homeless, this God dwells among us! Through these agonizing words
Jeremiah expresses the 'centrality' of God better than any planned speech
about the centrality of God. This God, of whom we may be able to see only
his back, is the God who gives humanity its essential identity. 'We are called
by thy name.' Is it not a 'strange paradox' that God who behaves like 'an
overnight wayfarer' is in truth at the centre of all things and the one who
gives humanity the full identity of salvation? This God does not appear to
us with the splendour of the light of a thousand suns. It is this God that we
cannot grasp in our hands. This image of God is so different from the
picture our contemporary religious culture has of God. The prestige we
expect at the centre is not there. The centre is portrayed in the image of 'an
overnight wayfarer'. What an unexpected centrality! What a paradox!

5. Centre symbolism and ideology

Wherever humans are there are ideologies. We cannot live without having
some kind of comprehensive view about our own life and history.

> Ideology is an emotion-laden, myth-saturated, action-related system of
> beliefs and values about man and society, legitimacy and authority,
> acquired as a matter of routine and habitual reinforcement.[11]

Ideology tends to feel itself competent to say the last words about human
life, human existence and human community. It is 'an emotion-laden,
myth-saturated, action-related system of beliefs and values'. It is laden with
tremendously powerful psychological and philosophical impact. Ready to
stand at the centre of all other thoughts, it assumes a position from which it
can dominate and subjugate them. Ideology speaks about the beginning and
the end. In the ideology of *apartheid* race policy of South Africa we are
encountered by an ideological message which declares that 'in the beginning
was pigmentation' which directly confronts the opening passage of the
Gospel of John: 'In the beginning was the word'.

As we have seen the Japanese ideology of the imperial cult dominated and
subjugated all other human emotion and thoughts. This cult had its own
'complete' interpretation of world history that the world should come under

the Benevolent Rule of the Divine Emperor. It was certainly myth-saturated. Capitalism is an ideology. It makes the claim that profit is the key to blessing and abundance. Ideology that claims to know the beginning and the end has an unambiguous message to the world. The following words of *The Communist Manifesto* are very forceful and clear. There is no ambiguity.

> The history of all hitherto existing society is the history of class struggles. ... Our epoch, the epoch of the bourgeoisie, possesses, however, this distinctive feature: it has simplified the class antagonism. Society as a whole is more and more splitting up into two great hostile camps, into two great classes directly facing each other: Bourgeoisie and Proletariat.[12]

These words indeed indicate 'an emotion-laden, myth-saturated, action-related system of beliefs and values'. A forceful interpretation of human history is suggested.

Theology, in contrast to ideology, if it is to be theology, must find itself under the judgment of God. This is a strange idea to the perspective of ideology. Ideology is judged by the historical experience of humanity. For instance, the ideologies of 'White Man's Burden', 'Manifest Destiny', 'Superiority of Aryan Race', 'Emperor Worship Cult', 'Omnipotence of Science-Technology' and so on may be judged by the general moral sensitivity of humanity. But ideology does not need to find itself under any judgment in order to be an ideology. The concept of 'limitation' is not a part of its structure. It behaves only in self-assertion. That it should not be allowed to see 'the face of God' is of no concern to ideology. Ideology is self-sufficient. Theology is not. Ideology demands the prestige of being at the centre of human thought and life. Domination or oppression of one section of humanity by another is usually guided and done by ideological understanding of humanity and history.

Theology becomes an ideology when it loses the dimension of the strange paradox and makes a claim that it is at the centre, thus pushing aside the living God. An ideologized theology is more pernicious and sinister than ordinary ideologies. That Christian nations should protect themselves by any means at any cost – even a hundred million human lives – because the Christian civilization is the highest value in the world is an ideologized theology. This we hear too often from Christians! The suggestion that nuclear bombs in the hands of a Christian United States will protect world peace, while in the hands of the Soviet Union will bring world destruction has the odour of ideologized theology. It is a theologically fabricated self-righteousness. The 'theological' idea that nuclear destruction will expedite the Second Coming Christ is an ugly ideologization of theology. On the occasion of the United States Supreme Court's eight to one decision of 24

May 1983 holding that the Internal Revenue Service may deny federal tax exemptions to church-affiliated schools that discriminate on the basis of race, Bob Jones III, the president of Bob Jones University, North Carolina, said: 'I have pity for the heathens who sit on the Surpreme Court, pity for their damned souls and their blighted minds,...'[13] In all these examples there is a 'centre complex' which makes people involved incapable of engaging in critical self-examination. Ideologized theology is a theology in captivity of our centre complex. There is unfortunately an easy two-way-traffic between theology and ideology. In fact, a question regarding the possibility of un-ideologized theology is ever with us, and there is no easy answer to this challenge.

Ideology is 'religious' whether it is capitalism, communism, patriotism, racism, or emperor worship in its desire to utter the last word. All ideologies behave like religions, including atheistic communism and theistic capitalism. People at Lenin's Mausoleum in Moscow behave as religiously as the muslims at the National Mosque in Kuala Lumpur in Malaysia. Even 'godless ideology' has its own 'god' who would solemnize its ideological system. In this context 'god' signifies. 'centre complex'.

In biblical theology 'God' means the rejection of our centre complex. It is this that keeps theology from falling into ideology. The centre complex appears when we are tempted to say the last words about human destiny in the world. It then begins in our 'faith and confidence'. To be precise what is meant here is a deluded self-confidence that we think we can utter the last words. Our self-image here is no longer the seeker of the truth, but the possessor of the truth. Our self designated place is the centre of all things. The ideological use of centre symbolism is destructive to the welfare of humanity. Many genocides have been committed in the name of centre complexed ideologies and ideologized theologies. Such a centre complex constantly 'schedules God' and thus genocides!

But are there not good ideologies? Not all ideologies are like emperor worship or *apartheid* race policy. This is not an easy question to answer. To be 'good', they must at least support and nourish the basic human values, such as life, happiness and freedom. 'Good' ideologies are thought systems which safeguard and foster these values. They are not self-sufficient. They point to the values outside them. So long as they function in the act of 'pointing to', they do not say the last word. In this way good ideologies are protected from falling into the idolatry of self-aggrandisement. The ideology which points to the higher value is not controlled by centre complex.

But why is it that when God says the last word – 'In the beginning was the Word' – it is not frozen into an ideology? Why is it that when God is confessed as the Unconditional One we are not in idolatry? Or are we? Is theology, in a quite serious sense, a sublime form of idolatry? I shall return to this issue in chapter 20 where I discuss the theology of the cross. In the theology of the cross I see critical reappraisal of centre symbolism.

This chapter began with the image of the mountain as *axis mundi*. We have compared, and sought an interaction between, cosmological and theological concepts of centre symbolism. The cosmological perception is psychologically and aesthetically fundamental to our concept of centre symbolism. Apart from the cosmological sense of the proportion and framework of space, we cannot have a concept of centre. Naturally, there is a theological use for centre symbolism. But theological speech about God remembers that God must not be confined in centre symbolism. In theology there is something within the nature of God that makes it impossible to say that 'God is the centre' without feeling spiritual tension and disturbance. With this image of God we have travelled to a theological criticism of the ideological use of centre symbolism.

This section (Part II) is moving from the cultural to the ethical. At the end of chapter 6 I indicated the direction the discussion would take towards meeting the challenge of 'misfortune and terror of history'. Now we are ready to discuss this subject. What does this challenge mean to the world of Mount Fuji and that of Mount Sinai? Faced by 'misfortune and terror of history' how do the two traditions understand the words of the psalmist: 'Help comes from the Lord who made heaven and earth'? This is the theme of the next chapter.

9

The Cauldron in which a Spider Spins its Web

When we speak of the struggle against human greed,
we are in the area of history, not nature.

In the silence of the temple compound a frog makes a solitary jump into the pond. In this simple figure the cosmological religions see a symbol of the hidden secret of salvation. But, as we have seen in tracing the history of such spirituality, whether this secret can answer our human need can be questioned. The question was raised by the seventh-century poet, Yamanoue no Okura (660–733) in a poem which appears in *Manyoshu*. This is one of the few which are seriously 'history' oriented. It is called a poem on poverty.

On the night when the rain beats
Driven by the wind
On the night when the snowflakes mingle
With the sleety rain,
I feel so helplessly cold.
I nibble at a lump of salt,
Sip the hot, oft-diluted dregs of *sake*.
And coughing, sniffing,
And stroking my scanty beard.
I say in my pride,
'There's none worthy, save I!'
But I shiver still with cold.
I pull up my hempen bedclothes.
Wear what few sleeveless clothes I have,
But cold and bitter is the night!
As for those poorer than myself,
Their parents must be cold and hungry,

Their wives and children beg and cry.
Then, how do you struggle through life?
Wide as they call the heaven and earth,
For me they have shrunk quite small;
Bright though they call the sun and moon,
They never shine for me.
Is it the same with all men
Or for me alone?
By rare chance I was born a man
And no meaner than my fellows,
But, wearing unwadded sleeveless clothes
In tatters, like weeds waving in the sea,
Hanging from my shoulders,
And under the sunken roofs,
Within the leaning walls,
Here I lie on straw
Spread on bare earth,
With my parents at my pillow,
My wife and children at my feet,
All huddled in grief and tears.
No fire sends up smoke
At the cooking-place,
And in the cauldron
A spider spins its web
With no grain to cook,
We moan like the 'night-thrush'.
Then 'to cut' as the saying is,
The ends of what is already too short',
The village headman comes,
With rod in hand, to our sleeping-place
Nothing but pain and shame in this world of men,
But I cannot fly away,
Wanting the wings of a bird.[1]

Okura has observed carefully the lives of people in poverty. Karl Marx, who observed child labour in the lucifer factories, would have appreciated this seventh-century Japanese poem. What a painful human existence! Okura, a country district chief, did not share the lot of these poor but he pondered upon the subject of human dignity and poverty. He wants to fly away from this world of pain and shame. 'Wanting the wings of a bird', he cannot escape. He would be ready to 'jump into the pond' and forget the misery, submerged in the great cosmic ocean, but he cannot ignore this historical reality of dehumanization. Rather he must seek the betterment of society so that the village headman will no longer 'come with rod in hand to our sleeping place'. Okura, in this poem of poverty, recognizes that there is something that the embrace of heaven and earth cannot heal. How can the cosmos deal with the misfortunes and disasters of history? Can heaven and earth 'house' (ecologize) social injustice and heal it? What will heaven and earth say to the question of Jeremiah?

> Why does the way of the wicked prosper? Why do all who are treacherous thrive? (Jer. 12.1)

Can we jump into the bosom of cosmic tranquillity with this disturbing question in mind? The whole world is imaginatively divided and united in the realms of hornbill and watersnake. Or the world is understood in terms of the interaction of *ying* and *yang*. The Chinese see in every mountain a sunlit side and a shadow side. According to Indian thought there is a grand cycle of creation, maintenance, destruction and slumber in the cosmos. One of the profound poems of Taittiriya Upanisad sings with mystical joy, 'I, who am food, eat the eater of food'.[2] There all distinction between food and eater disappear. All is one in the primary human act of eating. What can these grand cosmological images of salvation which arise in the Eastern totality religions say to the question of poverty in the human community which destroys human dignity? What can the rapturous experience of union 'I, who am food, eat the eater of food', say to the hard human pain expressed in the image of the 'cauldron in which a spider spins its web because there is no grain to cook'?

Rice comes from heaven and earth. Soil, water, and heat are required for the seed to grow. In the cultivation of rice, people also must participate. Heaven and earth do the mysterious inner work and men and women add the external work by laying the seeds, controlling the water, pulling weeds and fertilizing the field. This is the basic structure of human culture. The mysterious life of rice itself comes from nature. Therefore the ancient Chinese called rice and ancestor 'heaven' symbolizing that rice is a gift from our ancestors who are in heaven. No human external work can 'create' even one grain of rice, nor can the gods produce it. It is the gift of nature, of heaven and earth. This marvellous work of nature is, in turn, called the work of the gods.

The ancient Japanese understood that there is a cereal god for cereal, a fish god for fish, a tree god for trees. There is a concept of 'god' or ancestor behind all things. Nature, personalized, has become a matrix of ritual. The basic relationship among inner work, external work and the gift of the gods indicates that in all cultures humanity is in dialogue with the cosmos. This dialogue takes on the quality of religion. The relationship between cosmos and religion can be seen in two ways; we can see cosmos within the structure of religion or religion within the structure of cosmos. Hosea makes reference to heaven and earth in order to introduce the character of God.

> Let us know, let us press on to know the Lord; his going forth is sure as the dawn; he will come to us as the showers, as the spring rains that water the earth (Hos.6.3).

For Hosea the workings of the natural world are a simile to describe God's behaviour and character. The natural world itself is neither deified nor worshipped. In the words of the Psalmists, 'The heavens are telling the glory of God; and the firmament proclaims his handiwork' (Ps. 19.1).

When, on the other hand, religion is seen in the structure of nature some aspects of nature will necessarily be deified. Thus the Indian god Indra is an atmospheric deity of storm, Surya is a solar god, Agni is the god of fire and Soma is the god of narcotic beverage. The line of distinction between these orientations is subtle but real. In the Hindu mythology the sun itself has been personified in the god Surya. We have seen that Hosea uses the sun and the rain in a simile to describe the character of God. Jesus' well known words go further and express the relationship of sun to God as that of servant or functionary.

> Love your enemies and pray for those who persecute you, so that you may be sons of your Father who is in heaven; for he makes his sun rise on the evil and on the good, and sends rain on the just and on the unjust (Matt. 5.44f.).

There is a clear discontinuity between God and nature in the biblical orientation which is not found in the cosmic nature religions.

The figure of the frog submerging into the cosmic embrace, and the ecstatic line of the Upanisad, 'I, who am food, eat the eater of food' are examples of the sense of religious experience which participates in cosmic awareness. Drought, flood, storm or earthquake made the ancients think that gods were angry with them. Certainly drought, flood, storm and earthquake can cause famine and bring 'the cauldron in which a spider spins its web'. Therefore we must placate and please the gods. But at this point the biblical position on the relationship between God and nature comes out with a new cutting edge to the culture and religion of nature orientation.

This God is not identical with the cosmic embrace. This God is not a cereal god or tree god. There is a distance and distinction between this God and the world of nature. One of the ways in which this distinction is expressed is that this God is ethics oriented. 'Love your enemies and pray for those who persecute you.' Practise the mind of God in history! Famine can also come through the combination of human greed and mismanagement, violence against fellow humans and against nature. The awareness of human factors in tragedy is the beginning of the awareness of history. There is not much history awareness, then, in saying ecstatically that 'I, who am food, eat the eater of food' or 'a frog plunged into a pond'. It is an awareness of human greed that opens up our mind to the awareness of history. And the biblical God intimates to us that he is 'very aware' of it, to put it awkwardly. Human greed is a destructive spiritual energy which cannot be explained in the cosmological context. Because of human greed unnecessary and unexpected disasters visit humanity. These disasters are 'unnatural'. A historical awareness causes the cosmological mind to feel at a loss before the human cause of the 'cauldron in which a spider spins its web'.

At its core, human greed is a misuse of human freedom. There is no way to be human without exercising freedom. Both the use and misuse of freedom arise within human nature. When we speak of the struggle against human greed we are in the area of history, not nature. The remarkable quality of Okura's poem is that he is asking a question relating to history, not nature. In the world of nature no 'village headman comes with rod in hand to our sleeping-place'.

The prophet Hosea announces the poignant complaint of God;

> She did not know that it was I who gave her the grain, the wine and the oil, and who lavished upon her silver and gold which they used for Baal (Hos. 2.4).

All these good things come from God through nature. They do not come simply from nature, 'it was I who gave her the grain ...' The grain, then, must be distributed according to the will of the One who has given it to us. If we did so the spider would far less often spin its web in the cauldron. 'It was I who gave her the grain' is a declaration of war against the human greed that destroys the proper distribution of grain and other human necessities. Again, 'it was I who gave her the grain' are words that raise history awareness within us because they excite our ethical sensitivity. Ethics which does not fight against human greed is not worthy to be called ethics. All elaborate moral theories and systems are empty exercises if they fail to fight against human greed, just as all foods go to waste if they are not eaten.

Historical thought is impossible apart from ethical implication. History takes place within the cosmos, yet historical thought has something within itself that goes beyond thoughts inspired by nature. When cosmological time is challenged by critical time which opposes human greed it becomes eschatological time; and when cosmological space is challenged by the mind that battles against human greed that cosmological space will become eschatological space, space reconstructed to have a new possibility. Human greed – this unfortunately negative concept – can be named as a bridging element that takes us from the world of nature to that of history. This will not happen if greed is accepted by us as a non-problem, but when we start fighting against it, we will move into history. The awareness of eschatological time and space is the awareness of history.

What is human greed? Greed (*pleonexia* in Greek) means, first of all, 'having more'. Then 'receiving more' and finally 'wanting more'. In Thucydides of Athens (*c.* 460–369 BC) the word meant 'taking the great share', 'to increase one's possessions', 'seeking aggrandisement', 'taking advantage of', 'seeking political gain', 'pressing one's advantage' and even 'selfishness'. In the Jewish literature in Greek, this word meant 'dishonest gain', 'unlawful enrichment', 'seizing the property of others', 'immoderation'. In the New Testament this word group *pleonexia* appears chiefly in the writings of Paul. It generally means 'striving for material possessions'. The greedy person is called an idolater (Eph. 5.5) and is placed together with 'robbers and idolaters' in I Cor. 5.10. *Pleonexia* is one of the basic facts which make humans unable to recognize God so that they bring upon themselves the destiny of being forsaken by God (Rom. 1.28f.).[3]

Why are people greedy at all? Why are we passionately interested in acquisition? Is the drive to greater possession a biological necessity, or is it something we have learned by living in a certain cultural context? Why is it that all human systems whether political, economic or even religious are caught in the net of human greed? Emil Brunner, the Swiss theologian, wrote the following words on capitalism in 1932.

> It is that system in which all that we can see to be the meaning of the economic order from the point of view of faith is denied; in which, therefore, it is made impossible for the individual to realize, in any way, through his economic activity, the service of God and of his neighbour. This system is contrary to the spirit of service; it is debased and irresponsible; indeed, we may go further and say; it is irresponsibility developed into a system[4].

Whether we agree with this intense criticism of capitalism or not, we must admit that greed plays a dominating motif for capitalism, also that greed is by definition irresponsible. It is not difficult to detect the presence of human greed in communism, racism and militarism. There are two historical incidents, one from the world of Mount Fuji and the other from the world of Mount Sinai, which illustrate how the religious edifice (religious symbolism) can by itself become the occasion for oppression in human history. Both show how human greed is tragically present in the composition of human history.

In eighth-century Japan the peasants were exploited by the aristocratic class. Their labours were conscripted, heavy taxes were laid upon them, they were required to present to their rulers, at specified times, their allocation of silk. It was a time of dehumanization for the peasants. In 747 the emperor Shomu began the building of the imposing temple to house the immense image of the Buddha Vairocana, a solar manifestation of the Buddha. Anesaki writes of this Buddha in *Todai-Ji*, in Nara:

> ... he is represented in a bronze statue more than fifty feet in height, seated on a gigantic lotus pedestal. The enormous halo is studded with minor statues of Buddha and saints, while on the petals of the pedestal are engraved scenes of the twenty-five realms of existence with the figures of celestial and terrestial beings – all united in adoration of the central figure and glorifying the majesty of the Supreme Enlightened.[5]

It was an irony of human history that the cost for the building of the image itself was the source of an added affliction upon the people, especially upon the poor of the time. While the cosmically benevolent image of the solar Buddha is being built, the number of the cauldrons in which the spider spins its web increases. I believe this has happened repeatedly in human history.

The temple of Solomon, the pride and glory of the Jewish nations, was built on just such exploitation.

> King Solomon raised a levy of forced labour out of all Israel; and the levy numbered thirty thousand men. And he sent them to Lebanon, ten thousand a month in relays. ... Solomon also had seventy thousand burden-bearers and eighty thousand hewers of stone in the hill country (I Kings 5.13–15).

King Solomon built the temple close to his royal palace. Exactly so the Todai-Ji was built in proximity to the palace of the Japanese emperor Shomu. Palace and temple have always been found in an ambiguous relationship, but they share a cosmological orientation. 'The prestige of the centre' is fundamental to the ideological structure of both. Often palace and temple are merged when the king assumes the function of priest or when the king is declared to be divine (*deva-raja*) as in the history of kingdoms in South East Asia and also in the more recent history of the Japanese emperor cult. This merger is usually done by the kings to enhance their glory. As the ruler's glory increases (greed), the people suffer more, and the number of cauldrons that have spider's webs increases. The world of religion is not free from the snares of greed. When we feel critically the power of human greed we are moving from the cosmological to the historical.

Okura's cauldron is a constant reality in human society, a destructive fact of history. The concept of history, as indicated above, is intimately related to the awareness of social injustice. For history the brutal massacre of Koreans in Japan which took place after the Great Earthquake in Tokyo Plain in 1923 is far more crucially important than the earthquake itself. Historical thought is impossible apart from ethical consideration. Greed is an ethical and not a cosmological concept. It is anthropological, not natural, because we have freedom to be greedy or not greedy. Both king Solomon and emperor Shomu had freedom not to exploit the labour of the masses to accomplish their aims, but they chose to place a great number of people under forced labour.

Since human greed is related to human freedom its history does not fit into the neat formula of the alternative *kichi* and *kyo* principles. It is unpredictable. It always produces violence, a violence initiated by the freedom to will greed. Self-serving power is called violence, or, we may say that the self-righteous use of power is called violence. Greed is often propelled by the strong emotion of self-righteousness. The cosmological culture of Mount Fuji dislikes self-righteousness, but the awareness of salvation in nature cannot quite handle this situation of self-righteousness, the human freedom to will greed. The culture of Mount Fuji lacks a higher point in reference to which one can examine the tragedy of human greed.

'In the beginning God created the heavens and the earth' (Gen. 1.1). These words must not be understood simply to mean the creation of the cosmos. It is in truth the beginning of history. It declares that God in freedom, without any coercion, exercised freedom and created the heavens and the earth. These opening words of the Book of Genesis are God-centred eschatological words. It is in this God that the worlds of nature and history are united. The moment God created the heavens and the earth – the moment we confess this – history has begun. When we say, 'in the beginning God ...' we are to see the meaning of the heavens and the earth in the light of this God. It is important to know that this God does not use freedom for the satisfaction of greed. The Creator God is a self-giving God. God rejects greed. This is the meaning of history. And in this rejection is the possibility of right appreciation of nature. We come to a new understanding of history when we see it in the light of the God who rejects greed.

I have said that the culture of Mount Fuji dislikes self-righteousness. People in this culture know that self-righteousness is destructive, if not immediately then eventually, to human community. They understand that self-righteousness is not interested in sympathy, in 'suffering together' with people in spiritual and material need. In terms of the health of human community they object to greed. I believe this, by itself, is significant. But they are historically distanced from the idea that the Creator God in his freedom rejected greed as a viable option for human history. Okura was deeply pained and tormented by this sight of the poor. He wanted to fly away from this world of suffering. 'But I cannot fly away, wanting the wings of a bird.' The poem of Okura is impressive because it is one of the earliest expressions of the deep felt pain in the heart of Japanese when encountered by historical misfortune.

I have suggested that the critical awareness of human greed bridges between the cosmological and the historical. If so, the fundamental message of Buddhism must be studied carefully against the simplistic view that 'Buddhism is not a history concerned religion'. The message of the Buddha concentrates in urging us to battle against our own human greed. This examination is the theme of the next chapter. In chapter 11 we will ask questions of technology's contribution to our history awareness. The value of technology to humanity is terrifyingly ambiguous. Is it not true that technology has been all too often used by human greed?

10

Human Greed and Human History

Buddhism is history concerned because it urges us to
battle against our human greed.

When we try to understand the spiritual and cultural world of Asia, the
understanding of Buddhism is critically important. Although Hinduism has
contributed immensely to the life and culture of Asians, it remains, with
nearly five hundred million adherents, basically an ethnic faith. Buddhism,
on the other hand, has broken through the confine of the Indian cultural
milieu and has achieved the quality of being a universal religion together
with Christianity and Islam. There are millions of Japanese Buddhists, but
hardly any Japanese Hindus. In this chapter we attempt to bring the
concept of history in Buddhism into a dialogue with the biblical
understanding of history in terms of the attitude of each to the subject of
human greed. The discussion will begin with the observation that greed
can never be 'non-historical'. It will proceed to a consideration of the
confrontation of greed with grace in both traditions. That is to say, in both
traditions human greed is criticized in a profound manner. Finally, ways in
which these two religious views differ will be discussed.

While Hinduism does not have a founder, Buddhism has its founder in
the person of Gotama Buddha, of whom tradition has handed down a great
many life stories and legends. Buddhism inherited from the Hindu world
such concepts as *dharma*, the fundamental law that governs human beings
in community and in the universe; *samsara*, the doctrine of repeated births
in this world; *karman*, action, reaction and retribution; and *nirvana*, the
ultimate realm of tranquillity, the state in which the 'flame of desire' is
'blown out'. Yet Buddhism was able, with remarkable originality, to
develop its distinct religious identity which is critically different from the
accepted Hindu religious view. It concentrated its spiritual and mental
energy in the search for the cause and solution of human suffering, *dukkha*.
This centring on the existential question has given Buddhism a profound
sense of tragedy.

The gospel of Buddhism begins with the life of Siddharta (*c.* 563–483 BC) who in his thirty fifth year achieved enlightenment and became the Awakened One, the Buddha. One of the most inspiring images of Asia is that of the Buddha, squatting in lotus position in extreme ascetic meditation.

> Because I ate so little, all my limbs became like the knotted joints of withered creepers; because I ate so little, my buttocks became like a bullock's hoof; because I ate so little, my protruding backbone became like a string of balls; because I ate so little, my gaunt ribs became like the crazy rafters of a tumble-down shed; because I ate so little, the pupils of my eyes appeared lying low and deep in their sockets as sparkles of what in a deep well appear lying low and deep; because I ate so little, my scalp became shrivelled and shrunk as a bitter white gourd cut before it is ripe becomes shrivelled and shrunk by a hot wind.[1]

This legend of extreme self-mortification indicates that the *dharma*, the truth, discovered by the Buddha, is not a cheap truth. Nor was it a revelation, in the manner of Judaeo-Christian or Islamic truth. After achieving the enlightenment the Buddha speaks confidently and triumphantly of his gospel on the basis of his hardly-won understanding. The Japanese Zen scholar, Hisamatsu Shinichi, characterizes the difference between Buddhism and Christianity as that of self-enlightenment-religion as over against belief-religion.

> In Christianity we are to believe in God who is the absolute other. But in Buddhism we are to achieve self-enlightenment, instead of believing in someone. ... The Buddha who is believed in is not a true Buddha, and by the same token the person who believes so is not a true person. Buddha appropriated through our own enlightenment is the true Buddha, and the person who is enlightened is the true person.[2]

Of his enlightenment the Buddha is reported to have said:

> My mind was emancipated, ...Ignorance was dispelled, knowledge arose, darkness was dispelled, light arose.[3]

I doubt whether we can know today what was exactly the contents and experience of Gotama's enlightenment. Buddhist tradition, however, in speaking of it, refers repeatedly to the concept of 'Conditional Arising', *paticcasamuppada* (Pali, *paticca*, 'grounded on', *samuppada*, 'arising'). Conditional Arising, then, is to be understood as 'the manner of arising of a certain phenomenon when it arises through various conditions'.[4] The famous fundamental idea is expressed as follows:

> This being, that comes to be; from the arising of this, that arises; this not being, that ceases; from the ceasing of that, that ceases.[5]

The doctrine of Conditional Arising is the answer to the question, 'why do we suffer?' or, to use the terminology of the answer, 'Out of what does suffering arise'? There are various formulations of Conditional Arising, but the standard one enumerates 'Twelve Conditions'. We are not sure whether this formulation was done during the lifetime of the Buddha or posthumously.

> Conditioned by ignorance activities come to pass, conditioned by activities consciousness, conditioned by consciousness name-and-shape, conditioned by name-and-shape sense, conditioned by sense contact, conditioned by contact feeling, conditioned by feeling craving, conditioned by craving grasping, conditioned by grasping becoming, conditioned by becoming birth, conditioned by birth old age-and-death, grief, lamenting, suffering sorrow, despair come to pass. Such is the uprising of this entire mass of ill. This, brethren, is called /causal/ happening.[6]

This same message can be expressed in terms of 'ceasing':

> But from the utter fading away and ceasing of ignorance [comes] ceasing of activities; from ceasing of activities ceasing of consciousness; from ceasing of consciousness ceasing of name-and-shape; .... Such is the ceasing of this entire mass of ill.[7]

Obviously this is the core of the Buddha's gospel as we know it. This is the law that governs human life, and it was there always independently of the Buddha. It was not his creation. He only discovered it.

> Conditioned by rebirth is decay and death: – whether, brethren, there be an arising of Tathagatas, or whether there be no such arising, this nature of things just stands, this causal status, this causal orderliness, the relatedness of this to that. Concerning that Tathagata is fully enlightened, that he fully understands. Fully enlightened, fully understanding he declares it, teaches it, reveals it, sets it forth, manifests, explains, makes it plain, saying 'Behold'.[8]

Before we study the message of the Conditional Arising, we must consider four fundamental marks of Buddhism which provide a background to the Conditional Arising.

1. All things are changeable and transient (*anicca*). According to Buddhism there is no such thing as independent, imperishable substance. All of the phenomenal world is changeable and transient, including the human mind. 2. All is no-self (*anatta*). *Anatta* means 'the quality of insubstantiality, or of having no true self-nature, or of having no continuing identity'.[9] According to Buddhism all things exist only as interactions with others, and there is no independent substance that exists by itself. The Buddhist anthropology sees human beings as an aggregate of

five elements; body, feeling, recognition, imagination and discrimination. There is no substantial 'I' then, there is only Five Aggregates ever in mutual interactions. 3. All is suffering (*dukkha*). *Dukkha* means evil, suffering, sin, imperfection and unsatisfactoriness. The realization that all is *dukkha* is the beginning of the religious life. 'If these things were not in the world, my disciples, the Perfect One, the holy Supreme Buddha, would not appear in the world; the law and the doctrine which the Perfect One propounded would not shine in the world. What three things are they? Birth, old age, and death.'[10] And 4. *Nirvana* is tranquillity. This is the description of the ideal state in contrast to 'all is suffering'. *Nirvana* is the highest good, perfect salvation.

The first two of the marks of Buddhism speak about the fundamental way with which the Buddhist looks at the world – through *anicca* and *anatta*. The last two are concerned about the contrasting values, *dukkha* and *nirvana*. Conditional Arising sees the human life through *anicca* and *anatta*, and it moves from *dukkha* to *nirvana*.

Masutani Fumio, the Japanese Buddhist scholar, says that most likely at the moment of the enlightenment the Buddha was not thinking in terms of the chain of twelve causations but in a simpler form, as simple as ignorance (*avijja*), greed (*tanha*) and suffering (*dukkha*).[11] Ignorance causes greed and greed causes suffering. Eradicating ignorance, greed disappears, with greed ceasing, suffering disappears. It is possible that this simple form was elaborated later into more sophisticated form.

Ignorance is not just any sort of ignorance but it is ignorance of *anicca* and *anatta*. This ignorance will create greed chasing that which is unreal, changeable, impermanent, and of no substance. This greed brings forth suffering, evil, and unsatisfactoriness. In *dukkha* we experience the opposite of *nirvana*. In whatever forms it expressed itself, the thought of *paticcasamuppada* was the contents of the enlightenment, but what it meant to Gotama himself at the moment of his enlightenment we will never know. We may wonder why it took Gotama six years of strict ascetic meditation to reach such a fundamentally simple formula. Yet the tradition says that this doctrine is an extremely difficult one to understand.

Must I now preach what I so hardly won?
Men sunk in sin and lusts would find it hard
to plumb this Doctrine, – up stream all the way,
abstruse, profound, most subtle, hard to grasp.
Dear lusts will blind them that they shall not see,
– in densest mists of ignorance befogged.[12]

The teaching of Conditional Arising is difficult for the people because they are 'sunk in sin and lusts' and they are 'in densest mists of ignorance befogged'. For we are in the grip of our own *tanha*, desire, coveting, craving, greed and lust. *Tanha* obstructs our way to the highest good, *nirvana*. Conditional Arising speaks far more concrete language than we may readily accept. And clearly the progression from ignorance to 'old age-and-death, grief, lamenting, suffering, sorrow, despair' goes through an involved chain, represented by the drive of craving. For the primitive message of Buddhism, ignorance, greed and suffering are the central three words. They are understood to be fully empirical. It is not abstract at all to say that ignorance begets greed, and in turn greed produces suffering. In this sense Buddhism is, in its core message, history-concerned. I was deeply impressed by the seriousness and dedication with which Thai Buddhist monks fought against their own *tanha*. They have shown to me a Buddhism different from the one presented in Christian textbooks on Buddhism. Buddhism takes history seriously because it takes up the problem of *tanha* seriously. Not in terms of a Christian view of history, but in its own way, it defines history and takes it seriously.

Masutani Fumio suggests that probably the Buddha realized that the truth of Conditional Arising would be too difficult for the people and therefore he worked out the formula of the Four Noble Truths for popular evangelism. The Four Noble Truths certainly reflect the fundamental orientation of Conditional Arising.

This, O Bhikkus, is the Noble Truth of Suffering; Birth is suffering, decay is suffering, illness is suffering, death is suffering. Presence of objects we hate is suffering. Separation from objects we love is suffering; not to obtain what we desire is suffering. Briefly, the fivefold clinging to existence is suffering.

This, O Bhikkus, is the Noble Truth of the Cause of Suffering; Thirst, that leads to rebirth, accompanied by pleasure and lust, finding its delight here and there (this thirst is threefold), namely, thirst for pleasure, thirst for existence, thirst for prosperity. [13]

These first two Truths describe the predicament of humanity. They are Buddha's diagnosis of the human sickness. The First Truth tells us how fundamental and inescapable is the reality of suffering in human life. 'The fivefold clinging to existence' means our clinging to existence through each element of five aggregates; body, feeling, recognition, imagination and discrimination. 'Happy is he who lives in this world free from passion, has overcome sensual enjoyment, and who has attained mastership over the conceit of "I am". This indeed is the highest happiness.'[14]

The Second Truth goes beyond the plain description of the suffering to the investigation of the cause of suffering (conditional arising). The cause of suffering is defined as thirsting greed (*tanha*). The Third and Fourth Truths are concerned about salvation.

This, O Bhikkhus, is the Noble Truth of the Cessation of Suffering; (it ceases with) the complete cessation of this thirst – a cessation which consists in the absence of every passion – with the abandoning of this thirst, with the doing away with it, with the deliverance from it, with the destruction of desire.

When greed ceases, then suffering ceases (conditional arising). The Fourth Truth reads;

This, O Bhikkus, is the Noble Truth of the Path which leads to the cessation of suffering; that holy eightfold Path, that is to say; Right Belief, Right Aspiration, Right Speech, Right Conduct, Right Means of Livelihood, Right Endeavour, Right Memory, Right Meditation.[15]

The first two concerned with diagnosis are responded to by the last two, which offer therapy. This form suggests the spirit of Conditional Arising. Why is this particular diagnosis given, and not some other way of looking at the fundamental ill of human existence? This is a difficult question to answer. It must go back to the original contents of the Buddha's enlightenment and the whole story of his search for salvation previous to it. It also must reflect the way life was generally perceived in the ancient Hindu world. The question whether this diagnosis can claim universal validity is also a difficult question to answer. Can we, who live in today's world, understand this diagnosis of the Buddha in the way that the Buddha intended is also open to question. My own inclination is to agree that the concept of human greed as the cause of human suffering has a profoundly universal ring. The contents of the word *tanha* is not just ordinary greed, but intensified 'thirsting greed'. Ordinary greed may contribute to the formation of culture and civilization, but 'thirsting greed' does not. This diagnosis can be applied to the personal as well as the community life of humanity. The thirsting greed of humanity is the point at which the Buddhist proclamation anchors itself deeply in history.

The central issue in Conditional Arising and also in the Four Noble Truths, then, is that greed causes suffering; and that if we want to be free from suffering, we must destroy greed. The Buddha gives us practical advice as to how to eliminate our greed by following the Holy Eightfold Path. As we have seen the path of Conditional Arising can go in both ways, through 'arising' and through 'ceasing'. Greed and suffering are both value concepts. How greed – a certain value concept in the orientation of life – is related to suffering – also a certain value concept in the understanding of life – must be a very complicated story. There must not be mathematical precision, as it were, between them, as two plus two is four. Why is it that greed causes suffering? Conversely, why is it true that when greed ceases suffering ceases? And is this true in spite of the incredible complexity of life? Can we say so simply that greed is the cause of suffering?

If this is the fundamental truth of Buddhism, then its doctrine is simple, direct and easy to understand intellectually and emotionally *and* at the same time 'abstruse, profound, most subtle, hard to grasp'. The question whether Buddhism is history-concerned faith or not is also 'abstruse, profound, most subtle, hard to grasp'. The simple answer which has been given, in particular onesidedly judged by Christian theology, says that Buddhism is not history-oriented faith. As I have indicated, the difficulty to give a clear answer to this question is increased by our awareness that there is no way to reach the sayings of the historical Buddha to know how he understood his own enlightenment.[16] All we know about him is derived from the tradition of his community in much the same way as the story of Jesus Christ was passed on by his believing community.

Three brief comments may be permitted here to explain why it seems to me that Buddhism is far more history directed than it is generally understood to be.

First, it is very possible that people saw in the Buddha a man of remarkable depth of wisdom and mercy, who had achieved emancipation from the power of greed. He must have demonstrated something of a 'breakthrough' in his life. It is most likely that this primary 'breakthrough' is related to the thought of Conditional Arising. Buddhist faith is an impossibility apart from the inspiring historical presence of this human person called Gotama. In terms of this impressive historical presence, Buddhism cannot be simply described as a faith which has no interest in history.[17] There must be the personality of the historical Buddha behind a saying such as this one found in the *Dhammapada*:

> Should a person commit evil, he should not do it again and again; he should not find pleasure therein: painful is the accumulation of evil.[18]

Second, the enlightenment of the Buddha was not a gift from a higher being. It was a self-awakening. The Buddha rejected dependence upon others in the achievement of enlightenment. He viewed the practice of making sacrifice to gods to be of no value for the destruction of greed and the emancipation from suffering. Only by an all-out personal battle against greed are we freed from suffering. As one who rejected the religious value of sacrifice twenty-five centuries ago, the Buddha's name stands out in the history of religions. Rejecting sacrifice he turned his back on the general religious philosophy and ritual of the Vedic Hindu spirituality and took a radically critical attitude towards the magical. He demanded careful thinking and well founded practice. Buddha's rejection of the magical suggests his move towards the concept of historical responsibility. We are responsible to control, and if possible to eliminate, our own greed.

For the same reason that he rejected sacrifice, the Buddha rejected the caste system prevalent in his society. the tradition tells us that he is reported to have said:

No brahman is such by birth
No outcaste is such by birth.
An outcaste is such by his deeds.
A brahman is such by his deeds.[19]

That a 'brahman is such by birth' is a cosmological concept supported by the Vedic myth of Primeval Man (*prusha*).

The Brahman was his mouth,
The arms were made the Prince,
His thighs the common people,
And from his feet the serf was born.[20]

The Buddha declares his independence from the cosmological sociology and moves in the direction of the modern world in which the worth of a person is decided morally rather than cosmologically. This is obviously a direction towards historical thinking. That 'an outcaste is such by his deeds' implies the concept of freedom and thus, also of history. Buddhism thus maintains a critical relationship with the cosmologically elaborated political power, such as, *deva raja* kingship in south east Asia.

The third indication of an emphasis on history is found in the Buddhist understanding of ignorance. Ignorance is ignorance about the relationship between human greed and human suffering, and it is a confused mind, darkened and without understanding. This connection between ignorance and suffering is fundamental, as we have seen, in the doctrine of *paticcasamuppada*. This transition is historical and empirical. And transition (movement and change), and not no-movement nor unchangeability, is the central category of the Buddhist thought. Everything flows and changes! At least this indicates psychological and intellectual tendency towards history. Ignorance fails to understand this transition from ignorance to human suffering. Buddha asks that we be awakened in our mental and intellectual life. He would agree with Pascal that the proper dignity of the person is to be found in the ability to think critically.

Man is but a reed, ... but he is a thinking reed. ... All our dignity consists, then, in thought. By it we must elevate ourselves, and not by space and time which we cannot fill. Let us endeavour, then, to think well; this is the principle of morality.[21]

These two thinkers, living in such different times and places, agreed that the basic value of humanity is in our ability to dispel ignorance. I would like to add to this observation that both thinkers seriously involved themselves in the understanding of history. The concept of ignorance is, for the Buddha,

historical and empirical. What sense is there if the concept of ignorance has
nothing to do with this historical world? How a-historical ignorance can
produce a historical greed, 'thirsting greed'? And how the thirsting greed
can be a-historical?

These are three brief comments directing our attention to the history
oriented nature of Buddhism.

It seems to me that the Buddha is saying that human intelligence must be
able to make a critical appraisal of the impermanence of all things. What is
impermanent is changeable, and that which is changeable must not be
allowed to shackle our minds. 'Is the body permanent or impermanent?' the
Buddha asks his disciples.

> 'Impermanent, Lord.'
> 'What is woeful, impermanent, by nature changeable is it proper to
> regard that thus: "This is mine; this am I; this is the self of me"?'
> 'Surely not, Lord.'
> 'So with feeling, perception, the activities, consciousness, is it proper
> thus to regard it: "This is mine; this am I; this is the self of me"?'
> 'Surely not, Lord.'
> 'Wherefore, brethren, whatsoever body, be it past, future, or present,
> inward or outward, gross or subtle, low or high, far or near, –
> whatsoever body there be, thus must it be regarded in its real nature by
> perfect insight: This is not mine; this am not I; this is not the self of me.[22]

The final line of the quotation is the fundamental insight that would lead us
to the *nirvana*. When 'I' is understood this way, it must be renounced.

> His sum of life the sage renounced,
> The cause of life immeasurable or small;
> With inward joy and calm, he broke,
> Like coat of mail, his life's own cause![23]

At this point it is usually said that such teaching shows weak or even anti-
historical orientation; and thus Buddhism is branded as a religion which has
no interest in history. Rather, it was through an intense and critical
observation of history that the Buddha came to the position of 'renouncing'
the self. Thirsting greed and *nirvana* are in strong contradiction. Whatever
we may say about the essence and character of the *nirvana*, one thing is
clear; it is the ultimate opposite of human greed. And whatever we may say
about greed, it is non-sensical if greed is not historically defined. *Nirvana* is
the complete elimination of greed. As long as it is so *nirvana* cannot be
completely free from the touch of this history of ours. This must be the
reason why there are profound ambiguities attached to the concept of
nirvana. Can we achieve *nirvana* in this life? The answer is yes and no. The
struggle towards the achieving of *nirvana* begins in this world, where we
live. 'With inward joy and calm' we must overcome our ignorance, and thus

greed, and thus suffering. This is the meaning of the line; 'His sum of life the sage renounced'.

There is, then, in the fundamental message of Buddhism, that which coincides with the spirit of the prophet Jeremiah of the biblical world.

Woe to him who builds his house by unrighteousness, and his upper rooms by injustice; who makes his neighbour serve him for nothing, and does not give him his wages; who says 'I will build myself a great house with spacious upper rooms,' and cuts out windows for it, panelling it with cedar and painting it with vermilion (Jer. 22.13,14).

The Buddha would immediately see that the root of King Jehoiakim's trouble is his greed, which is the cause of injustice and unrighteousness. In his expensive palace he would be far removed from the highest good, *nirvana*, in this life and beyond. Should the Buddha encounter king Jehoiakim, he would tell the king that he is enslaved to the idea that 'this is mine; this am I; this is self of me'. Social injustice and unrighteousness, according to the Buddha's teaching, derive from human greed.

The Buddhist thought of renouncing self means, in fact, destroying greed. It is of no use, put it awkwardly, to renounce self if greed remains active, since the value of renouncing self is found in none other than the elimination of greed. The Buddha, thus interpreted, is speaking a different message from the Vedantic (Upanisadic) formulation of salvation. In Upanisads the salvation is presented as the union between *Atman*, our inner world, and the *Brahman*, the world outside of us. In the sublime words of the pre-Buddhist Chandogya Upanisad:

This is myself within the heart, smaller than a grain of rice, than a barley corn, than a mustard seed, than a grain of millet or than the kernel of a grain of millet. This is myself within the heart, greater than the earth, greater than the atmosphere, greater than the sky, greater than these worlds.[24]

What a strange self! The smallest self is 'greater than the earth...' This is nothing but the union of the *Atman* and *Brahman*. The subtle essence of the great outside world of objectivity, 'that are thou', *tat tvam asi*![25] But in this philosophical scheme no fight against one's own greed is suggested. The Vedantic doctrine of salvation is constructed more upon the cosmological image than historical involvement. It speaks about the 'subtle essence' of cosmological mystery than 'cause and elimination of suffering' in history.

Thus Buddhist thought of renouncing self must be brought to dialogue with the sayings of Jesus, such as this in the Gospel of Matthew:

If any man would come after me, let him deny himself and take up his cross and follow me (16.24).

I am not suggesting that this teaching on Christian discipleship and Buddha's doctrine of the destruction of greed are identical. Rather I am suggesting that there is a certain spiritual correspondence between them. The Buddha speaks about the destruction of greed which moves in the same direction with Christian self-denial. These words of the gospel are clear and powerful. In Buddhism these words of Jesus may find correspondence in the Conditional Arising. Any one who would like to reach *nirvana* must live intelligently according to the teaching of the Conditional Arising. Life under the instruction of the Conditional Arising involves the battle against human greed. This interpretation of the fundamental message of Buddhism reveals the historical character of Buddhism. It is not simply concerned about tranquillity outside of history. It makes a strong call for the elimination of human greed, historical greed.

The progression in Conditional Arising; ignorance – greed – suffering, can be seen as parallel to three stages of history in Hindu philosophy; creation – maintenance – destruction. That the creation of the world of phenomena and multiplicity derives from ignorance is an idea that is not without precedence in the Hindu tradition. Creation is understood to be the fall from one to many. This is the time of ignorance. The period of maintenance can be thought of as a time of struggle with human greed. Destruction, then, is the period of suffering resulting from the power of human greed.

But the doctrine of Conditional Arising does not address itself to the overview of human history in forms such as the Hindu three periods or Augustine's *City of God*. It is more in the line of an existential diagnosis of the individual human being. This diagnosis is not in the tradition of the cosmological scheme in which hope is expressed in terms of the continuity and renewal of cyclical time. There is something in the Conditional Arising which transcends cosmological circularity. In that sense the doctrine of Conditional Arising has its own transcendental mystical quality in spite of its basically rational nature. I am suggesting that in the doctrine of Conditional Arising there is a rare union of rational analysis and mystical integration. That greed arises from ignorance and suffering from greed is neither a completely rational nor a completely mystical concept. Conditional Arising is constructed rationally and mystically and therefore cannot be limited to either category. The thesis is something we can understand and yet cannot understand. It is not an ordinary structure. I believe this is the secret of the fascination of the Conditional Arising and it is at the same time the strength of its argument. Something so deeply rational may take on the character of the mystical. Such a meeting in depth of the rational and the mystical can be deeply historical. Human greed is rationally and mystically treated and such treatment contributed to demonstrate the historicity of human greed.

The law – *dharma* – of the Buddha has rational as well as mystical depths. Again, from greed comes suffering. It may be argued, however, that from greed comes happiness and fulfilment. In the judgment of the *dharma*, however, greed will create suffering. Yes, even while the greedy are enjoying the fruits of their greed, actually under the light of the *dharma* they are suffering. This *dharma* is not an abstract concept. Since it governs our history, it is as real as the history we know. The religion of self-enlightenment is mystical and rational, and has its own serious relationship with history. I notice such mystical rationality or rational mysticism in the 'Fire Sermon' of the Buddha:

> Monks, everything is burning. And what, monks, is everything that is burning? The eye, monks, is burning, material shapes are burning, consciousness through the eye is burning, impingement on the eye is burning; in other words the feeling which arises from impingement on the eye, be it pleasant or painful or neither painful nor pleasant, that too is burning. With what is it burning? I say it is burning with the fire of passion, with the fire of hatred, with the fire of stupidity; it is burning because of birth, ageing, dying, because of grief, sorrow, suffering, lamentation and despair.[26]

Human history is 'burning' with the fire of passion, hatred and stupidity. This view of history is far more 'historical' than the Japanese view of history as 'next-next-continuously-becoming-by-momentum' or as the alternatives of *kichi* and *kyo*. But this 'burning' suggests more than this. It can disturbingly suggest that our human rational understanding and structure of salvation can be subjected to burning and reduced to ashes. Our rationality may not be free from passion, hatred and stupidity if we are under the control of greed. Greed can disfigure our rationality. This realization cannot come from our own rationality alone. It takes more. It takes a union of the rational and the mystical to come to such realization. This may be the reason why the Buddha said: 'Men sunk in sin and lusts would find it hard to plumb this doctrine...'

It is important to notice that this Buddha's admonition against human greed is not originated in the 'Lord who made heaven and earth'. It came from his own self-enlightenment. And it has its own serious study of history.

The Buddhist admonition to fight against human greed finds expression in the Buddhist monastic movement. Theravada Buddhism prescribes for the monks a life of strict discipline. There are 227 training rules or injunctions, called *patimokkha*, 'that which binds, obligatory', which they are required to observe. The first four of these 227 injunctions are, as we have seen, *parajika*, 'suffering defeats'. Those who violate them are defeated and must be expelled from the monastery. In Thai Buddhism they are as follows:

1. Sexual intercourse
2. Taking anything worth more than five 'masok' without the owner's consent (A 'masok' is a negligible amount, like five cents.)

   3. murder
   4. falsely claiming to possess the highest truth.[27]

The rule is rigorous. To be defeated in any of these first four injunctions is to be put out of the monastery without possibility of reinstatement. Here a moment of discontinuity is expressed in Buddhist thought and practice. Some deeds are so decisively unacceptable for the achievement of *nirvana* that they mean defeat. It is important to notice that these four defeats are basically to do with human greed, starting with sexual intercourse to claiming the possession of the highest truth.

Sexual intercourse, in whatever context, is strictly forbidden for the monks. Sexuality as the gift of God is an overarching concept of the biblical tradition. Only its misuse, adultery, is condemned. In cosmological religions it is commonplace to find that the gods are sexually paired. Cosmic life is experienced and expressed as an image of sexual union. We have seen that in the case of the God of Israel this is completely absent. As ruler of the universe, God oversees all its activity, including its sexual polarity and vitality, but God is not identified as cosmic vitality or sexuality.

What is the reason for the proscription of sexual intercourse in the first *parajika*? The Buddha must have associated sexual acts with lust and greed. If the *nirvana*, the most desirable state of mind, must be free of lust and greed, then sexual intercourse must be forbidden those who would specialize in reaching *nirvana*. The fundamental decision is taken in order to achieve the highest good, the *nirvana*. The Buddhist negation of sexuality, then, is not nihilistic. *Nirvana* is tranquillity itself, while sexuality is intense agitation. Distancing ourselves from the excitement of sexuality or greed does not mean that we are taking distance from the reality of history. It is possible to be deeply involved in history without involving ourselves in lust and greed. The New Testament is completely silent about the sexuality of Jesus who is, in the apostolic view, most profoundly involved in the history and destiny of humanity. The character of the God of Israel has inspired the same possibility in a dramatic way. In spite of confusions and misuses in history of the Christian monastic tradition, the noble aspiration of that tradition is for deep involvement in history without sexual involvement. In recent history the Indian, Gandhi, has illustrated this possibility. The identification of sexuality with historicity eventually produces a tendency to worship lust, which is called paganism. By fighting against lust and greed we come closer to the core of history, and thus can become more authentically historical than otherwise. Marianne Katoppo, an Indonesian woman theologian suggests that virginity of Mary must not be understood in medical terms but in her freedom for others.[28]

There is a positive interaction between the disciplined life (asceticism) and history. I believe Buddhism has made a significant contribution in this. If we see the First Defeat in this way, it reveals a somewhat similar character to the saying of Jesus, 'If any man would come after me, let him deny himself and take up his cross and follow me' (Matt.16.24). He was speaking of deep historical involvement by way of self-discipline and self-denial. I am tempted to say that it is this orientation which makes religious faith noble and inspiring. It may be one of the important elements that contributes to make a religion a universal religion.

Monastic discipline is not the only expression of Buddhist spirituality. Side by side with monastic discipline there was developed in Buddhism a response to the people's need for salvation. This is the expression of grace religion, in contrast to monastic religion, within Buddhism. The religion of grace must be able to say that even the greedy and lustful person can be saved. Those who cannot leave the world to enter the monastic discipline must also have some hope of salvation. The affirmation of grace must find a way to make possible an emotional and philosophical identification between the noise of lust and the tranquillity of *nirvana*. In Buddhism this grace religion is called *Mahayana* (the greater vehicle) because it is a way for the many, while monastic Buddhism, which only a few are able to follow, is called *Hinayana* (the lesser vehicle).[29]

Grace religions, such as Mahayana Buddhism and Christianity, have a serious problem in relation to human morality. They say that the grace is more dependable and powerful than all human self-discipline. Thus, inevitably, is opened up a way of easy morality. To say that even the lustful can be saved is a threat for spiritual discipline and morality. Yet, one way or other, grace must risk this 'dangerous' position. The relationship between grace and morality resists simple solution. It will remain a relationship of conflict and ambiguity.

The tradition of Mount Sinai rejects any identification between human lust and the mind of God. It is clearly indicated that God does not approve human lust and greed. At the same time God is ever creating a new possibility within human history.

> I will put my law within them, and I will write it upon their hearts; and I will be their God, and they shall be my people (Jer. 31.33).

I will recreate them! This is grace. Yet this grace does not cancel out ethical responsibility from them. They must live practising the law of God which was placed in their minds by God. This combination of grace and ethics does not present us with easy salvation but with a more deeply painful historical experience. God is presented as 'helpless' in the face of human greed. Quell comments on Hosea 11.8,9; '"How can I give you up, O Ephraim!" God indicates his helplessness that comes from his profound love for his people. God would not be so helpless if he did not love his people so intensely'.[30] This is the painful 'helpless' depth of biblical grace and ethics. This is the way God experiences history. Here the profound character of the grace religion reveals itself. Biblical ethics would be far simpler if it spoke ony of discipline and moral excellence. In the Bible, ethics is not an independent concept. It is rooted in the nature of God who is involved in history. Inevitably, then, history is the confusing interaction between grace and ethics. History continues because God continues to be in search of humanity. This search, the secret of grace and ethics, takes place in history. *God in Search of Man* (Abraham Heschel) is deeply rational and mystical, revealing the core of history as the biblical experience presents it.

Because both Buddhism and the biblical faith urge us to struggle against human greed, both faiths involve us inescapably in the experience of history. In comparison to the biblical stance, however, there is no discussion in Buddhism of the 'helplessness' or 'frustration' of the Buddha. According to Buddhist teaching the final word about history lies with us.

> And whosoever, Ananda, either now or after I am dead, shall be a lamp unto themselves, and a refuge unto themselves, shall betake themselves to no external refuge, but holding fast to the Truth as their lamp, and holding fast as their refuge to the Truth, shall look not for refuge to any one besides themselves – it is they, Ananda, among my bhikkhus, who shall reach the very topmost Height![31]

The followers of Buddha are exhorted to live this history, replete with human greed, by holding fast to the Truth as their lamp, careful not to seek any external help in their struggle. Buddhism, which does not speak of the 'helplessness of the Buddha', demonstrates the simpler, yet serious, understanding of history. History must be experienced responsibly, 'betaking ourselves to no external refuge'. The historical Buddha conquered his greed. He must have conquered it through the insight of Conditional Arising. This is the inspiration of the Buddhist. But each one must realize for himself or herself what the Buddha accomplished. There is no one to help 'either now or after I am dead'.

> Decay is inherent in all component things! Work out your salvation with diligence![32]

There is nothing external to all things that support and protect them. Therefore, through our adherence to the Conditional Arising and Four Noble Truths, we must battle diligently against our own greed, and attain salvation with our own power and insight.

The teaching of the Buddha comes neither from 'the Lord who made heaven and earth' nor simply from 'heaven and earth'. Without 'the Lord' it reveals to us the nature of human life and history. Its message cannot be dealt lightly. .

In the Conditional Arising and the Four Noble Truths, I understand the Buddha to be speaking of individual, personal greed. My suffering comes from my greed. My ignorance of this truth about myself is the source of greed that produces my suffering. Did Buddha speak at all about collective greed? Can we understand the Conditional Arising as a social analysis? Is there in Buddhism any philosophical ground for revolution? Is there in Buddhism a principle on which power comes under criticism?

Between 29 May and 5 June 1966, nine Buddhists in South Vietnam burned themselves to death in political protest. The name of the Buddhist leader, Thick Tri Quang, became well known for his outspoken criticism of President Johnson's South Vietnam policy. The king of Thailand is defined as a Buddhist according to the constitution of the kingdom. He is a *deva-raja*, god-king, in the manner of the ancient tradition. As defender of the Buddhist faith he enjoys immense spiritual prestige. He lends his religious prestige to the government's anti-communist campaign. One of the major events in the Japanese religious and political world in the post-war years has been the emergence in the Nichiren School of a Buddhist political party, *Komeito*. Millions of Buddhists are actively engaged in political actions. Buddhism is a social force which the secular power cannot ignore.

These historical examples, even including the self-immolation of the monks in Vietnam, do not answer the question whether Buddhism has a clear principle of social revolution. Is the Conditional Arising addressed to social ills? There is an episode in Buddhist literature in which the Buddha draws social consequences from personal greed.

'Now what do you think, Kalamas, when greed arises within a person, does it arise to his profit or to his loss?'
'To his loss, Sir.'
'Well, by becoming greedy or being overcome by greed and thereby losing balance of mind, does he not indulge in killing, commit theft, go after another's wife, tell lies and not only that, mislead others into evil and immoral acts which lead to his own loss and misery for a long time?'
'Yes, he does, Sir.'
'Likewise, when hatred or malice, delusion or ignorance or such other evil states arise do they not make people lose control of their minds and thereby lead them to perform all kinds of evil and immoral acts which end in loss and suffering?'[33]

This is a popular application of Conditional Arising to social ethics. It is, in fact, a kind of social analysis but it falls short of dealing with the relationship between greed and political power, greed which is systematized and impersonalized. Realizing the hazard of making any sort of general comment upon so broad a subject as the social ethics of Buddhism, I am compelled to observe that Buddhism is primarily interested in personal ethics rather than in social ethics. But the relationship between the two is not that of polarization. It is a profoundly complementary relationship. The rational and mystical elements in Buddha's discourses on the human ills can equip us better as we take up study of social ills and social salvation. That is to say, the Buddha, who gave the 'Fire Sermon', would have been very much in one mind with Jeremiah's 'Temple Sermon' (Jer. 7.1– 15).

> For if you truly amend your ways and your doings, if you truly execute justice one with another, if you do not oppress the alien, the fatherless or the widow, or shed innocent blood in this place, and if you do not go after gods to your own hurt, then I will let you dwell in this place, in the land that I gave of old to your fathers forever (vv. 5–7).

The image that 'the eye is burning with greed and lust' is not unrelated to 'execute justice one with another'. If our eyes are burning with greed, we would most likely not execute justice one with another. 'If your eye is sound, your whole body will be full of light' (Matt. 6.22). I believe that the ethics suggested by Conditional Arising is not foreign to the biblical ethics since it speaks about *human* greed which is by definition both personal and social.

But at this point we must ponder whether the two traditions suggest the same connection between greed and suffering or not. When we have greed in our mind we are likely to will social injustice. Social injustice, no matter how we cover it up with inspiring rhetoric, will result in the suffering of people, even the ruin of the community. The connection between greed and suffering may be said to be not through Conditional Arising but through human *will*. Now, following the teaching of the Conditional Arising and the Four Noble Truths, it is indeed hard to believe that the social ills caused by the arms race could not be alleviated if the terrible greed for national power, prestige or 'security' were to disappear. Our national greed is implemented through planned mechanisms and strategies. Here is a delicate point of connection between ignorance and will. Suffering comes from ignorance. Granted. But human greed arises in human will and has willed consequences. Is it possible that at that point we might resist the appearance of such will? How do the Conditional Arising and the Four Noble Truths look if we see them in the light of the freedom of human will? Does the mystical nature of the Conditional Arising deal sufficiently with the issue of human freedom? How are ignorance and will related to each other when we see them in the light of the ancient words of the psalmist; 'My help comes from the Lord who made heaven and earth'?

Both Buddhist and biblical traditions are history oriented since they deal with historical human greed. The former speaks about history calmly – rationally and mystically – through the Conditional Arising, while the latter speaks passionately in the image of God who loves the world and history. This observation poses a great challenge to Christian theology. The relationship between Buddhism and Christianity is not that of 'true religion' and 'false religion'. It is to do with two different yet intertwined understandings of the history of human greed. God 'did not leave himself without witness' (Acts 14.17).

11

Technology Occasions a Conflict between Efficiency and Meaning

Idolatry is subjugation of meaning to efficiency by the power of human greed, thus it represents a reckless approach to, and relationship with, the holy.

Our battle against our own greed and lust is hard and painstaking. It cannot be carried out with technological efficiency. Yet in this battle is located the possibility of human meaning. The historical cannot be subsumed under the category of technological efficiency. There is a relationship of irritation between the historical and the technological. As Buddhism indicates its own history concerned character, it would resist to be treated in the perspective of the technological efficiency.

In chapter 9 we referred to the temples of Solomon and of the Emperor Shomu. Their temples are the visual symbolism of the centre, the *axis mundi*, located at the meeting point of heaven, earth and hell, that is, of meaning. Meaning is being cultivated when different messages intersect. The point of meaning is the sacred point at which people offer their prayers to 'God'. I have pointed out that the construction of those temples over the oppression of the people demonstrates a problem in the relationship between human greed and human meaning. Greed is efficient because it has no compunctions about using others for one's own glory. Technology is not inherently destructive to human well-being. But when technology is used to serve human greed, its compounded efficiency will certainly impoverish and destroy the meaning of human life. The coming of highly efficient science based technology challenges us to ponder the relationship between efficiency and meaning today. In this context I propose that one of the ways we allow ourselves to fall down before idols is through the subjugation of meaning to efficiency.

Religion is to do with experience and expression of the sacred. That experience takes place within a particular cultural context. As culture changes, our imagination and perception of the sacred will be influenced. As we move into a new cultural environment of technology we must expect some significant changes in our religious experience. This does not mean that the Buddha will be seen in the pilot seat of a Jumbo Jet with earphones over his ears and his two feet busily pushing pedals and valves. The Buddha will remain under the Bo Tree. The cross will remain as the central symbolism for Christians. The Upanisadic speculation about the unity of the cosmos and human being will remain. But our appreciation of them will change, as it has changed. Religious symbolism does not dictate meaning in a totalitarian fashion. It allows space for the human spirit to move, imagine and sing.

The relevance of religious symbolism derives from our commitment to the truthfulness of the religious message itself. Religious symbolism, be it the 'jealous God' of the Book of Exodus, 'My Rock' of Psalm 28, the cross of the New Testament, the Bodhisattva of the *Lotus Sutra* or the Paradise of the Qu'ran, must speak relevant language if we are to find truth in it. When religion makes a truth claim it also makes a relevance claim. The *arhat*, the bodhisattva, the Christ must make sense in the world of science-technology.

Finally, religion promises salvation. Salvation is a future-linked concept. It suggests a dimension beyond. The future and the beyond of religion cannot be fully explained in terms of the religious experience of the past alone. The religious 'present' is a future-leaning present. Technology also is future-leaning. It suggests to us that its amazing efficiency will replace the meaning that we have traditionally found in religion. It is not religion but science based technology which can put a person in New York in immediate conversation with another in Tokyo through the telephone. It is not religion but medical technology which is able to save the lives of hopeless patients. Technology challenges religion through its astounding performance.

A south east Asian example will illustrate this challenge. The Thai Buddhist monk, Buddhadasa, characterizes the *nirvana* as 'a state of everlasting radiant smiles with nobody smiling'.[1] This poetic expression points to the transcendental and paradoxical character of the *nirvana* concept. In it tranquillity and activity are united. This world and the world beyond are in dialogue. The analogy of the 'smile' is eloquent in terms of the accommodation to Buddhist truth of the Thai people. It is the value to which the community adheres. In this definition of *nirvana* the smile is negated and affirmed. I have observed the monks on the jet flight between Bangkok and Rangoon. They find themselves, even though it is a matter of less than one hour, in the comfortable technological environment. I noticed smiles on their faces, but they were 'nirvanic' smiles. 'A state of everlasting radiant smiles with nobody smiling' was there, at the altitude of 33,000 feet and at the speed of 600 miles an hour. For the specialists of the *nirvana* ideal, science-based-technology is a new experience. They place it between 'smiles' and 'non-smiles' as they appreciate it. The monks seem to say that the appreciation of technological efficiency must be placed in the context of the appreciation of the *nirvana*. Theravada monastic Buddhism raises the issue for us as to the relationship between the two values, *nirvana* and technology, religious salvation and the technological possibilities. Often the tension between them refuses to be obediently placed between 'smiles' and 'non-smiles'.

Thus, religion is to do with our experience of the sacred. This experience will be influenced by the power of the dominant cultural element, such as technology. And there is an ongoing tension between the salvation by technology and salvation by religion. When I reflect upon this tension between salvation by technology and salvation by religion, two important concepts come to me; cosmos and history. Religion interacts with cosmos and history, and so does technology. That both of them interact with the same cosmos and history creates a situation of ambiguity. As they 'mould' cosmos and history by engaging in intense dialogue with them, both religion and technology, shows their similarity and dissimilarity. Religion and technology encounter each other on the question of relationship between 'efficiency and meaning'.

The cosmos provides us with an ordered image of nature. It is an image of wisdom. There is in cosmos a mysterious unity of *eikon* (image, that which can be seen, 'river') and *logos* (word, rational understanding of what is happening in a given *eikon*, such as rational explanation on 'the movement of water'). The water in the river flows with a certain reliability, giving us image and word, and providing a certain sense of security to us. Whenever cosmos is perceived by us we will come into contact with *eikon* and *logos*. The cosmic image awakens our imagination. The cosmic word instructs us, giving us understanding and rationality. Embracing and instructing us, the cosmos inspires us to make symbols, thus also pointing us to the sacred. The cosmos is religious. The mystery of the unity of *eikon* and *logos* rejects secularism.

Technology arises from an efficient administrative 'image-writing' (iconography) upon nature. It is an expression of the experimenting, adventurous and aggressive mind. Wherever technology touches it leaves technological *eikon*(s), be it in the kitchen, the street, the hospital, the school, or even in the mind, morality, philosophy, or religion of people. The ability to engage in this powerful image-writing derives from the inspiration technology receives from the original cosmological *eikon* and *logos*. Aeroplanes, even the most advanced ones, retain the image of a bird. Both the simple Dyack canoes paddling on the streams of North Borneo and the nuclear submarine point to the image and rationality of fish.

Technology is a kind of enlightenment which creates enormous efficiency on the basis of image and word of the cosmos. The ground is fertile. Technology produces fertilizer to increase its productivity. This act of 'enhancement' in efficiency by the human mind produces the possibility of an enlightened relationship with the cosmos. *Efficiency is enlightenment.* This is the spiritual and religious message of technology to humanity. In this sense our technological age is an enlightened age. If we confess 'efficiency is enlightenment' we become 'religious' in the technological sense.

Technological enhancement is, however, ambiguous. It has the ability to 'rebel' against the cosmological *eikon* and *logos*. Technology can be creative or destructive to our home, the cosmos. It makes the field greener by the administration of fertilizer and it also places humanity under the threat of annihilation of the destructive use of nuclear energy. The ability to enhance or to destroy humanity lies in the way we make use of the technology we have produced. At this point technology is deeply involved in history. The relationship between the two is not direct, however. It is mediated by people. Technology is related to history by the way we make use of it, whether creatively or destructively.

The ambiguity of technology is rooted in our own spiritual ambiguity. Technology and humanity, efficiency and meaning are in a dangerously precarious relationship. The vast increase of technology raises a serious question as to the relationship between technological efficiency and human meaning. It has become, perhaps, the most grave challenge humanity has encountered in the course of its history. Technology used by human greed will destroy humanity.

Before we come to the biblical view of the relationship between technological efficiency and human meaning, we should pay attention to how it is in the traditional cultures.

1. Traditional cultures are acquainted with the paradoxical image of an 'inefficient posture' that makes space meaningful

Traditional cultures breathe in space personally created. It is a space of myths and symbols. Tane, the mythical god and father of forest of the New Zealand Maoris, is a hero who gave his people personalized living space. In the beginning Rangi (Father Heaven) and Papa (Mother Earth) clung together and there was no space between them for their children to grow and enjoy freedom of movement. After a series of failures on the part of the children to separate their parents it is said that Tane was able to rend apart Rangi and Papa. ...he paused; firmly he planted his head on his mother Papa, the earth, and his feet he raised up against his father Rangi, the sky; he strained his back and his limbs in a mighty effort. Now were rent apart

Rangi and Papa... The posture ('heading' instead of 'footing'!) with which this hero accomplished his mission is mytho-technological. Space is gained painfully by the strain of his back and limbs.

The up-side-down posture in which the god engaged in his work is technologically awkward and inefficient. The glory of the traditional cultures is found in its insight that some form of 'inefficient posture' must be retained to safeguard the sense of human value in the community. Even while they may welcome it, they are suspicious of streamlined efficiency because they know the high human value of the symbolism of inefficiency which makes space and community meaningful. That it took six years of meditation for Gotama Siddharta to reach the enlightenment – what an 'inefficient' process! – is significant.

One of the most notable and paradoxical of the 'inefficient postures' in the history of religion is asceticism. I may say that asceticism is the search for human meaning through an inefficient approach to the sacred. Ascetic postures are inefficient postures. The nude Jain, Mahavira, is certainly inefficient in his defence against insects and dogs. An ascetic who is starved cannot live efficiently. The meditation posture of the Buddha is not technologically promising. The Shiva standing on one foot is beautiful but not productive. The monk's denial of sexuality is a total inefficiency in terms of the future.

The Buddhist *patimokkha* contains the rules for the *sangha*, the community of the monks, which are binding. The monks are bound people. The first of the 227 states that 'sexual intercourse of any kind is forbidden'. This injunction sets the tone of the whole monastic tradition of Buddhism, the way of the *arhats*. The power to achieve *nirvana* is symbolized by the ability to free oneself from sexuality. Creativity is dialectical. It reaches affirmation through a moment of negation. In personal radical inefficiency is found the efficiency to achieve *nirvana*. This is the paradox of asceticism. Traditional cultures are familiar with the paradox of ascetic efficiency. The presence of the Buddhist monks in Thailand and Burma, through their 'inefficient posture' makes the space of the countries religious. Human space and human possibility are made meaningful through asceticism. This is a secret fascination of the traditional cultures which I see reflected in the wisdom of the cosmos. That the cosmos is ascetic we shall see later.

2. Cosmos-oriented, traditional cultures are enchantment-cultures

For much of Asia the benevolence of nature is symbolized by the regular coming of the life-giving monsoon. Without the monsoon, how would it be possible to cultivate the fields? Whether cultivation is done by tractor or by waterbuffalo, the technology waits upon the monsoon. The monsoon is primary and technology is secondary. The feeling of the primacy of the monsoon arouses an 'enchantment emotion' with the cosmos.

In Thailand, society is ordered by two cosmos-oriented institutions; Buddhism for religion and the monarchy for political life. Thai Buddhism is a Buddhism of the monks, who are 'religious virtuosi' in the terms of Max Weber. The ordinary people gain their religious merit and find their place in the Buddha's cosmos by supporting these specialists for the nirvana. These virtuosi become the silent centre of the enchanting cosmos. The king at the supreme head of the religion, stands at the centre of Buddha's cosmos. He is able to accumulate a vast amount of merit. He is the cosmic tree and Mount Meru, mythical mountain at the centre of the universe, in person. His authority lies in being at the centre of the monsoon cosmos *and* the Buddha's cosmos. The king is an extremely enchanting person, a living mythological person. He is the symbol of the unity of religious and cosmological centres. The beauty of his wife, the queen, is both cosmological and religious.

In such a cosmos-oriented society people are not lonely. They are surrounded by mythic and symbolic stories which identify themselves through symbols. It is an enchanting world in which the community is in dialogue with the cosmos. The dialogue is not disturbed by the slow, gentle technology of the waterbuffalo ploughing in the fields. But the pressure of scientifically applied high technology can strain the dialogue to the breaking point. That to which scientific technology is applied suffers the loss of enchantment. The problem of the traditional cultures facing transition is to know how to have the abundance technology gives without losing the enchanting world.

3. Traditional cultures are liturgy-oriented

They are acquainted with the holy. From their long experience with the holy they know how to approach that which contains the holy. The Shwedagon Pagoda stands on Rangoon's Singuttara Hill. Those who would approach the Pagoda remove their shoes at the foot of the hill and come barefoot to the presence of the holy. Every step is a liturgical step. The long slow climb to the top of the hill is an experience of liturgical time. The sweat one feels on the forehead under the hot afternoon sun is liturgical sweat. The holy must be approached slowly, carefully, humbly and even painfully, that is, liturgically (inefficiently). Traditional cultures abound with holy places, holy temples, holy icons, holy men (monks, *saddhus*) holy days, holy trees, holy caves and so on. Always the holy is liturgically approached. The monk who presents in person the doctrine of the Buddha must be approached carefully. The monk upon receiving food from the laity is not to express gratitude to the donor since the holiness he represents transcends the daily human context of life. News that American astronauts had rocketed to the moon and walked on the sacred face of the moon was not welcomed by the Balinese people. How could the moon, the holy heavenly deity, be thus approached technologically?

Technology is characterized by controlled power. An appropriate symbol of technology is the train, which can move at great speed and over great distances, over mountains as well as in valleys, but only where its tracks are laid. The technologist has an inner drive to control and systematize. This is the point at which technology and the holy conflict. That which is controlled cannot be holy. The holy, in its dignity, rejects to be controlled and scheduled. Technology, by its very function, seems to foster secularization. When one looks down on the famed temple of the Sacred Tooth of the Buddha in Kandy, Sri Lanka, from the comfortable window seat of a jet plane, the holiness of the Sacred Tooth is seen from a new perspective, that of technological mobility and altitude. It is 'viewed from above' – 'at the speed of six hundred miles per hour' – diminished, controlled. Can the holy be experienced non-liturgically? ... from the air? How can we enjoy the fruits of technology yet retain the meaningful experience of the holy?

The role of technology cannot be ignored in the interpretation of spiritual values because it stands between cosmos and history, deeply affecting both. It is becoming very clear in high-technology societies, as problems of pollution and waste disposal mount, that the way in which technology affects history will depend very much on the way in which it influences the cosmos. Must the use of high technology be a completely destructive influence upon cosmos and history? When does technology, whether primitive or advanced, become a danger to humanity's welfare? This danger comes to us when we misuse our technology.

The end result of misuse is that we no longer have technology in our hands but technology has us in its hand. In this preposterous situation we are engaged in idolatry by throwing away our own human dignity (holiness) and subjecting it to the symbol of efficiency. It is usually the power of greed that motivates us to take a disrespectful attitude towards our own holiness. Therefore this symbol of efficiency is generally not neutral but poisoned by the breath of human greed.

However, only we, who can have some awareness about the tensionful relationship between meaning and efficiency, can engage in idolatry. We must have some idea about the distinction between use and misuse of technology or of human holiness if we are to speak about the subject of idolatry meaningfully. Idolatry means that meaning is in the hands of efficiency. The holy must be approached carefully and liturgically. Disrespectful approach to the holy is called greed.

I have suggested that the cosmos is ascetic. It may seem awkward to speak of the 'asceticism of the cosmos', but the orderliness of nature suggests to me the concept of 'discipline' which is characteristic of the cosmos. The cosmos embraces us in an orderly, disciplined way. The cosmos 'keeps' more than '227 rules' in order to remain disciplined. In this sense, it can be said to be ascetic. So the albatross at the Taiaroa Head of Otago Peninsula in New Zealand schedules its life activities according to the wind. The sun rises according to its schedule, never too early or too late but always different from yesterday or tomorrow, and the plants respond to its warmth according to the season. So also the human community is influenced by the asceticism of the cosmos.

Technology is also highly structured. Much of its structure is derived from the cosmos as we can see if we think of the aeroplane, the submarine, the caterpillar and the crane. The system of cosmic discipline has been copied, enlarged and enhanced in technology. Think of the jet engine. It is built with demanding precision and staggering complexity. The whole mechanism is highly 'disciplined'. The 'posture' of the engine is technologically designed to generate efficiency. Technology in this sense is 'ascetic'. It too participates in the 'arhatic monastic' psychology. Through this asceticism technology earns the right to influence human life to a high degree. We are impressed, consciously or unconsciously, by the 'asceticism of technology' as the Thais are impressed by the presence of the ascetic monk, or the naturalist by the 'ascetic' albatross. In nature to be ascetic and to be efficient are united. There is no greed in the world of nature. There is no awareness of distinction between use and misuse of power in nature. In the human world efficiency is usually invaded by greed, and therefore the meaning of asceticism is distorted.

The world of the cosmos does not effect the disenchantment of the cosmos. It is rational yet poetic. It is scientific yet religious. Let us once more think about the frog in Basho's *haiku*. Frog plunge. It does so according to nature. As it plunges it represents the image of the cosmos. It points to the rational orderliness of the cosmos. There is gravity in this world. There is strong muscle if frog's legs. But the nature of the frog to plunge must be interpreted in terms of the Mahayana philosophy of *tathata* ('thusness') as Basho himself intended. A frog plunges according to the 'thusness' of being a frog. Thus the *logos* of the cosmos is expressed as both rational and poetic. While the *logos* is thus appreciated the cosmos remains enchanting. There is a striking similarity in depth between Basho's 'old point' and 'the omega point' of Teilhard de Chardin in that both concepts are simultaneously rational and religious. The *logos* of the cosmos from which technology has developed itself is the *logos* which resists the disenchantment of the cosmos which technology tends to introduce. The *logos* of the cosmos does not allow a disfigurement of the *eikon* of cosmos to take place. Man, between the *logos* and *eikon* of the cosmos, is a cosmically enchanted person. The cosmos is able to enchant us scientifically as well as religiously. Can the cosmos with its *logos* and *eikon* prevent technology from becoming a destructive tyrant over us? Can the enchanted person provide the check?

A similar observation can be made with regard to the liturgical nature of the cosmos. That the cosmos is orderly means that it is liturgical. It is carefully programmed and performed. The liturgy of the cosmos – sunrise, sunset, cycle of life, hierarchy of being – influences us to be liturgical. We find symbols of centre, archetypes, repetition and regeneration in the liturgical performances of the cosmos. If the holy is 'wholly other' that is, 'wholly' located outside the *logos* and *eikon* of the cosmos, it can carry no meaning. The holy may come to us as disturbing the order of the natural world, as – God descends upon Mount Sinai in fire or as a 'virgin birth' – but it cannot come to us wholly apart from the world of nature. There must be 'Mount Sinai' and 'a woman' in order for the holy God to come to us. The Temple of the Sacred Tooth, viewed from the window seat of a jet plane, may give us a different approach to the holy, yet that approach is not outside the 'ascetic' cosmological possibility. It still happens within the orderliness (liturgy) of the cosmos. I may indeed feel strange seeing the great National Mosque in Djakarta from the air, but my feeling is still within the cosmological framework. The *eikon* and *logos* of the cosmos is the primary and universal agent which safeguards the human experience of the holy. Technology, including the sophisticated Pioneer 10 of the American Space Programme which finally in 1983 escaped the confine of the solar system, must function by the scientific-technological use of the *eikon* and *logos* of the cosmos. In both the concept of technology and of the holy there is the presence of the cosmos. It is as though the cosmos does not like to hear the words, 'wholly other'.

The holy must be approached slowly, carefully and respectfully. If we approach the holy recklessly, wantonly and disrespectfully, we will eventually destroy ourselves. The *tanha* approaches the holy in this destructive manner. These two possibilities are with us whether or not we have advanced technology. The choice is there for people who can travel six hundred miles an hour as well as for those who move at three miles an hour. It is possible that a person with a powerful technological means can be more 'pious' and 'respectful' before the holy than the person without such means. The reverse is also a possibility. But when technology is no longer seen to be a means to an end, that is, when technological efficiency decides the meaning of human life, then we have idolatry of technology. Here technology is 'boosted' to the realm of the unconditional to use the words of Paul Tillich. When this takes place it is difficult to maintain a dialogue between us and technology which has been absolutized. We will be in the hands of technology. This will be contradictory to the cosmic *logos* and *eikon*. The stick must be in the hands of people, not people in the 'hands' of the stick! It seems to me important to notice that a cosmos which does not feel happy to hear the words 'wholly other' forms the background of this discussion, psychologically and philosophically. When we allow anything or any event to be 'wholly other', we are not really paying sufficient attention to the richness of the life-giving surroundings called the world of nature, and with it the *logos* and *eikon* of the cosmos. The close relationship between the cosmos and religious symbolism must be repeatedly appreciated in order to avoid the dangerous absolutizing of so many things and ideas. The *logos* and *eikon* of the cosmos dislike such absolutization.

When greed approaches the holy recklessly and disrespectfully then it is in fact absolutizing itself. Absolutization is then not simply a philosophical concept. It is a concrete reckless act we witness in our life situations. The reckless relationship with the holy is idolatry, and there is absolutization hidden in it. Traditional cultures which are acquainted with the paradoxical meaning of 'inefficient posture', which try to maintain the quality of enchantment in the cosmic *logos* and *eikon*, which are appreciative of liturgical approach to the holy – advise us against the reckless relationship with the holy. Behind these advices of the traditional cultures is their centuries old observation of the world of nature in which they found the inspiring unity of asceticism and efficiency not paralysed by human greed. It is important then to know that in order to be able to say that 'my help comes from the Lord who made heaven and earth', we must learn carefully and humbly about what kind of help we may be able to obtain from 'heaven and earth'. When we respect 'heaven and earth', we may be led to the depth of the biblical proclamation; 'my help comes from the Lord who made heaven and earth'.

In this context I find the Buddhist bodhisattva image of many hands instructive in showing how meaning is protected from the attack of efficiency. The many hands of the bodhisattva represent many technological possibilities. They approach different situations with different forms and methods of appropriate technology. The bodhisattva is an image of technology presented in the value form of a religious image. Imagine that one of the forty hands of a Japanese bodhisattva is holding a box of laundry soap. Technology is serving us in the general area of cleaning. Cleanliness has been made possible by technology but it must not be understood simply 'technologically'. That it carries religious connotation will become clear to us if we are able to 'see' the box of laundry soap in the hands of the bodhisattva. This 'seeing' is a religious experience in the technological context. Again, imagine that one of those hands holds a pill for family planning. Technology offers a practical method to combat the impending crisis caused by the explosive increase in human population. The pill comes from the pharmacy, a place of medical efficiency, but its meaning is not confined there. In society it raises not one, but many questions of human meaning. Placed in the hand of the bodhisattva, the pill can bring a special importance to those questions of meaning.

I think one of the hands may hold nuclear power but it would refuse to hold a nuclear bomb. The bodhisattva is a symbol for a healing relationship between efficiency and meaning. Nuclear energy directed to annihilation does not fit with the ability to enhance the efficiency which is in the cosmos. It threatens the *logos* and *eikon* of the cosmos which the bodhisattva expresses. The image of the bodhisattva carries the message of mercy to front stage. It does so basing itself upon the perennial cosmological elements of *logos* and *eikon*. Here, then, is a remarkable ancient image which can stand up to the challenge of today. Technological efficiency is controlled by the meaning of mercy. The image of the bodhisattva warns us not to have a reckless relationship with the holy. We must place nuclear energy in the context of mercy and justice. Religion and technology must engage in a dialogue.

The tradition of Mount Sinai warns us of subjugation of meaning to efficiency. At the foot of Mount Sinai, in the prolonged absence of Moses, Aaron received gold from the people and 'fashioned it with a graving tool and made a molten calf; and they said "These are your gods, O Israel, who brought you up out of the land of Egypt!"' (Ex. 32.4,5). This whole episode of the production of a molten calf is a very efficient story in which technology participates. The absence of Moses, the leader, made the people insecure and lonely. Together with Aaron they decided to solve the problem quickly and efficiently by producing gods there at that moment to fill the vacuum! In this story theological impatience and technological efficiency went nicely hand in hand. This move, made by Aaron and the people, seemed to have solved the problem. But it had not. It produced, instead, the disfigurement of their own history and the loss of their own identity. The meaning of their historical life was destroyed by this efficient quick move. The measure they dared to take was not one which could properly be called 'theological'. It was, in fact, 'magical'. In this process technology participates in magic. 'Let us make a golden calf!' 'Let us make a divine emperor!' In magic meaning is subordinated to efficiency. Magic is, in this sense, inevitably aggressive. It is reckless. The straight borders, efficiently drawn between African nations by their European masters were 'magical' lines that subordinated the life of the peoples involved to arbitrary lines. When the inescapable impact of Western modernization hit Japan in the nineteenth century, it set in motion a burst of magical efficiency in many levels of Japanese life. One of the efficient measures the leaders of Japan took was the deification and absolutization of the person of the emperor. 'Deification' is an eloquent example of magic concerned more about efficiency than the meaning. This magic necessarily produces violence. Violence is power magically used. Aaron and his people did violence against their own history, faith and identity when they magically produced a molten calf. It is a fundamental function of theology to criticize magic.

Technology occasions in our minds questions relating to how efficiency stands to meaning. This question has become acute since technological efficiency has reached the degree of incredible efficiency in recent years. Unfortunately this aspect of technology is most obvious in the area of military technology. 'The World War II submarine could sink only passing ships; now a single sub can destroy 160 cities as far away as 4000 miles.'[2] writes Ruth L. Sivard. She makes this telling contrast:

> Nuclear missiles can go from western Europe to Moscow in 6 minutes, but the average rural housewife in Africa must still walk several hours a day for the family's water supply.[3]

Her concluding words on 'World Military and Social Expenditures' is that 'the 9 trillion spent for "defense" in the last decades appears to have diminished rather than strengthened world security'.[4] The walk the African housewife takes – a slow and dusty walk – contributes more to human meaning than the incredible efficiency of the missiles that can travel a great distance within short minutes. The nine trillion dollars have been spent most 'inefficiently' for 'defence'. The more we have spent the more precarious we have become. The more we have poured the money to arms in the name of humanization (!) the faster we have made ourselves dehumanized. Greed blinds human minds. 'They took bribes and perverted justice' (I Sam. 8.3).

The subordination of meaning to efficiency by the power of human greed has produced dehumanization, or in the picture language, 'wilderness'. Greed ignores and even despises the wisdom of the traditional cultures and today's religious criticism. Technological efficiency in the hand of human greed is causing the life-and-death situation in the world today. 'My help comes from the Lord who made heaven and earth.' This means that humanity's salvation is hidden in the Lord who represents the subordination of efficiency to meaning. That is the meaning of the name of the Lord.

In this section of Part II, we began with a discussion on the cosmological reed-shoot culture of Japan. The *ashi-kabi* culture is optimistic and the concept of continuity is central to it. Does the 'help come from heaven and earth' for the Japanese people? 'To dust you shall return.' Is this the last cosmological word of comfort we hear? Or does it come from the Lord who made heaven and earth? We then looked at this tension between the cosmological and the eschatological in the light of human greed. Buddhism is presented as a 'history concerned religion' since it urges us to battle against our own greed. No greed is a-historical or non-historical. The tension between salvation by technology and salvation by religion is discussed in the image of conflict between 'efficiency' and 'meaning'. The demonic appears when meaning is subordinated to efficiency. In this section, then, the continuity culture of Japanese people has been examined and it has been brought to the critical moment of the confrontation between God (meaning controls efficiency) and Baal (efficiency controls meaning).

In Part III under the theme; 'You shall not take the name of the Lord your God in vain', we move on to describe some significant historical 'points of contact' between the spiritual tradition of Mount Fuji and that of Mount Sinai. Strangely these words of the commandment can be meaningfully applied to Japan, the nation that does not know the name of the Lord, as we have seen with the biblical themes of the previous two parts. The words of God come to us with particular *and* universal relevance.

PART III

You Shall Not Take the Name of the Lord Your God in Vain

(Exodus 20.7)

12
World of Spirits

Nature-spirits and History-spirit.

We now take as our main theme the words of the commandment; 'You shall not take the name of the Lord your God in vain'. When we take 'the name of the Lord our God in vain' we are engaged in idolatry. What else is idolatry but to quote the name of God for our own advantage? Thus using the prestige of God for our own glory? How does it come about? In what way can a theological discernment such as this be applied to the Japanese situation? And when do we 'take the name of the Lord our God in vain' in the historically Christian nations and cultures? Such a study demands a full treatment of the history and culture of the nation concerned. With regard to Japan, I am compelled, however, to be selective for two reasons; The scope of full treatment is far beyond the aim of this book. I also think that the illumination of certain critical spiritual events in Japan may suffice to illustrate in a basic sense what this particular commandment means to the Japanese spiritual world. My approach to this part of our study is historical. I must then begin with the ancient spiritual world of the Japanese people.

Muraoka Tsunetsugu, a scholar of Japanese classics, says that the Japanese people lived without philosophy until cultural stimulation from overseas reached them. They were a simple, happy, nature loving people who accepted the reality of birth and death without much thought. The word for 'way', according to Motoori Norinaga (in his *Naobinomitama* — Righteous Spirit), in the ancient time meant only a road upon which people walked and was deepened as a philosophical concept only later.[1] The first mention of *Shinto* (The Way of Kami) appears in the *Nihonshoki* (Chronicles of Japan) compiled in AD 720. The record in the *Nihonshoki* is that the emperor Yomei (*c.* 585–87) 'accepted the Buddha's doctrine and was respectful also to Shinto'. The emperor Kotoku (*c.* 645–54), on the other hand, was 'respectful to the Buddha's doctrine but disdained Shinto'.

He cut sacred trees in the compound of the shrines. The word 'Shinto' itself comes from the Taoist tradition in China. It is interesting that the expression at first included some Buddhist and magical practices. The name Shinto does not appear in *Kojiki* and *Manyoshu* to which we have referred already.[2]

The Japanese scholar Ueda Masaaki says that it is not easy to determine what constituted the pure Japanese religious experience in ancient time. However, he finds three words playing an important role in ancient Japan: *tama* (spiritual being), *mono* (something strange or awesome) and *kami* (divine being which is 'above'). Each of these points to some spiritual being or power.

Tama refers to spirit and soul. It is used in *hito dama* to mean human spirit and *koto dama* to mean the spiritual power that resides within words. The focus of the religious ritual of the community when sickness or death takes place is also *tama*. The weakened spirit is strengthened by *tamafuri* (shake the spirit). *Tamayobahi* is to 'call back' (*yobahi*) the spirit to the body. *Tamafure* is for one spirit to 'touch' (*fure*) another. When the *tama* of a departed ruler is 'touched' by the *tama* of his heir the authenticity of succession is spiritually confirmed. *Tamafuu* means the 'increase' (*fuu*) of the spirit. *Tamashizume* means the 'pacification' (*shizume*) of the spirit. In all these ritual practices the spirit of the dead will become spirit of the ancestors after thirty-three or forty-nine years and submerge among the ancient gods. In general there are two kinds of *tama; mitama* and *aramitama*. *Mitama* are the peaceful spirits of the ancestors. The *aramitama* are the spirits of the recent dead, unsettled, dangerous spirits that can take revenge on the living.[3]

Spirit of all things other than human is called *mono*. The implication is that *mono* is an animistic spiritual substance, uncanny and strange, which can threaten people. *Mono ga tsuku* (*tsuku,* possessed by) means being possessed by an evil spirit.

Kami is the power of the spirit that sends fortune and misfortune. It resides in the emperor, the imperial ancestor, the deified spirits of the dead, in thunder, also in anything which is 'above'. Recent research tends to place emphasis also on anything fearsome, such as the snake. In the words of Motoori Norinaga, 'evil and mysterious things, if they are extraordinary and dreadful, are called *kami*'.[4]

Kami are not to be invited into any empty space. They may be invoked at a great rock (*iwakura*) or at a tree which then becomes sacred (*himorogi*). At the centre of the Shinto shrine stands a 'divine pillar' (*shin tsyu*) which probably represents the *himorogi*. This leads scholars to believe that the *himorogi* may have been the origin of the Shinto shrine.

The ancient spirits inhabit the mountain to protect the welfare of the villages below. From about the second half of the third century tumuli were being built with a stone room at the top. This may have been the beginning of the 'spiritual mountain belief' (*reizan shinko*), since the mountain is thought to belong to the other world. These stone rooms provided a place for the *tama* of the clan chiefs of successive generations.[5] This is an early expression of ancestor veneration. The clan gods (*Uji-gami*) were the ancestral gods of the clan. Each major clan had its protective ancestral *kami,* according to the Census Registry of the early Heian period (tenth century). Significantly, these kami were of two main groups; *musubi kami* (procreative gods) and *hi kami* (solar gods). The favour of these two groups was basic to agricultural life. They were worshipped together. It was said that *hi kami* (Hikohononiniginomikoto) was sent to the Reed Plain, (the mythical name for Japan) to rule together with the *musubi kami* (takamimusubinomikoto). Throughout the centuries the procreative power and the solar power were looked upon as one by the people who depended upon rice as their staple food.

In the history of the imperial household the most important ritual is the Ritual of *Nihiname* (the rite of eating the newly harvested rice) in which the emperor will stay overnight with the spirit of rice (*kokurei,* a female spirit) in symbolic procreative presence. Only in going through this rite will the emperor genuinely qualify himself as the emperor. This is the reason that philosophically Japan cannot have an empress to govern the nation. The night before the *Nihiname* Ritual the ceremony of the pacification of the departed imperial spirits is held. In this ceremony the emperor is divinized. As we can see there is no clear demarcation line between the human and the divine, or between human and other beings, including spirits.

People who officiated at the religious rituals of *tama, mono* and *kami* used the occasions for the enhancement of their own political power and prestige. Thus a local *kami* of the people of the district of the Sea of Ise became a dominant solar god from which was developed a *kami* called *Amaterasu Omikami,* the Heaven Illuminating Great Deity, the ancestral *kami* of the imperial household. So it came about that the Japanese people heard their emperor saying, in 1941, in the Imperial Rescript declaring war: 'Hallowed spirits of our imperial ancestors guarding us from above ...'. These imperial spirits are the *tama* that have become ancestral *kami* and have been integrated into the scheme of the *musubi* and *hi* powers. This is emotionally and philosophically satisfying to the Japanese mind since it lies very close to the idea of the concrete presence of the *tama* of the departed. The Japanese people did not conceive of a heaven or a sheol to which the *tama* would go. They thought of the *tama* as still among them but with invisible bodies, without breath or momentum (*ikioi*). The personal *tama* continue to be in a concrete way. Buddhism poses a fundamental difficulty to this *tama* centred spirituality. It denies the concept of soul as a constant and identifiable entity. There is not a soul, there are only interactions of five elements that make up the human being and consciousness. This Buddhist anthropology is one of the most sophisticated theories that Asian religious philosophy has produced. In Japanese Buddhism this doctrine had to be adjusted to the culture of *tama*. The followers of Honen and Shinran of whom we shall speak later, for instance, believed that the *tama* goes to the Pure Land or Western Paradise, after death.

These three basic Japanese concepts, *tama, mono* and *kami* are animistic and pantheistic. They make up the original contour of the Japanese spiritual and cultural world which is radically different from that of the monotheistic tradition such as we find in the Bible. *Tama, mono* and *kami* are, by themselves, far less 'history oriented' than the biblical concept of spirit (*ruah*). Literally *ruah* means 'wind' or 'stream of air'. 'The breath of God' represents life. Here it may resemble a bit the Japanese *tama* such as in the case of *tamafuri* and *tamayobahi*. But in the Bible *ruah* is not self-existent. It comes under the power of God. Not only the life begins with the breath of God (Gen. 2.7) but in the vision of Ezekiel it revives. 'Thus says the Lord God to these bones; Behold, I will cause breath to enter you, and you shall live'. (Ezek. 37.5). God alone is called 'the God of the spirits of all flesh' (Num. 27.16). The breath of God gives inspiration to the prophets to receive God's instructions.

> Woe to the rebellious children, says the Lord, who carry out a plan but not mine; and who make a league, but not of my spirit (Isa. 30.1).

> I have put my spirit upon him, he will bring forth justice to the nations (Isa. 42.1).

It is the breath of God that inspires prophets to speak the judgment of God in history. *Ruah* is thus a radical element of history. This is the important difference between the animistic and pantheistic *tama* and the biblical monotheistic *ruah*. *Tama,* as well as *mono* and *kami,* are not complicated because they are natural concepts which do not impinge upon our confusing human history as a word of judgment. They lack ethical and historical content. This does not mean that they are unrelated to ethical and historical realities. Human greed has a way to make use of them for its own self-glory and increase. *Tama, mono* and *kami* are open to misuse, particularly in the political context when they are ideologically defined. But ideology comes from a more 'historical spirit' than *tama, mono* and *kami* which are fundamentally animistic. It is one thing to speak about *tama* and quite another to say that the imperial ancestral spirits guard Japan's destiny 'from above' as she was heading towards the war. The latter is an ideological use of the *tama* concept. Ideology aims to give a comprehensive picture of human life and world, and is therefore more 'historical' than the animistic *tama* can be.

In the biblical tradition the *ruah* of God inspires people to see history critically. In the context of Mount Fuji culture ideology enabled people to see their own history and that of the world 'critically' to their own advantage. This ideology was built upon the exploitation of *tama, mono* and *kami*. The Japanese emperor cult was an ideological misuse of *tama, mono* and *kami*. In fact, it is impossible to see how the emperor worship cult came to be apart from this primitive Japanese spirit world. And this misuse ruined the nation.

In relation to this subject of misuse, we find a strange story in the Bible (I Kings 22.1–36). The king of Judah, Johoshaphat, and the king of Israel, Ahab, were not sure whether they should go up and strike the city of Ramothgilead and recapture it. Four hundred prophets advised them to 'go up to Ramothgilead and triumph; the Lord will give it into the hand of the kings'. One prophet, the prophet Micaiah, dissented. This is what he says to the kings:

> Therefore hear the word of the Lord: I saw the Lord sitting on his throne, and all the host of heaven standing beside him on his right hand and on his left; and the Lord said, 'Who will entice Ahab, that he may go up and fall at Ramothgilead? And one said one thing, and another said another. Then a spirit came forward and stood before the Lord, saying, 'I will entice him'. And the Lord said to him, By what means? And he said, 'I will go forth and will be a lying spirit in the mouth of all his prophets. And he said, 'You are to entice him, and you shall succeed; go forth and do so'.

In this unusual story of a dialogue between God and the spirit, the secret about the unison prophecy of the four hundred prophets is exposed. The kings will be enticed to go to war by the influence of the lying spirit 'in the mouth of all his prophets'. The spirit suggests this strategy and God approves the plan and promises success. It is the mystery of evil that a spirit that has become a lying spirit can carry out the will of God in the world. Why is this strategy approved by God? There is no easy answer to this. When it was debated among the leaders of Japan whether she should go to war against the United States, all the Japanese 'prophets' said in unison that the spirits (*tama*) of the imperial ancestors would give the United States into the hand of the emperor. There is an uncanny similarity between what happened in the ninth century BC in Palestine and in the twentieth century in Japan. The similarity is that in both cases the court prophets spoke under the influence of a lying spirit. The difference is that Japan did not have a 'Micaiah' who could tell the theological background of what had happened. Micaiah's story begins with the vision of the throne of God. The spirit which inspired him was not a nature spirit but the spirit that had understanding of the meaning of the throne of God for human history. The

Japanese *tama, mono* and *kami* are rooted in a nature to which the concept of the throne of the history-concerned God is foreign.

With what justification then can we speak of the Japanese experience in the light of the episode of the prophet Micaiah? I think this possibility is positive and constructive to the welfare of the Japanese nation. It is an extremely illuminating way to look at the tragedy of the last war. The image of a lying spirit is a very picturesque way to bridge these two important concepts; the throne of the history concerned God and our human history. A spirit comes to the presence of God. With the approval of God this spirit will become a lying spirit on the lips of the prophets. Here is suggested the rule of God over the work of the spirits. The spirit world is controlled by God. This is no doubt, a new idea for the Japanese interpretation of history which will enable it to go beyond the thought of the protection of the spirits of the imperial ancestors to find the point of transcendence by which history can be judged. In an absorbing way Micaiah's story invites the Japanese mind to this possibility. Responding to the invitation, they can gradually come to the moment when they appreciate the connection between the throne of God and human history. It is in this theological context the commandment 'you shall not take the name of the Lord your God in vain' will become meaningful to them. In the culture dominated by *tama, mono* and *kami* this commandment cannot really function. However, the biblical understanding of *ruah* is 'historicizing' the Japanese concepts of *tama, mono* and *kami* through many events in the recent years, in particular through the experience of 1945. The spirit of the post-war constitution is radically different from 'the spirits of the imperial ancestors'. The spirit with which Japanese people debated the possibility of national repentance is different from the traditional behaviour and concept of *tama, mono* and *kami*. Since 1969 leading religious groups in Japan, Buddhist, Christian, New Religion, have been active in opposing the government's effort to nationalize Yasukuni Shrine of pacification of the war-dead. This opposition has been conducted with the history-spirit rather than nature-spirit. The spirit with which the people fight against land and air industrial pollution is no longer *tama, mono* and *kami*. It is much closer to the biblical history-spirit. These events are challenging the Japanese people to reformulate the traditional concepts of spiritual beings. The spirits must be historicized and must assume ethical quality. 'I have put my Spirit upon him, he will bring forth justice to the nations.'

The next chapter is to do with the coming of the spirits of the universal religions to the spiritual and cultural world of Japan. This story begins in the sixth century. It is a great story of religious experience of the people of Japan as the messages of the universal faiths have reached Japan one by one. This chapter will attempt to give a historical perspective to the cultural and religious life of Japanese people today.

13
The Coming of Universal Civilization

'I see men; but they look like trees, walking.'
(Mark 8.24)

1. This world is transient

Prince Shotoku (574–622) was born thirty-six years after the introduction of Buddhism to Japan. He became regent for the empress Suiko. The key position of this great prince in Japanese culture is recognized by scholars. 'His reign of thirty years was the most epoch-making period in Japanese history, and it was marked by the striking advance of Buddhist influence and continental civilization as well as of a united Japanese nation.'[1] 'It was through prince Shotoku that Buddhist thought and civilization, accompanied by those of Confucianism, came to clear interaction with Japan's primitive naturalistic outlook.'[2] One of the most outstanding achievements associated with the name of the prince is the first constitution of Japan, known as the Seventeen Article Constitution (604). In this constitution there is an inspiring unity between law and morality. Fundamental to prince Shotoku's legal and moral concepts are those of harmony, justice and mercy, concepts which are supported by the sense of veneration of the Buddha. The First Article speaks about the principle of *Wa*; harmony, coming together, unison, peace, tranquillity.

> Harmony is to be valued, and an avoidance of wanton opposition to be honoured. All men are influenced by partisanship, and there are few who are intelligent. ... But when those above are harmonious and those below are friendly, and there is concord in the discussion of business, right views of things spontaneously gain acceptance.[3]

The *Wa* that appears at the beginning of the constitution represents the fundamental orientation of the whole constitution. The constitution aims to build up a harmonious human community through democratic discussion, not by subjugation of 'those below'. Article Ten is significant in describing the value of self-criticism in public discussion.

> Let us cease from wrath, and refrain from angry looks. Nor let us be
> resentful when others differ from us. For all men have hearts, and each
> heart has its own leanings. Their right is our wrong, and our right is their
> wrong. We are not unquestionably sages, nor are they unquestionably
> fools. Both of us are simply ordinary men. How can any one lay down a
> rule by which to distinguish right from wrong? For we are all, one with
> another, wise and foolish, like a ring which has no end. Therefore,
> although others give way to anger, let us on the contrary dread our own
> faults, and though we alone may be in the right, let us follow the
> multitude and act like them.[4]

Discussion must not be conducted with 'angry looks'. Instead it must be
engaged in with the mind of *Wa* which rejects absolutism of one's own
position. 'We are not unquestionably sages, nor are they unquestionably
fools.' Prince Shotoku is surprisingly silent about the question of power
and what power can do to the possessor of it. He does not speak about the
destructive *hybris* (pride) which is in human mind. His assessment of human
sinfulness or limitation is far more tolerant than one given by Christian
thinkers such as Augustine, Luther and Reinhold Niebuhr. Prince Shotoku
who asks 'how can any one lay down a rule by which to distinguish right
from wrong?' belongs to a thought world radically different from the
biblical world.

The Second Article refers directly to the contribution the Buddhist
tradition can make to the nation.

> Sincerely reverence the three treasures. The three treasures, viz. Buddha,
> the Law and the Monastic Order, are the final refuge of the four
> generated beings, and are the supreme objects of faith in all countries.
> Few men are utterly bad. They may be taught to follow it. But if they do
> not betake them to the three treasures, wherewithal shall their
> crookedness be made straight?[5]

Only through the teaching of the Buddha can the crookednes of the people
be made straight. Yet the prince Shotoku begins the constitution with the
Confucian concept of *Wa*. According to Watsuji, the prince must have
preferred to give the *Wa,* rather than the three treasures of Buddhism, prior
position, thus making it the first principle of the art of Japanese
government. This relationship between Confucian harmony and Buddhist
mercy (*jihi*) has dominated Japanese political philosophy ever since.[6]

The subject of impartial justice is taken up in the Fifth Article.

> Ceasing from gluttony and abandoning covetous desires, deal impartially
> with the suits which are submitted to you. ... If the man who is to decide

suits at law makes gain his ordinary motive, and hears cases with a view to receiving bribes, then will the suits of the rich man be like a stone flung into water, while the plaints of the poor will resemble water cast upon a stone. ...[7]

These words of the oriental prince can be compared with the saying in the Book of Deuteronomy;

The Lord your God is ... not partial and takes no bribe (Deut. 10.17).

Article Six begins with these words:

Chastise that which is evil and encourage that which is good. This was the excellent rule of antiquity. ...[8]

The constitution does not aspire to organize a nation ruled by laws and institutions. It rather aims to achieve a moral state through appealing to universal morality and religion of Buddhism. The value of Buddhism implicit in the constitution is, according to Inoue Mitsusada, the doctrine of 'self-denial'.[9] Is not this an unusual constitution!

Prince Shotoku was a devoted Buddhist scholar. He studied the doctrine under the learned Korean Buddhist scholar Eji. It is said, though the tradition cannot be confirmed, that he wrote commentaries on three scriptures; Hokke-Kyo (*Saddharma-pundarika-sutra*), Shoman-Kyo (*Shrimaladevi-simhanada-sutra*) and Yuima-Kyo (*Vimalakirti-nirdesha-sutra*). The commentary is called *Sangyo Gisho* or Three Sutra Commentary. The central emphasis in *Sangyo Gisho* is the image of the bodhisattva of Mahayana Buddhism who practises mercy. The bodhisattva identifies himself with all the deeds of humanity in his infinite mercy and purifies them. In particular the bodhisattva portrayed in Hokke-Kyo is one who empties himself for the salvation of others. If *Sangyo Gisho* were not the writing of the Prince Shotoku then it must be the product of the group of scholars who associated with the prince. Here we find the spirit of Mahayana Buddhism admirably grasped by an eminent Japanese scholar. The commentary concentrates on the image of the selfless saviour figure of the bodhisattva.

Since the time of Prince Shotoku Buddhism has been with the Japanese people for thirteen centuries. It has inspired philosophy and rich art; painting, sculpture, architecture and literature. It has been a guide through the confusing course of history. Remarkable religious personalities appeared and impressed upon the people the profound insights of Buddhist salvation. It is far beyond the scope of this book to describe the rich experiences that Buddhism has made possible in the history of Japan. For the purposes of our discussion it is important to consider one very significant aspect of Buddhism which has profoundly influenced Japanese spirituality.

Buddhism brought to Japan the concept of the negation of life. That this life must not be simply accepted, but must be negated if the higher life of bliss is to be attained, was a completely new idea to the Japanese people. For the first time, Japanese people were encountered by dialectical thinking. Life must be negated first, then it may be affirmed on the higher level of value scale. As we have seen prince Shotoku is attributed with the saying *Seken Koke, Yuibutsu Zeshin,* 'This world is empty and passing away. Only the world of the Buddha is true'. Prince Shotoku said in his commentary on Shoman-Kyo that emphasis upon life and death should be reversed, and that only 'the *tathagatagarbha* – the possibility to become buddha which resides within the souls of ordinary people – is true'. According to Okuda Jio these words of prince Shotoku expresses the fundamental thought of Japanese Buddhism. Okuda calls attention to the echo of the philosophy of the prince's Buddhism in the medieval Zen Buddhist master, Dogen, who said, 'Meeting Buddha in life and death, there is no longer life and death'.[10]

It was in this realization that the Japanese came into contact with religious thoughts that were far in advance of their own. A dialogue between an outlook of life in terms of nature and the negation of life according to the doctrine of the Buddha came into being in the intellectual and spiritual life of the people.

Previously only death had been seen as a negation of life. The sight of loved ones who ceased breathing was no doubt a painful experience, yet even death was thought of as a part of life since the life of the *tama,* as we have seen, continued in the *kami.* Now the profound suggestion that life might be negated even during life came through Buddhist thought. It was a negation which was not natural as death is natural. This religious negation was couched in the form of religious meditation. This concept of negation introduced to the Japanese continuity orientation the possibility of discontinuity and opened the way for dialectical thinking to develop. Affirmation could assume a deeper dimension through negation. It was no longer simple affirmation but one that found a breakthrough by way of negation. Salvation could be conceived of as not only affirmation of life as perceived in nature but of life, that is, continuity, in spite of full knowledge of the reality of death, that is, discontinuity. The introduction of dialectical thinking to Japanese thought through Buddhism was a profound experience for Japan. The universal religion, Buddhism, taught the creative value of negation.

The Second Article of the constitution commends the three treasures which are called 'the final refuge of the four generated beings' (that is, those generated through embryo, through egg, plants in the moist places, and all living beings that change their forms). The doctrine of the Buddha is the refuge to all living beings. The concept of refuge itself is of fundamental importance in our understanding of Buddhist negation. Life is now viewed as something that needs 'refuge'. It is thought to be transient, precarious, painful and threatened by disintegration. Human life is grasped as something of *dukkha,* unsatifactoriness and suffering. If life is free from negation why should we seek to take refuge? Is not 'taking refuge' a dialectical concept?

Prince Shotoku's *Seken Koke, Yuibutsu Zeshin* corresponds to the biblical story of the fall.

> The eyes of both were opened, and they knew that they were naked; and they sewed fig leaves together and made themselves aprons (Gen. 3.7).

This is the realization of the self through negation. Naive natural life comes to an end. Having disobeyed the command of God – the negation of God – they came consciously to know that they were naked – they were negated. 'For the first time, in their shame they detect something like a rift that can be traced to the depths of their being.'[11] 'The eyes of both were opened and they knew that they were naked.' This is a dialectical knowledge, a knowledge that has gone through negation. Prince Shotoku found negation of this life in the world of the Buddha. Through the perspective of the transcendent, God or the Buddha, both traditions came to the realization of the true self. This is not to say that the biblical tradition and Buddhism are in any sense identical. They exhibit a similar structure with regard to this particular point.

Universal faiths, in comparison to nature religions, are dialectical. They instruct humanity not to 'take the name of God in vain'. When prince Shotoku said *Yuibutsu Zeshin* he was not taking the name of the Buddha in vain. He exhibited a deep sense of humility before the Buddha. The giver of authentic negation and thus of the profound affirmation of life is the Holy. Martin Luther says that man is 'savingly killed' (*salubriterque occiduntur*) by God.[12] God kills us (*opus alienum,* strange work) in order to save us (*opus proprium,* proper work). One of the four causes for 'defeat' (*parajika*) in the Buddhist monastic injunctions corresponds to the 'taking of the name of God in vain'.

The fourth defeat:
A monk who, though not having the higher knowledge of possessing the superhuman qualities, shall give out with regard to himself that he knows and perceives that complete knowledge and insight has arisen, and then at another time, whether on being pressed or not, desiring to be purified, says, 'without knowing, friends, I said I know, without perceiving, I said I perceive, speaking vainly and falsely', unless it was through undue assurance – he is *parajika,* he is no longer in association.[13]

In the Thai Buddhism tradition this *parajika* is simply stated as 'falsely claiming the possession of the highest Truth of mankind'. It is understood that it takes a great deal of mental concentration to achieve superhuman qualities (*uttarimanussa*). To claim falsely to have done so is to risk the most serious censure of expulsion from the order. Superhuman qualities or the highest truth of mankind is attainable by monastic endeavour, but one must not make a false claim to it. Though with a difference, we can speak intelligently about the danger of 'taking the name of God in vain' in both great spiritual traditions. To use the name of 'God' or of 'Enlightenment' for one's own purpose of prestige is not permissible. When the highest value is used in this way and not adored, self-aggrandisement which is self-idolatry will appear whether the context is Buddhist or biblical.

Prince Shotoku's *Seken Koke, Yuibutsu Zeshin* reveals the fundamental structure of creating religious existence. The negation that comes from the Buddha whom he adores is the philosophical principle that can preclude self-idolatry. These ancient words of Prince Shotoku can be seen in promising dialogue with what Richard Niebuhr said of the radical monotheism:

> Radical monotheism dethrones all absolutes short of the principle of being itself. At the same time it reverences every relative existent. Its two great mottoes are: 'I am the Lord thy God; thou shalt have no other gods before me' and 'Whatever is, is good'.[14]

'Only the Buddha is true' (*Yuibutsu Zeshin*) 'dethrones all absolutes'. And this 'dethronement inspires the words in the constitution; 'We are not unquestionably sages, nor are they unquestionably fools'. The Buddhist civilization, however, to which Prince Shotoku belongs, does not positively 'reverence every relative existent'. It is not ready to proclaim that 'whatever is, is good'. Rather, it would say that 'whatever is, is *koke* (without substance)'. The Western culture has 'two great mottoes' while the Buddhist east has the one motto *Yuibutsu Zeshin,* which moves in the direction of 'I am the Lord thy God ...' There is some spark of monotheism observable in the Buddhism of Prince Shotoku! It is not identical in force and definition with the Western mottoes, but it is also too narrow to deny a connection between the dictum of Prince Shotoku and the analysis of the Western culture given by Niebuhr.

The Seventeen Article Constitution of Prince Shotoku highlighted the Confucian concept of *Wa* (harmony) and the Buddhist concept of *Jihi* (mercy). And this noble combination of the two is spiritually supported by the Buddhist doctrine of self-negation. Here we witness a brilliant and grandiose philosophical architecture which has spoken meaningfully to the depth of human mind for centuries. What this constitution meant to Japanese culture is comparable to what the Ten Commandments meant to the Jewish civilization. The Japanese constitution of this ancient time addresses itself in the name of *Wa* and *Jihi,* while the Ten Commandments of Moses comes to us with the words of its preamble.

I am the Lord your God, who brought you out of the land of Egypt, out of the house of bondage (Ex. 20.2).

Wa and *Jihi* are philosophical and political virtues. These noble and desirable virtues must be concretized in the context of human history. Failure to do so would entail harm and destruction to humanity. In the tradition of Moses, the story of salvation has a strong focus. It is to do the will of 'your God, who brought you out of the land of Egypt, out of the house of bondage'. From this proclamation of salvation, the Sinai Traditon moves immediately to say:

You shall have no other gods before me (Ex. 20.3).

Why is it that the proclamation of salvation immediately followed by this proclamation of 'no other gods' is, to the religious thinking of the east, not necessarily obvious. Why does God emphasize 'I' of God – 'I am the Lord your God ...' – to the exclusion of possible help from 'other gods'? Why is it so important to know that it is this God and *not* that God that 'brought you out of the land of Egypt'? Why does this God make such a demand of exclusivity upon humanity and human history? Has it not caused an unnecessary nervous tension throughout the history of human civilization? What is the historical value of the commandment; 'You shall have no other gods before me'?

In the perspective of prince Shotoku, we may say that the question with regard to 'this God and not that God' is hardly significant. It is important to practise the principles of *Wa* and *Jihi* in the context of human community. Can this God who 'brought you out of the land of Egypt' help us to practise *Wa* and *Jihi* in our everyday life? Or, does this God bring in 'theological debates' which produce hate and misunderstanding among humanity? In either case, the primary importance is not attached to God's presence and work in history, but rather in the concrete application of the ideals of *Wa* and *Jihi* to human situations.

But how can we successfully apply *Wa* and *Jihi* to human situations without the help of God? the God who embodies these virtues? Any honest attempt to answer this question will be encountered by the complexity of history that surrounds this question. Human history of the last three millennias tells us that the people who believed in the God who embodies the ideals of *Wa* and *Jihi* have not necessarily been more successful in implementation of these values in history than other people who try to practise *Wa* and *Jihi* without such theological understanding. Confusion in history is that in both civilizations, Buddhist East and Christian West, *Wa* and *Jihi* have not been practised as they should have been. It is the civilization of 'no other gods' that produced the nuclear bombs and actually dropped them on the cities fully inhabited by human beings, and it is equally the civilization of 'any gods welcome' of Japan that engaged in one of the most brutal killings of people during the war. It is again the civilization of 'no other gods' that issued the Emancipation Proclamation in 1863 through the person of President Abraham Lincoln, and it is the Hindu civilization of polytheistic orientation that was able to infuse the value of *ahimsa* through the person of Mahatma Gandhi.

The confusing information we receive from history does not imply that both the Ten Commandments and the Seventeen Article Constitution are meaningless. They give us much needed insights to check and fight against the human drive towards violence and destruction. The Ten Commandments do it explicitly by warning humanity of the danger of idolatry, while Prince Shotoku's Constitution does so by calling our attention to the great values of *Wa* and *Jihi*. The 'theological implication' of the words of the prince; 'We are not unquestionably sages, nor are they unquestionably fools' is significant. With these words, it seems to me, the prince warns of 'the boosting of human' to someone more than human. This anthropology of humility propagated by the prince is sound in the perspective of the biblical tradition. The tradition of prince Shotoku is aware of the 'problem that is suggested by idolatry' though, of course, the prince does not speak of it explicitly, living in a different cultural and religious milieu from that of the biblical world.

2. Taking refuge in Amida Buddha

Buddhism was a formative power in the cultural and spiritual life of Japan from the time of its introduction in the sixth century. It burst into a new phase of creativity in the twelfth and thirteenth centuries. The great religious figures of the Kamakura Shogunate period were Honen of the Jodo school (1133–1212), Eisai of the Rinzai Zen school (1141–1215), Shinran of the Jodo Shin school (1173–1262), Dogen of the Sodo Zen school (1200–53), and Nichiren of the Lotus Sutra school (1222–82). They represent a transition from scholastic learning to existential faith, from institutional religious life to personal charismatic depth, from aristocratic patronage to ministry to the people. They also placed a new emphasis on transcendental values. Frequently these reformers are compared with the sixteenth-century religious leaders in Europe. Such a comparison is justifiable in spite of the difference in religious and cultural context since the depth of their reinterpretation of Buddhism represents a rare moment of creativity in the history of religions.

Kamakura Buddhism is a demonstration that the Japanese people, through their own religious thinking and experience, had digested the unfamiliar contents of the universal religion, Buddhism. Watsuji Tetsuro, one of the foremost of Japanese scholars in religion, history and culture, describes the richness of Kamakura Buddhism:

> The doctrine of *Nembutsu* (recitation of the name of Buddha) of Honen and Shinran intimates a faith of absolute trust in mercy which is understood to be the Absolute. This doctrine has profound similarities with Christianity which teaches absolute trust in God who is love. The Zen tradition of Eisai and Dogen is a religion of practical knowledge which begins with the insight of absolute emptiness. This orientation presents Buddhism as a religion of enlightenment. Nichiren's Lotus School, with its emphasis on absolute trust in the *sutra* and on intentional practice of what the adherents believe, is more like Islam with its confidence in the Qur'an and submission to god. Thus in Kamakura Buddhism we discern three types which reflect the spirit of world religions. That these manifestations arose out of the soil of Japanese Buddhism must be seen as one of its unusual achievements.[15]

All of these masters studied at Mount Hiei monastery (Enryakuji), outside Kyoto, which from early in the ninth century, was the most prominent centre of Buddhist studies. There they came upon the great Mahayana Buddhist doctrine *Hongaku* which had achieved a profound religious expression in China. Our world is made up of changing and precarious everyday reality and of unchanging and stable eternal reality. The former is often called illusionary and profane, while the latter is true and sacred. According to Tamura Yoshiro, Buddhism understood changing reality primarily in the form of contrast such as; self – other, man – woman, old – young, thing – mind, life – death, good – evil, pain – pleasure and beauty – ugliness. These contrasts, in truth, are not really existing as solid substance since they are always changing because of their relationship to emptiness. This Buddhist viewpoint is called the doctrine of *anicca,* non-permanence or *paticcasamupada,* dependent origination. What is said is that the contrasts are an illusory appearance of reality, and in the eyes of truth, they are identical. In our everyday experience these contrasts make sense, but in the light of eternity and unchangeable reality, self is other, man is woman, old is young, thing is mind and so on. This is the fundamental line of the *Hongaku* thought developed in Mahayana Buddhism.

It is able to affirm the contrast in everyday life in the light of the eternal unity of opposing concepts. In about the fourth century the idea of *tathagata-garbha* – that buddhahood is innate to all human beings and that enlightenment is a possibility for everyone – was identified as the meaning of the unchangeable reality. *Hongaku* (*hon* – 'native to', *gaku* – 'enlightenment') is different from *Shigaku* (*Shi* – 'to begin') which understood salvation to be achieved only be great spiritual effort.

Mount Hiei expanded the *Hongaku* thought and began to espouse the view that this world is none other than the Buddha world. *Klesa* (human greed, anger and stupidity) is *klesa* and *bodhi* (enlightenment) is *bodhi*. The two are distinct and yet they are one. There is a difference between the sacred and the profane, yet this world is the Buddha world. *Hongaku* does not say simply that *samsara* (this world of repeating births) is *nirvana* (the ultimate realm of tranquillity). The distinction must be preserved, yet the two are one in spite of their radical differences. 'When we free ourselves from the discriminating thought about life as life and death as death, but see life and death simply as they are, then we come to affirm life and death as the unchangeable eternal reality.'[16]

Tamura points out that this *Hongaku* insight appears in the understanding of time. We are to see the true eternity on the other side of the contrast between temporality and eternity. That is to say, eternity can be grasped in a moment. It is the thought relative to 'Eternal Now'. This insight leads us to see space in the perspective of transcendence too. The eternal world (the pure land) is the space which is beyond the space of our profane world, and therefore, it is affirmed that this world of ours is the pure land world. About an ordinary person and the buddha, the *Hongaku* thought would say that the true absolute buddha is found beyond the contrast between an ordinary person and the buddha, that is, at the point where an ordinary person is identical with the buddha. One may look back from this point and see the difference between the two, but then one sees as one who is an ordinary person who is also identical with the buddha.

Hongaku thought recognizes a sharp dualistic truth about the world and human life, then moves to affirm the unity of the two. It thus implies the invalidation of the way of monastic effort over 'many aeons' to reach *nirvana*. The moment we realize we have buddhahood within us is the moment of enlightenment. The *Hongaku* thought makes a breakthrough in the dualistic way of thinking and reaches a level of creative absolute monism. Therefore it is able to affirm life.[17] The *hongaku* thought gave Japanese Buddhist thinkers an important logic of salvation.

In his sixty-sixth year (1198) Honen wrote a book called *Senchaku Hongan Nembutsu Shu*. In this work Honen forcefully expresses his conviction that the way of reaching salvation by the recitation of the name of the Buddha (*nembutsu*) is the only proper Buddhist faith in this time of the *mappo* – the last hours in history in which the Buddhist doctrine is fast disappearing. He rejected all other ways as *zogyo* (unimportant deeds). The way of the *nembutsu* is the sure way for all, learned and unlearned, rich and poor, man and woman, to be saved. The foundation for this sure salvation is found in the vow that the Amida Buddha made. The Buddha of the Western Quarter, called Dharmakara when he was still a bodhisattva before he became a Buddha, made forty-eight vows. The eighteenth vow states that the bodhisattva Dharmakara would not become the Amida Buddha unless all people could be brought to the land of happiness and comfort (*sukhavati*) – the Pure Land of the Western Quarter – by the recitation of the name of the Amida Buddha. This eighteenth vow is called by Honen 'the king of all vows' and the vow (*gan* in Japanese) of *nembutsu ōjō* (*ōjō* – dying to salvation). Honen came to know this gospel of the *nembutsu* through the writing of the famed Chinese pure land Buddhist Shan-tao (613–81). Honen made his own existential selection to devote himself in the way of salvation by *nembutsu*. According to him the name of the Buddha contains all the merits, virtues and power of the Buddha. And this *nembutsu* way is easy for all. If he had taken the vow that only by way of building stupas or making images of the Buddha we may be saved, then only the rich could have salvation. Honen's *Catechism in Twelve Articles* reads:

> There shall be no distinction, no regard to male or female, good or bad, exalted or lowly; none shall fail to be in His Land of Purity after having called; with complete desire, on Amida. Just as a bulky boulder may pass over the sea, if loaded on a ship, and accomplish a voyage of myriads of leagues without sinking; so we, though our sin be heavy as stone, are borne on the ship of Amida's primeval vow and cross to the other shore without sinking in the sea of repeated birth and death.[18]

This is a remarkable expression of 'grace religion'. In the *nembutsu* doctrine of Honen there is a distant echo of the *Bhagavadgita:*

> And at the hour of death, on Me alone
> Meditating, leaving the body
> Whoso dies, to My estate he
> Goes; there is no doubt of that.[19]

The apostle Paul writes thus to the church in Rome;

> For there is no distinction between Jew and Greek: the same Lord is Lord of all and bestows his riches upon all who call upon him. For 'every one who calls upon the name of the Lord will by saved' (Rom. 10.12,13).

The spirituality expressed in these words of Honen carries an intensity of faith and sincerity which corresponds to that of Paul:

> For as many of you as were baptized into Christ have put on Christ. There is neither Jew nor Greek, there is neither slave nor free, there is neither male nor female; for you are all one in Christ Jesus (Gal. 3.27,28).

Honen died in his eightieth year uttering his last words in praise of the Buddha:

His light pervades the worlds in all the ten directions.
His grace never forsakes any one who invokes His Name.

Ishida Mizumaro, the Japanese scholar in Buddhism, however, points out a
limitation in Honen's Pure Land Buddhism. Ishida recognizes Honen's
decisive emphasis on the grace of Amida Buddha. Yet the fact that Honen
encouraged people to recite the name of the Buddha '60,000 times a day'
and he himself engaged in '70,000 times a day' suggests, according to
Ishida, that 70,000 times is somehow 'better' than 60,000 times, the more
the better. Human judgment and measurement invades the decisive
framework of grace. To be a good person and go to the pure land is 'better'
than to be a bad person and go to the pure land. In spite of his profound
grasp of the sinfulness of humanity, Ishida says, Honen was still not
completely free from the thought of 'what we can do'. 'Honen may be
likened to a person who successfully made sweet persimmon from the tree
of bitter persimmon by grafting. ... but the character of the original tree is
still not completely eradicated. It is there.'[20]

One important way to understand the universal religious significance of
Honen is to appreciate his words on grace of Amida Buddha. His is a grace
religion. Yet it is important to know that his grace religion did not say that
this world is the pure land according to the fundamental insight of the
hongaku thought. Honen's emphasis is placed upon the duality rather than
the unity of *samsara* (the defiled land) with *nirvana* (the pure land). He
asked the people to leave this world behind and move on to the pure land.
Here we see a grace religion creating a remarkable contrast to the dominant
oriental thought-style expressed in the *hongaku* orientation. Buddhism has
brought in the concept of negation. With Honen this universal religious
heritage of 'negation' has been given profound expression in the thought
and experience of the Japanese soul. 'Negation' has affirmed 'Grace'!

Shinran, a disciple of Honen, poses a radical challenge to *hongaku*
thought. While *hongaku* views that within everyone there is, as it were,
hidden enlightenment and our experience of enlightenment is to make it
explicit to ourselves, Shinran, following Honen, says that our life is so
hopelessly entangled in sin and depravity that there is no possibility of
salvation within us at all. Shinran's battle, like Augustine's, was against his
own sexual lust, *concupiscentia*. Honen took the position that celibacy is
not necessary for the monk of the *nembutsu* way. The European Luther, for
whom the doctrine of the justification by faith alone was decisive, took the
similar viewpoint. It is said that Shinran, seeking the solution to this hard
problem of *concupiscentia,* went into a one hundred day meditation at one
of the temples of bodhisattva in Kyoto. On the ninety-fifth day he received
the revelation that, as a monk, he could have a wife. When he was twenty-
nine years old he decided to become a disciple of Honen who was then sixty-
nine years old. Within four years after he identified himself as a monk of

the *nembutsu* school, he was instructed with the *Senchaku Hongan Nembusu Shu.*

The great religious figures of the past spoke about their battle against their own *concupiscentia.* Shinran was certainly one of them. In my reading of Asian theology today, I do not encounter the theme of *concupiscentia.* 'Liberation' is an important theme. Liberation from social oppression has been the centre of theological reflection of the Third World theologians. In these discourses, we do not meet the subject of *concupiscentia* in the way Augustine and Shinran talked about. Is this because *concupiscentia* is too embarassingly personal? Or is it irrelevant to the concern of the liberation from socially structured oppression? Have we moved from an age in which religious persons fought against *concupiscentia* to an age in which such persons fight against social injustice? But then how does personal *concupiscentia* relate to social injustice? Is there no relationship whatsoever? If classical religious experiences are bound up with the spiritual battle against personal *concupiscentia* then are we who live today losing the contact with the religious world of the past? Since we today tend to think that *concupiscentia* cannot be an important subject of religious life?

The Buddhist establishment was not pleased with the 'easy way' of the *nembutsu* school. The leadership of the group was exiled from Kyoto to the country. Shinran spent some thirty years in exile. The amazing thing about Shinran is that the bulk of his great writings were done after he was eighty-three years old.

Shinran emphasized that the recitation of the name of the Buddha must be done simply and honestly without any thought of calculation for merit-making. The *nembutsu* free from all calculation is the true *nembutsu* which though it may seem folly to the wise, is the power of the Buddha for those who trust in him. Shinran did not recognize any power innate in the human being which can do good. All good belongs to the Buddha only and we are to receive it from him, including the very ability to recite the name of the Buddha. Thus Shinran expounded the most radical doctrine of *tariki* (the power of the other, of the Buddha) in contrast to *jiriki* (self-generated power). Salvation happens to us 'naturally' that is, according to Buddha's nature, and not through any human effort or contrivance. 'Naturally', here means 'through *tariki*'. All salvation is found in the Buddha and the Buddha saves us 'naturally' through showing abundant mercy while having really no reason to be so merciful. Just as *nembutsu* must be free from human calculation, so must the mercy of the Buddha. Before the vow of the Buddha there is no distinction between old and young, good person and bad person. The Buddha is not biased. The Buddha is not calculating.

(Our salvation is) 'natural, as it is', in the sense that it is not due to our own device or intention but provided for by Buddha Himself. It is 'natural', because we need not think of our own good or bad; everything has been arranged by Buddha to receive us into His Paradise. It is 'natural', because His grace is intangible and invisible and yet works by 'naturalness' to induce us to the highest attainment.[21]

According to Shinran, then, we are saved by the simple act of trust in the Amida Buddha. This trust, however, must not be interpreted as a requirement or condition for salvation. It is a creation of the Buddha himself that works within our mind. The famous words 'Even a good man will be received in Buddha's land, how much more a bad man' appears in *Tanisho,* a posthumous collection of the sayings of Shinran (*c.* 1200).[22] This saying does not mean that Shinran simply accepted the state of the bad man. There are two kinds of 'bad man' in the mind of Shinran; the bad man who knows that he is bad, and the bad man who is ignorant of the fact that he is bad. Here the profound dimension of religious irony appears as it is indicated in the words of Jesus Christ; 'Those who are well have no need of a physician, but those who are sick; I came not to call the righteous, but sinners' (Mark 2.17). The 'naturalness' of the Buddha's salvation belongs to the bad man who knows that he is bad and needs Buddha's help. 'We need not think of our own good or bad.' This does not mean that the bad man who does not realize his own badness can be saved.

Shinran realized that the strong grace of the Buddha may cause people to be 'vainly proud' (*hongan bokori*) of the vow of the Buddha. He quotes his master Honen saying that we must not take poison because we know there is a medicine to cure poison. This is a sharp insight of strong grace religion. 'Are we to continue in sin that grace may abound? By no means! How can we who died to sin still live in it?' (Rom. 6.1,2).

For the Japanese Shinran to arrive at such a deep sense of his own depravity, as profound as that of Augustine and Luther, is an exceptional event in the history of religion. He confronted himself relentlessly and found that he was caught in the snare of his own lust. But the power of lust and greed alone was not able to lead him to such a deep sense of the sinfulness of the human being. He was able to see his own sinfulness in the light of the Buddha. It was this that saved Shinran from being vainly proud of the Buddha's mercy. He grasped the naturalness of Buddha's salvation against the background of the intensity of human depravity. These two are constantly in dialogue within the soul of Shinran. Human depravity is *met* by the Buddha's mercy! The sinner is *embraced* by the Buddha. And thus he moved from the moral world to the religious world.

Here is drawn a delicate line between the *hongaku* thought and that of Shinran. Shinran does not say the sinner is the Buddha. Nor did he say that this defiled land is the pure land. The pure land is the land *beyond* this land. Yet it is in this defiled land that we are met by the Buddha and embraced by the Buddha. The following words from the Gospel of Mark describe the similar 'religious' situation. Jesus the holy son of God eats with sinners in *this* world.

> And as he sat at table in his house, many tax collectors and sinners were sitting with Jesus and his disciples; for there were many who followed him. And the scribes of the Pharisees, when they saw that he was eating with sinners and tax collectors, said to his disciples, 'Why does he eat with tax collectors and sinners?' (Mark 2.15,16).

There is a difference between saying an ordinary person *is* the Buddha and saying that he/she is *met* by the Buddha. Shinran's critique of the *hongaku* thought is subtle yet powerful. Salvation does not begin in the realm of beyond; it begins right here in the sinful confusing world of humanity. The grace of the Buddha comes to a person who is enslaved by the power of *concupiscentia* right now in this world. Grace and lust are not identical. They are different. The Buddha and Shinran are not identical. They are different. Yet they are not unrelated to each other. Grace meets lust. The Buddha embraces Shinran. In the biblical world the holy God in his holiness – that is in his set-apartness – comes to the sinful unholy world. The holy God is God coming into this sinful world. Honen and Shinran are looking in the direction of the God who comes to the tax collectors and sinners. I find this one of the most inspiring moments in the history of Buddhism. And it is here I see a delicate yet powerful challenge to *hongaku* thought.

The religious event associated with these two great names, Honen and Shinran, is the moving articulation of the mercy of the Buddha as it was experienced by them. The mercy of the Buddha came to meet and to save a man enslaved by the power of lust. The narration of such a deep spiritual struggle indicates that Japanese religious life has gone far beyond primitive naturalism to reach the level of universal religious consciousness.

Honen and Shinran lived before the coming to Japan of Francis Xavier who brought the message of the holy God coming to sinners to save them. Within the cultural and religious world of Mahayana Buddhism they were able to bear witness to the mind of a God they did not know. They spoke of the triumph of grace over human sin. Is not this one of the great themes of the universal faith? They have participated, from their own religious and cultural world, in the truth relating to the universal concern of human salvation. In them the Japanese people achieved a religious depth which can confidently echo the spiritual depth of the universal faiths. Honen and Shinran did not take the name of the God of Israel. They did not know that name. Yet it could be said that they participated in what the name of God rightly implies. 'God did not leave himself without a witness' (Acts 14.7).

3. God created the heavens and the earth

In the sixth century Japan came in contact with thoughts culturally and philosophically far in advance of its own which originated in India and China. Through them the Japanese came to a way of thinking which broke through the limits of immediate time and space to a profound philosophical meditation. They learned how to construct the meaning of human life within the vast reality of the cosmos, how to relate human virtue to the exercise of political power, how to find salvation within the radical transitoriness of life in this world.

In the sixteenth century, a millennium later, Christianity came to Japan. This historic encounter between the nation of Shintoism, Confucianism and Buddhism and a religion deeply involved in the history of the peoples in the West took place through the work of the remarkable Catholic mission society, the Society of Jesus. The name particularly associated with Japanese evangelization is that of Francis Xavier (1506–52). Xavier landed in Japan at Kagoshima on 15 August 1549 and remained in Japan for only twenty-seven months.

The Jesuits found Japan philosophically sophisticated and religiously experienced. More than three hundred years had passed since the death of Honen. Without exaggeration it can be said that this new encounter had the character of a world historical event. Here, in the country farthermost from the West, Christianity was meeting with a people tutored by three major religious traditions. This does not mean, of course, that the people were living on the spiritual level of Honen and Shinran. The movement begun by these masters had by this time lost their original vivid inspiration. The sixteenth century was a time of warring feudal lords, of famines and epidemics. The lives of the people were treated as a thing of no value. The people suffered, waiting for a message that could save them from the despairing world.

The motto of the Society of Jesus; 'For the greater glory of God' (*ad majorem Dei gloriam*) derives from the commitment of the founder of the Society of Jesus, Ignatius Loyola (1491–1556) to the two passages from the gospel:

> Go into all the world and preach the gospel to the whole creation (Mark 16.15).

> For what will it profit a man, if he gains the whole world and forfeits his life! (Matt. 16.26).

Into the Japanese spiritual world Xavier brought this great theology of Christian humanism. That the value of one human person should exceed everything else in this world was a completely new thought for the people of Japan just as the Buddhist message of the transitoriness of life had been ten centuries before. Now the preaching of the Jesuit mission brought a new contrast, that between the concept of the transitoriness of life and the concept of the infinite value of the human person. The teaching of Honen and Shinran had emphasized the supremacy of the compassionate Buddha and the importance of absolute dependence upon the efficacy of the saving vow of the Buddha, but they had not inspired a meditation on the relationship between the great mercy of the Buddha and the worth of the individual soul.

Zen Buddhism appeared to emphasize the value of human worth. The Zen paradox that complete negation is complete affirmation comes close to the statement of Matthew 16.25: 'For whoever would save his life will lose it' But Zen did not proceed to the next sentence which Xavier brought to Japan: 'For what will it profit a man, if he gains the whole world and forfeits his life?' (v. 26). For Zen this would be an undesirable attachment to selfhood, hindering the realization of the final emancipation. For the final emancipation is the eradication of the self altogether. For Christianity Matthew 16.26 expresses the basic spiritual orientation, while for Buddhism it would mean the final hindrance to the achievement of *nirvana*.

The *hongaku* thought is one of the prominent oriental religious dialectics. Here an opposition is emphasized and yet the opposition comes to unity forming absolute monism. Thus the realm of the sacred and that of the profane are clearly demarcated, yet the dialectic moves on to say that the sacred is the profane. The religious orientation that was introduced to Japan through the Jesuit mission has given another dialectic to the Japanese people. It rejects the direct monistic form of unity between the divine and the human. The reason for this is that God is the creator of all things and that the all things have not just come to be by themselves. Thus the fundamental demarcation is between the creator and creature. All other distinctions such as day and night, male and female, good and evil, life and death, and the buddha and ordinary person must be seen in the light of the fundamental distinction between the creator and creature. This view challenges the basic Asian religious and philosophical outlooks, including Zen orientation too. It challenges the whole psychology and metaphysics of the *Ashi kabi* culture.

The great story of the coming of Christianity to Japan is an ever challenging subject of study. Here I have limited myself to making a few observations relevant to our study from the letters of Xavier. On 1 February 1549 he wrote from Cochin of his intention to go to Japan to Father Simon Rodriguez in Portugal.

> They say that all my friends and acquaintances wonder at me very much for trusting myself to so long and dangerous a voyage. I wonder much more at their little faith. Our Lord God has in His power the tempests of the Chinese and Japanese seas, which they say are as violent as any others anywhere in the whole world. To His power all the winds are

subject, all the rocks and the whirlpools and the quicksands and shoals, which they say are to be found in those seas in such great numbers, so dangerous, so sadly famous for the shipwrecks they have caused. He also holds in His sway all the pirates of whose numberless hordes they tell us, and who are exceedingly savage and are wont to put to death with exquisite tortures all whom they take prisoners, and especially all Portuguese. And as this our Lord God has all these things under His dominion, I fear nothing from any of them. I only fear God Himself,...[23]

Xavier invokes the great biblical theme of the power of the creator God over the power of nature (storm) and history (pirates). It is faith in the God who rules *all* things. With this faith we move into a world of thought which is radically different from the thought world represented by the *hongaku* dialectic. Xavier expounded this faith at length during his vogage from Malacca to Kagoshima which lasted from 2 June to 15 August 1549.

... the captain and the sailors were always, against our will and in spite of all our efforts to prevent them, offering abominable worship to an idol which they had with them on the poop, and consulting the devil from time to time, whether it would be advantageous or not to sail to Japan? ... our sailors offered many superstitious sacrifices to the idol, and fell again to casting lots, asking the devil whether we should have good winds? By chance the lot so fell as to promise us a very favourable wind, so that we were not to stay any longer where we were. So without delay we heaved up our anchor and set sail in high spirits; they relying on their idol, which they worshipped with great devotion, burning candles and sticks of aloe-wood on the poop; and we trusting in God Who rules heaven and earth and sea, and in Jesus Christ His Son, for the sake of propagating Whose religion we were on our way to Japan. ... What do you imagine we thought and felt during that part of the voyage, while the devil was being consulted by his own worshippers as to our voyage to Japan, and the captain of the ship managed the whole business just as the devil willed and chose?[24]

Immediately after the above story, Xavier records the event of a tragedy which occurred at sea.

... there came another roll of the ship and the daughter of the captain was cast overboard into the sea. The violence of the storm was so great that our efforts to help her were all in vain, and she sank in the waves in the sight of her father and of all of us, close to the ship. There was so much wailing and groaning all that day and the night which followed, that everything seemed very mournful and miserable, whether from the grief of the barbarians, or the danger in which we were.[25]

Xavier draws a sharp contrast between his own freedom from fear, since he fears only God, and the power of fear over the captain, who worshipped the idol who indeed had no control over nature and history. Though not articulated in his letter, this tragedy of the daughter of the captain in a dramatic way summarized the 'heathen's' question of Christianity; that is, if indeed the creator God has control over storms, was he not responsible for her death? Why did he not create calm instantly so that she could be saved? Does this creator God take joy in 'so much wailing and groaning all that day and the night which followed'? If neither the idols nor the creator God could help this child, what is the difference between them?

In reading the letter Xavier wrote from Japan we find him looking at the pagans and idolaters as enemies of God under the control of the devil.

> Everything here being in the hands of heathen and of enemies to the true religion, we have no one but God to hope in, no one but Him to have recourse to for protection.[26]

For Xavier the basis of his theology of mission was firm and clear; that the message of Christ be propagated to emancipate people from the power of the devil. This could only be done in this life. For those already in hell there is no possibility of salvation. This was a case of great sadness among the Japanese. Here is again the similar suspicion on the part of the 'heathens' about the difference between the 'true God' and idols. If neither the idols nor the God of Xavier could help anyone who is in hell, what is the difference? This question came to Japanese people for the first time with Christianity which proclaimed the transcendent creator God.

On 29 January 1552, Xavier wrote to the Society in Europe from Cochin, in India, about this problem.

> One of the things that most of all pains and torments these Japanese is, that we teach them that the prison of hell is irrevocably shut, so that there is no egress therefrom. For they grieve over the fate of their departed children, of their parents and relatives, and they often show their grief by their tears. So they ask us if there is any hope, any way to free them by prayer from that eternal misery, and I am obliged to answer that there is absolutely none. Their grief at this affects and torments them wonderfully; they almost pine away with sorrow. But there is this good thing about their trouble – it makes one hope that they will all be the more laborious for their own salvation, lest they, like their forefathers, should be condemned to everlasting punishment. They often ask if God cannot take their fathers out of hell, and why their punishment must never have an end. We gave them a satisfactory answer, but they did not cease to grieve over the misfortune of their relatives; and I can hardly restrain my tears sometimes at seeing men so

dear to my heart suffer such intense pain about a thing which is already done with and can never be undone.[27]

It was 'this painful thought', Xavier recorded, 'which, more than anything else, kept them back from the religion of the true God'. In the same letter he shows how he dealt with this problem.

> We began by proving to them that the divine law is the most ancient of all. Before receiving their institutions from the Chinese, the Japanese knew by the teaching of nature that it was wicked to kill, to steal, to swear falsely, and to commit the other sins enumerated in the ten commandments, a proof of this being the remorse of conscience to which any one guilty of one of these crimes was certain to be a prey. ... We showed them that reason itself teaches us to avoid evil and to do good, and that this is so deeply implanted in the hearts of men, that all have the knowledge of the divine law from nature, and from God the Author of nature, before they receive any external instruction on the subject.[28]

This 'satisfactory answer' seems to have been sufficient for the Japanese judging from the tone of this letter. I doubt it. Japanese people were then, and now, not interested in the discussion about 'all have the knowledge of the divine law from nature'. The question is about the 'integrity' of this great God who decided to keep the prison of hell irrevocably shut for eternity. This image of God is simply so destructive and repugnant to any normal human sensitivity. Undoubtedly Xavier took his authority from the words of the Apostle Paul.

> For all that may be known of God by men lies plain before their eyes; indeed God himself has disclosed it to them. His invisible attributes, that is to say his everlasting power and deity, have been visible, ever since the world began, to the eyes of reason, in the things he has made. There is therefore no possible defence for their conduct; knowing God, they have refused to honour him as God, or to render him thanks (Rom. 1.19–21, NEB).

There was 'no possible defence' for the Japanese ancestors for they 'knew' God and yet had refused to honour him as God. Is that what Paul and Xavier are saying to the sixteenth-century Japanese? They observed nature and indeed were impressed by it. But they failed to come to a monotheistic view of God. They saw many gods at work in nature. In their appreciation of nature they failed to come to the idea that nature is created by God. They composed many poems about the beauty of nature, but they did not see that nature displays God's invisible attributes, everlasting power and deity.

Indeed, though the Japanese knew somehow, by nature, not to kill, steal or bear false witness, it is questionable whether they could have known, by nature, the first commandment; 'You shall have no other gods before me', or 'you shall not make for yourself a graven image' or 'you shall not take the name of the Lord your God in vain'? In order to refuse God they must have had some clear idea about such a God. Has it been visible to the eyes of reason that there is a God who says, 'You shall have no other gods before me'? And how could the Japanese ancestors appreciate these Ten Commandments without knowing something about the historical background of the preamble of the Commandments;

I am the Lord your God, who brought you out of the land of Egypt, out of the house of bondage (Ex. 20.2).

In this line of thought it is possible to take a more sympathetic view of the Chinese captain whose daughter was washed overboard on the trip to Japan. Certainly he had not known the Ten Comandments. His culture was rich in images, each with its own religious speciality. There was a god for the cure of sickness, one for business success, and another for safe navigation. This latter was his own particular god, whom he feared and venerated with tremendous devotion. The plain truth was that this precarious existence on the stormy sea with his three hundred ton ship was permeated with fear. But the fear was not of his own making. He comes from a history of such fear and such an arrangement of gods. Generations of sailors before him had developed the cult of the god for safe navigation. This 'evil' which Xavier saw in him was not individual but historical.

The captain indeed worshipped the idols. But his humanity came to a full expression in wailing and mourning when his daughter was lost. Wailing and mourning, in such a context, exhibits far more directly the universal human experience than discerning the divine attributes in nature. The captain was a full human being capable of genuinely feeling sorrowful and hurt. Why not build a theology upon such an expression of humanity rather than on the discernment of the divine attributes in nature? The question Xavier left unanswered still remains today unanswered. Here I notice theology's imperialism against human experience.

Xavier drew a sharp contrast between the captain's attitude of fear and his own attitude of faith. We, today, would draw as sharp a contrast between the superstition of the captain and our own 'scientific' understanding of the work of nature. Thus we have successfully avoided, so far, facing up to the issue of faith in this world. In this situation most of us belong with the 'captain who has become scientific', and thus we have successfully avoided facing up to the question of faith. Who among us would say with conviction with Xavier that in the very concrete sense 'to His power all the winds are subject, all the rocks and the whirlpools and the quicksands and shoals ...'? Xavier believed in the creator God. For him that meant to believe concretely in the power of God over all things. It was this great thought that Christianity, the universal religion, brought to Japan.

What would Xavier's estimation of Honen and Shinran have been? Would he see that they, 'claiming to be wise, ... became fools, and exchanged the glory of the immortal God for images resembling man or birds or animals or reptiles'(Rom. 1.22f.)? On 29 January 1552, Xavier wrote:

> I earnestly beg all who read this letter of mine, ... to pray that our Lord Jesus Christ will give us the victory over these two demons Xaca and Amida.[29]

'Xaca' is the Buddha of the Shakya clan. I believe that Xavier shared the limitation of his day. It would be too simple to say that Honen and Shinran were idolaters. Such an attitude belies an ignorance towards the sincere toils of those who seek spiritual understanding. For the Japanese the issue of the 'two demons Xaca and Amida' was related to the concept of the creator God. They found it difficult to understand how such an omnipotent God could be so cruel as to leave whole generations of people ignorant of the true doctrine and also leave them in hell forever. How was it possible that this omnipotent creator God would leave minds like those of Honen and Shinran in idolatry? Yet, they appreciated the new exciting idea of the existence of the creator God.

The Jesuit mission affirmed the concreteness of the existence of the human being in their homilies. This was not an easy doctrine for the Zen Buddhists to contemplate. For them there is no 'I'. All is 'emptiness' (*Mu*); heaven and hell and even the concept of 'God' is 'emptiness'. So the battle for the soul of Japan seemed to be drawn between two opposing conceptions. To many of the Japanese the omnipotent God of the missionaries seemed a more cruel god than the 'God' of emptiness which they knew. Instinctively, through their own cultural sentiment, Japanese people put a theology of creator and a theology of salvation together. For them if God is the creator of all things, such a God who is not *Mu,* must be able to do something to save the ancestors who are caught in hell. This is a critical question posed to both Zen Buddhism and Christianity.

Xavier wrote that 'everything here [in Japan] is in the hands of heathen and of enemies to the true religion'. His attitude towards the captain of the ship and the religions of Japan is that of confrontation between good and evil, God and devil. Christianity brought then to Japan the strongest possible conflict dualism. Dualism had not been unknown to the Japanese people, particularly that of life and death. But now, in contrast to the dualism of nature, there came an extemely intensified dualism of the creator God against the devil and people under the power of the devil. Honen and Shinran pondered about human depravity, but they did not discuss depravity in the context of a creator God involved in dualism of conflict. Must a 'theology' of such intensified conflict dualism be necessary in order to present the gospel of Christ? This question has remained unanswered for the Japanese people since the time of Xavier. Is the attitude towards the captain of the ship on the part of Xavier a necessary part of Christianity? The history of Christianity has not given an answer to this 'painful question' with which the Japanese of the sixteenth century, hearing the gospel of Christ, almost 'pined away with sorrow'. There is only a very thin line of demarcation between the condemnation of idols and the concept of conflict dualism. The gospel condemns idolatry yet it avoids falling into a scheme of conflict dualism.

The Christian view of the supreme worth of the individual soul, which the Jesuits brought to Japan for the first time, was a concept of utmost importance for the continued development of Japanese religion. Even though the thought of an implacable God who ignored the plight of the mistaken ancestors seemed cruel, the new religion carried an important message for Japan. It came at a time when there was much grief in Japan over the needless slaughter of people in the wars of the feudal lords. There was a deep yearning for the affirmation of the value of human life. That the human soul should be lost forever was a serious problem for them, but in that discussion the emphasis was placed upon personal responsibility towards the God who rules the whole universe. The core of the message of Christianity was that humanity stands before God responsibly. Neither God nor human life is *Mu*. If God is portrayed as cruel it is to make the living responsible by making human decisions most serious in the face of God.

Almost exactly a millennium earlier Prince Shotoku expressed the Buddhist philosophy of transcendence: 'The world is empty and passing away. Only the world of the Buddha is true.' He suggested that people should transcend this world according to the truth of the Buddha. This transcendence was possible apart from explicit consideration of the value of human life. It is the transcendence achieved by acknowledging the non-substantiality of self. The Jesuit also spoke of transcendence, but this transcendence is achieved by the power of God who creates and rules all things, including this world. It is the transcendence not towards *nirvana* but a new horizon of life emancipated from the power of the devil.

It is important to notice that one of the two biblical passages that inspired the Jesuit mission; 'For what will it profit a man, if he gains the whole world and forfeits his life?' does not suggest the *nirvana* orientation. On the contrary it has led the Society of Jesus to take 'this world' with utmost seriousness. It is not through the 'gaining the whole world', which can be done only be way of making ourselves a god, that is the way of idolatry, but by way of finding our life before the creator God, that salvation comes to humanity. It is in 'this world' that we are to free ourselves from idolatry of 'gaining the whole world' and move on to new life before the creator God. It is also important to notice that Prince Shotoku who said that this world is empty and passing away, was the one who impacted Japanese history with his political and ethical thoughts. He has influenced the historical life of the Japanese nation profoundly. In both cases, then, 'this world' has been enriched though the nature of the transcendence they appealed to is respectively different. Both traditions were able to keep themselves at a distance from idolatry since both negated the ideology of the 'gaining the whole world'; one from the perspective of the non-substantiality of self, and other from that of the infinite value of the human individual.

For a time the propagation of Christianity begun by the Jesuit Xavier proceeded creatively and with promising results. The Jesuit mission went into a tremendous educational effort. Catechisms, Expositions of the Ten Commandments, devotional and doctrinal books were published in Japanese with a rapidity which proves the remarkable intellectual ability of the mission. This enterprise was strengthened by the arrival in Japan of Alessandro Valignano (1539–1606) a distinguished Italian Jesuit who was sent to Japan in July 1579 as Supervising Father (*visitador Padre*). He demanded of the missionaries a more ambitious effort to understand Japanese language and culture, and initiated a strong programme for the theological education of indigenous leaders. There was a real possibility that through the efforts of the Jesuit mission Japan would become a Catholic nation.

According to a study of Takase Kouichiro, most of the Jesuit missionaries adhered to the view that if necessary military power should be used to subjugate Japan physically and spiritually. Some Jesuits working in Japan went so far as to suggest that the Spanish fleet be called from the Philippines to resist the power of Hideyoshi, the then ruler of Japan. The suspicion of Hideyoshi continued into the Tokugawa Shogunate which took the policy of a closed nation from about 1620 onwards.[30] The Edict of 1635 ordering the closing of Japan stipulated that Japanese ships were strictly forbidden to leave for foreign countries and that any informer revealing the whereabouts of the followers of the foreign fathers was to be rewarded. Japan was closed for more than two hundred years (1635–1853).

The isolation of Japan had serious implications for the Japanese people. It took three hundred years, from the sixteenth century, for the West to incorporate the critical awareness of reason and the scientific view of life into its consciousness. During much of the time that this great event of the modernization of the human mind was taking place Japan cut herself off from contact with the outside world and confined herself to her own limited way of thinking. The phenomenal success of the Jesuit mission which emphasized mathematics instead of astrology, indicates that the Japanese mind was also ready for the modern way of viewing the world. Instead Japan retreated into intuition, an attitude which, according to Watsuji, pushed Japan into an irrational war against the Western powers in 1941.[31]

I agree with Watsuji that Japanese intuitionism created the irresponsibility which brought about the destruction of the nation in 1945. Japan threw herself headlong into war in spite of all the scientific data which should have warned her against that course. I observe, however, that the West, having expended much spiritual energy on the assimilation of the scientific world view, has staged two world wars and is now caught in a most irrational nuclear arms race. Japan lost two hundred years in appropriating the scientific view of the world, but its greater loss, I feel, was the isolation for two hundred years from the message of the Jesuit, the theology of the value and dignity of the human individual. More likely it was the lack of this outlook which led Japan to war in 1941 and the annihilation of the nation in 1945. The 15 August 1549, the day that Xavier landed at Kagoshima, has an important historical connection with 15 August 1945, the day of Japanese surrender to the Allied Powers, almost four hundred years later.

It is difficult to leave the picture of the Chinese sea captain. We see him worshipping his idol in the midst of the storm on the high seas. The picture is poignantly relevant to our world today. We are burning incense, making sacrifices, paying obeisance to and worshipping the idol of military might, the nuclear bomb. It dictates national policies. Fear of it puts whole populations on the face of this planet at the mercy of political threat. There must be a deep sense of repentance, a recognition that *all* engage in idolatry. Was Xavier free from subtle idolatry when he said that 'everything here is in the hands of heathen and of enemies to the true religion'? Without such a sense of repentance we will succumb to the convenient idea that the world is divided between the good and the bad, with the bad, of course, on the other side. No one, and certainly not the Christian, is free from the temptation of idolatry. The universal religions have given us the insight to make this humble acknowledgment. And it is basic to our understanding and practice of the propagation of the gospel. Whatever the theological implications of Xavier's report about the captain, I am deeply touched by this picture of a tiny ship caught in a violent storm, in which one of the greatest Christian missionary figures of all time is travelling while its captain tries to navigate by carefully following the indications of the idol whom he ardently worships. Had the ship gone down these two would have gone down together to the bottom of the Chinese sea! The difference was that Xavier was caught by hope while the captain lived by fear.

The commandment forbids us to take the name of God in vain. If we do so we will eventually destroy ourselves. The value of the human person is always threatened by the misuse of the name of God. The name of God brings two possibilities; destructive self-glorification or creative self-denial. One leads to idolatry, the other to discipleship. In the critical moment of encounter between two civilizations, such as the one we have just discussed, the name of God will be taken. It is most important to be aware of how it is taken. My concern with the letters of Xavier is with his concept of 'enemy of God'. To call someone *my* enemy is polarizing. To speak of the 'enemy of God' is another dimension. We should rather be confused than too certain about who the 'enemy of God' might be. Then, strangely, when such an enemy really appears on the horizon of human history, we may know. '... the Holy Spirit will teach you in that very hour what you ought to say' (Luke 12.12). In general, it seems to be good theology not to define who the enemy of God is. Let God decide if God has an enemy.

The cultural and spiritual history of Japanese people is deeply indebted to the influence received from abroad. In this brief survey we have dealt with two outstanding historical impacts upon Japan, those of Buddhism and Christianity. The former suggest basically the Way of Wisdom to salvation. Here the call from the Buddha (the Awakened One) is 'be awake!' to the transitoriness of this world. *Seken koke!* It defines the fundamental human problem as ignorance. Prince Shotoku grasped this fundamental truth of the universal religion, Buddhism. 'Be awakened!' implied in the most inspiring way the sentiment and metaphysics of the Buddhist negation. The Japanese people learned the religious meaning of 'negation'. Through the negation of ignorance there is a way to salvation.

Both Honen and Shinran achieved one distinctive expression of the Buddhist spirituality through their own religious experience and thinking. At the centre of their Buddhist existence they put the grace of the Buddha. It is not by our own works but by the grace of the Buddha we are saved. They were able to speak of an enhanced level of affirmation in salvation because of the keen awareness of human depravity. This dialectic of saving grace came to the Japanese people in the dramatic words of these two religious masters. They deepened the meaning of *Yuibutsu Zeshin,* 'Only Buddha is Enduring'.

Christianity brought to Japan the concept of the creator God who created all things with purpose and who rules all things with utmost personal love. It opened up a new horizon for interpreting individual as well as community life. It suggested the Way of Reconciliation. The call that the Jesuit missionaries extended to the Japanese people was 'repent!'. Have a new mind in trusting the creator God who came to us in Jesus Christ! Here the fundamental human problem is located in human relationship with this God. This message came through in spite of the painful and difficult discussion on the 'cruel God' which, by itself, was an extremely disturbing concept for the Japanese people.

The Japanese people have come into contact with two great religious outlooks; negation of this world and affirmation of this world; 'be awakened!' and 'repent!'. The task of bringing these two into a creative dialogue within their own cultural context was an important engagement for the spiritual life of the people. That task is even now only in its early stages. This important dialogue will be robbed of much of its potential if we take the name of God in vain. When the name of God is taken in vain no mutual understanding between divergent views can take place.

In the gospel story a blind man who is being cured of blindness says to Jesus: 'I see men; but they look like trees walking'. From the sixth century up to today, this saying of the blind man has expressed the spiritual pilgrimage of the Japanese people. I am not suggesting that the vision of the Japanese people is progressively becoming clearer throughout the centuries. I feel rather that since the impact of the universal religions such symbolic words of the blind man of the ancient time has become meaningful to the Japanese mind. The coming of universal civilization has awakened within the Japanese mind the critical awareness of history. They came to ask the question with regards to history for the first time. The answer to that is complex and ambiguous. The answer is partially given when the blind man makes this confession. None of us can have vision to see the entirety of human history and its value in the clear manner. Human history is something which always challenges us to see clearly. I like to affirm this as true for any culture and civilization of humanity.

14

Amalgamation of Religions

The commandment of God addressed to the
constantly changing religious situations.

Over the centuries the three great traditions which Japan received from
overseas, Confucianism, Buddhism and Christianity, have been 'digested
by a strong stomach' (Tamura Yoshiro) and have become, to greater or
lesser degree, part of Japan's own cultural and religious heritage. The
history of the interaction of the Japanese mind with these traditions is an
essential part of the story of Japanese culture and spirituality. It is a rich
and complicated story. The meeting, mutual influencing and mixture of
religions is a universal phenomenon which has particular characteristics in
each locality. In Japan this process has been called *shugō* or amalgamation
of religions. It has involved many combinations; the interaction of the
shinto tradition with Confucianism; the triple encounter of Buddhism,
Confucianism and Shintoism; the meeting of Shintoism with Christianity.
There is no 'theological' barrier among the Shinto, Confucian and Buddhist
traditions if they want to amalgamate. It was only with the tradition of
Christianity that a problem arose.

Shugo may seem to be a strange and irregular religious phenomenon to
casual observers from the monotheistic culture zone. Yet all religions are
open to such amalgamation with the practices and doctrines of other
religious traditions though perhaps some religions are more open to others.
Fundamentally the amalgamation of religions is syncretic. In the history of
Christian mission the word 'syncretism' has only a negative connotation.
Yet it must be recognized that the history of religions is a history of the
interaction of religions in which religions influence each other. There is no
'pure' or 'intact' religious tradition in the strict sense. The important
question is what are the spiritual forces which propel the process of
amalgamation. It can be expected that the new message will produce some
process of amalgamation. As we can imagine, this process involves a series

of delicate operations such as combination, selection and commitment. With what religious tradition does one tradition amalgamate? What aspect of a given religion should be singled out as a desirable element to be amalgamated with this or that aspect of the other religion? Is the amalgamation strong enough to inspire commitment?

Amalgamation is an ambiguous process. It is an inevitable process for religious life. It must be viewed critically. With what criterion the process may be viewed is a problem which scholars of religion have not yet clarified. Granted that we are in somewhat unexplored territory, I believe we can look critically at the process of *shugō* in the light of our dialogue between the cosmological Mount Fuji spirituality and the eschatological Mount Sinai spirituality. Perhaps we must suggest that some amalgamations, more than others, are able to point to the true God. Some take the name of God in vain less than others. There are degrees of intensity in idolatry. These are the thoughts which lie behind this chapter in which the development of religious amalgamation in Japan is traced.

The Japanese word *Jingu* is a shinto shrine. *Ji* is a Buddhist temple. In the year 766, at the order of the Imperial Court, a Buddhist image was installed in the compound of the shinto shrine of Ise. Thus the shrine of Ise was the first of many to become *Jingu-Ji* in a movement which was to amalgamate Buddhism, the more vigorous new religion, with shinto, the indigenous religion. As the number of *Jingu-Ji* increased in the following centuries, traditions arose that the shinto gods desired to achieve salvation by way of the Buddha's doctrine. The gods wanted to 'depart from the status of being gods'. They sought 'renunciation of the divine status' in order to become followers of the Buddha. One such *Jingu-Ji* was given the name *Shingan-Ji* which means 'a temple of granting the gods' wish'.

A tradition is recorded that a Buddhist priest in the Ise area whose name was Mangan received an oracle from *Tado Daijin* (the great god of Tado) on 20 December 763:

> I am Tado Daijin. From time immemorial I have accumulated sinful deeds. Now I am reaping what I sowed in the manner of the shinto. I desire now to follow the Buddha's Three Treasures in order to depart from this divine body.[1]

The priest Mangan built a small temple and made an image of a shinto god, calling it *Tado Daibosatsu* (Tado Great Bodhisattva).

In the agricultural community in which the *kami* of mountain and water were of central importance, these *kami* were looked upon as the source of agricultural harvests and at the same time the possessors of the awful power to obstruct fruition. The agricultural community was united in seeking benefit from these *kami* of nature. From the early eighth century there appeared wealthy owners and managers of private agricultural enterprise on a grand scale, probably city dwellers. The exploitative gigantic agricultural operations of the wealthy managers shook the foundation of the solidarity of the rural community so that it became increasingly difficult for the traditional nature-*kami* to maintain their religious authority.

The movement from the nature-*kami* to the Buddha-*kami* was also a movement from village agricultural *kami* to the *kami* of the more prestigious centralized government. It was a move sponsored by people of wealth and influence who were the natural recipients of the new Buddhist thought. Buddhist priests of the esoteric school (*Mikkyo* – that which is not obvious) also participated in this movement.

The year 763, when the priest Mangan built the *Tado Daibosatsu* was a year of famine, epidemic and natural calamity. The people understood this to be the expression of the wrath of the nature *kami* at what appeared to be a change imposed on the *Tado Daijin* which had stood at the centre of their community. Their social protest against exploitation was expressed religiously by ascribing the famine and epidemics to the wrath of the gods they knew. The wealthy class, however, saw the tragedies as a result of the many sins of the *kami* who now sought to submit to the way of the Buddha.

Perhaps as much instinctively as purposefully, the wealthy sought to change the *kami* who were angry to *kami* who would support their economic enterprise. This they did with the help of the esoteric Buddhist priests and by conferring the prestige of Buddhism upon the native deities. They built *Jingu-Ji*, they gave the title *bodhisattva* to the *kami* and they read the Buddhist sutras in front of the traditional *kami*. *Tado Daibosatsu* and *Hachiman Daibosatsu* are thus examples of the transformation of shinto deities into Buddhist deities in the eighth century. These gods of the *Jingu-Ji* became political tools of the powerful and of the government. *Hachiman Daibosatsu* soon became the model of *shin-butsu-shugō* (god-buddha-amalgamation) which contributed greatly to the increase of centralized political power in ninth-century Japan. Around *Hachiman Daibosatsu* arose the medieval ideology of *oho butsu ho* or Ruler's Law is Buddha's Law.[2]

Goryo-ye developed from the Shinto-Buddhist amalgamation in the eighth and ninth century. The *goryo* are 'the spirits of those who had suffered a violent death, believed to curse the living either by haunting them or inflicting a calamity on them'.[3] *Goryo-ye* were the 'rituals for the purpose of pacifying the vengeful spirits. Such rituals developed in the 9th century in Kyoto and gradually spread to the provinces. Significantly the *goryo-ye* was quite different in form and ethos from the earlier Shinto rituals centring around the kami of the clan'.[4] In 863 the government conducted a *goryo-ye* to pacify the spirits of the Emperor Suido and six others who met tragic untimely deaths in the court struggle for power. The *goryo-ye* were conducted by the aristocratic class but behind it there was a people's *goryo-shinkō* (belief that such vengeful spirits really are active). The *goryo-shinkō* was an expression of the people's protest against the exploitation of their rulers and of the wealthy. It lays blame for violent death and natural calamity on those who grasp power through violence. The new, vengeful *kami*, who came upon the stage of Japanese religious life in connection with political power struggle and economic exploitation, were *kami* of terrible character. Only the rites of the higher religion, esoteric Buddhism, were thought to be strong enough to pacify their spirits. The transition from the shinto *kami*, benevolent nature spirits, to the *goryo*, vengeful, and thought of as the *kami* who spread epidemics, can be traced through the ninth and eleventh centuries. It was a period in which rapid urbanization was accompanied by frequent and devastating epidemics. During the tenth century the association of epidemic with the vengeful *kami* became pervasive in the Japanese mind.

According to Ishida it was only in the thirteenth century that Shinto began to have any philosophical systems. During this period the Japanese mind began to rise from the ferment of thought and culture imported in previous centuries to express its own thought. These philosophical expressions of Shinto were in forms of *shugō*. Ishida lists five of them, the first of which arose in the Kamakura period:

1. Amalgamation of Shinto with Buddhism in Kamakura period: The Buddha appeared in the *kami* – *Honji Suijaku Shinto*, (Appearance – *sui* – of the primary reality – *honji* – into our historical world by assuming form – *jaku*. Kami is the appearance/*suijaku*/of the primary reality/*honji*/, the Buddha.) Specifically the one that interprets Shinto in the light of the Shingon (True Mantra) School of Buddhism.

2. Amalgamation of Shinto with Confucianism in the early Tokugawa period:
   Confucian Shinto propounded by Hayashi Razan (1583–1657) and Yamazaki Anzai (1618–1682).

3. Amalgamation of Shinto with *Kokugaku* ('National Japanese Learning' in contradistinction to *Kangaku* – Chinese or Confucian Learning – and *Yogaku* – Western Learning) in the later Tokugawa period: Shinto of Motoori Norinaga.

4. Amalgamation of Shinto with Christianity in the end of the Tokugawa period and at the beginning of Meiji Restoration: Shinto of Hirata Atsutane (1776–1843).

5. Amalgamation of Shinto with Nationalism in the Meiji, Taisho and Showa period (1868–1945): State Shintoism.

Thus two classes of amalgamation appeared; one with the foreign traditions such as Buddhism, Confucianism and Christianity; and the other between traditions within Japan such as *Kokugaku* and nationalism.

Professor Ishida points out that in the history of the Shinto amalgamation the fourteenth century marks the dividing line between (1) the period in which Shinto was explained through the imported religious traditions, and (2) the period in which Shinto began to make use of the imported religious thoughts in order to express itself. The first one is called *'Honji Suijaku'* as we have seen. The second is *'Han* (reverse) *Honji Suijaku'*.[5] In the former the Buddha appeared in *kami*, while in the latter *kami* appeared in the Buddha.

The fourth of Ishida's amalgamations, that of Shinto with Christianity, is of particular interest to this study. According to Muraoka, Hirata understood the Shinto god *Amenominakanushi no kami* (Heavenly Centre god) to be the god who rules all things in the universe, and *musubi kami,* the god who created heaven and earth and the human race, endowing humanity with spirituality of the highest order. He identifies the Japanese mythological deities, Izanagi as Adam and Izanami as Eve. This set of creative gods is contrasted in his doctrine with another shinto god, *Ookuninushi no mikoto*, Deity of the Great Land, the ruler of the spirits of the dead.

After death the human body will go back to the soil, but the soul will live without perishing. This Hirata concludes to be obvious since in this lifetime the complete recompense for good and bad is not satisfactorily carried out. Hirata believed that *musubi kami*, in creating humanity, gave its own spirit to people. Therefore the human spirit is able to distinguish good from evil. Evil arises because people are misled by the evil god. A right judgment will take place, he said, in the world of spirits. The good will then receive eternal blessing while the bad will have eternal tribulation.

The contrast in Hirata's 'theology' between the god of this world, Heavenly Centre god, and the god of the departed souls, Deity of the Great Land, is not a contrast between good and evil or light and darkness. He held that the god of the departed souls is superior to the god of this world. This is an unusual orientation for Japanese Shinto spirituality in which the emphasis has always been placed on the value of this world.

It is doubtful that Hirata ever had the opportunity to read the Bible in Chinese translation, the only Bible that would have been available to him. That he depended upon the Chinese writings of Jesuits is beyond dispute. He must have read, for example, *Tien Chu Shih* (True Doctrine of the Heavenly Lord) by Matthew Ricci.

Hirata's *shugō* was not a kind of Shinto Christianity. Muraoka writes:

There is the Ultimate Supreme Ancestor of the heaven and earth and of all things. It's name is *Amenominakanushi no kami*. This *kami* who sits in heaven, has no beginning and no end. This god is full of the virtue from which all things come. It does not work; it is stationary; it rules all that is. *Musubi kami* is the true master of all things. It inspired heaven, earth, people, *kami* and all things to appear. Over all these it rules; it nourishes all things. It is Our Great Parent. All our mind, body, personality and life are the gift of this god.[6]

Hirata used Christian theology to strengthen the Shinto deities. What he did with Christianity belongs to the line of thought called *Han Honji Suijaku*. The Son of God of Christianity, he said, is the imperial line of Japan. The god of Christianity is false; the shinto is the true religion. Hirata's thought supplied a basis for the nationalistic shinto revival which occurred at the time of the Meiji Restoration.

In the earlier Shinto-Buddhist amalgamation the god of Tado was understood to be renouncing divine status to become Buddhist in order to achieve salvation. This god confesses his sins! Obviously there is implied a superiority of the Buddhist gods over the indigenous Japanese gods. It also represents an appearance of a religious understanding of sin. The story of the god of Tado points in an awkward way to a transition from a naive awareness of sin in the agricultural society to a more advanced understanding of sin in the emerging urban social context. What had been fully accepted no longer worked and a god confessed his sins. As human societies become more complex, the occasions of conflicts of interests increase, and that in turn forces an expanded understanding of human sinfulness. There is certainly a difference between the native Japanese understanding of sin and that of Buddhism. It must have been quite an education for the god of Tado to hear the Buddhist sutras read for him!

I find the ease with which the god of Tado became the Buddhist *bodhisattva* of Tado is remarkable. Obviously, there was not much friction or confusion in the process. *Shugō* went on without any hindrance. This indicates that the Japanese mind is fundamentally pantheistic and therefore free from demarcation between 'this' god and 'that' god. Endo Shusaku, a Japanese Catholic writer, describes the Japanese mind as 'swamp' that can swallow all kinds of spiritual traditions apparently without much trouble. Up until 1945 for several decades the emperor was held to be 'divine'. The psychology and 'theology' that worked in this state ideology some twelve centuries later is very much like those that worked with the god of Tado. Curiously the fact that the divine emperor made 'confession' after the war before a more powerful American god in his Humanity Declaration resembles also the Tado incident. The Tado god was impressed by the Buddhist god. The emperor was impressed by the American god.

For the pantheistic Japanese the commandment; 'You shall not take the name of the Lord your God in vain' hardly makes sense. This commandment itself may be swallowed up in the 'swamp'. It seems that if this world is full of gods – birds, beasts, snakes, rivers and mountains are gods – the focus of the commandment that we must not take 'the name of God in vain' will disappear.

Secondly, as we have seen, however, the submission of the Tado to the Buddhist kami was not entirely without opposition. There was a disagreement between the wealthy and educated city people and the peasants who depended upon the assistance of the local kami as to which god was responsible for their problem, i.e. which was more powerful to help. What was essentially a power struggle between the classes became a power struggle between the gods. So also in this century there was a question of the relative power of the gods. In 1945 the Japanese people began to feel that the American god is stronger than their own god. Certainly there were those among the American soldiers then, and later in Vietnam, who perceived their god to be the more powerful. When Jerusalem was destroyed by the Babylonians in 587 BC the people of Judah felt that the god of the Babylonians was stronger, perhaps even superior, to their own God.

The struggle with the equation 'might is right' is a preoccupation of the biblical prophetic tradition. The prophets perceived idolatry in this dictum. They held to the difficult assertion that the God whose temple in Jerusalem was destroyed was, nevertheless, the 'right' and 'superior' God. Their assertion is no less difficult for us today than it was in the days of the prophets or of the Tado incident. But the important point is that in the Japanese mind a quick movement towards an amalgamation of the two 'gods' will suggest itself instead of the question of idolatry. When all kinds of gods are amalgamated – the gods of all different *curriculum vitae!* – then we will be relieved of the necessity to critically examine the gods or our idolatry. If the God of Israel and the gods of the Babylonians were, without any hindrance, amalgamated, then the question of idolatry would have been empty.

Thirdly, it is important to make some comment on the influence of the unpacified spirits or vengeful kami which continues to be an issue in Japan today. In the pacification of these spirits esoteric gestures and words are considered to be most efficacious. Esoteric rituals are 'mysterious'. Through such mysterious words and gestures the living approach the departed spirits to persuade them to submit to the teaching of the Buddha. The most intricate and complex symbols are employed. Such communication between the living and the dead is strictly forbidden in the tradition of Mount Sinai. From the standpoint of the history of religions it is truly remarkable that over so great a span of time as that required for the formation of the biblical account, the idea of spirit pacification which in other religions is a prevalent and fascinating subject, never appeared. The episode of King Saul calling up the spirit of Samuel through the help of a medium (I Sam. 28.3–19) was understood to be a violation of the law of God, but even in that story there is no suggestion of pacification of the spirit. What may be termed as 'unpacified spirits' appear in the New Testament.

> When he opened the fifth seal, I saw under the altar the souls of those who had been slain for the word of God and for the witness they had borne; they cried out with a loud voice, 'O Sovereign Lord, holy and true, how long before thou wilt judge and avenge our blood on those who dwell upon the earth?' (Rev. 6.9.10).

This is a disturbingly 'vengeful' passage in the Bible and it is hard to imagine that those who had given their life in witnessing for Jesus Christ could be asking that God avenge their blood. But these 'unpacified spirits' do not take vengeance themselves, instead they call upon the Sovereign Lord to do so for them. If the Lord does not consent to their request nothing will happen. In this sense, in their own words of prayer, the unpacified spirits are controlled. These words of Revelation, moreover, never gained any central importance in the Christian tradition. The more profound meaning of martyrdom, on the contrary, is found in the words of Jesus dying on the cross; 'Father, forgive them; for they know not what they do' (Luke 23.34) or in those of Stephen; 'Lord, do not hold this sin against them' (Acts 7.60).

One of the most refreshing theological innovations in Asia today is the introduction of the Korean concept of *han* into the theological discussion by the South Korean theologian Suh Nam Dong. *Han*, according to Suh Nam Dong, is 'an underlying feeling of Korean people. On the one hand, it is a dominant feeling of defeat, resignation and nothingness. On the other, it is a feeling with a tenacity of will for life which comes to weaker beings'.[7] According to David Kwang-sun, '*han* is a deep awareness of the contradictions in a situation and of the unjust treatment meted out to the people or a person by the powerful'.[8] The Korean poet Yang Sung-woo's *Slave Diary* contains typical expressions about *han*.'. . . the *han* which has been absorbed into the bones and muscles of the people of the country for 5,000 years is still breathing in the roots of the grass which covers the graves of the dead.'[9] *Han* 'can kill, cause revenge, destroy and hate endlessly'.[10] This *han* must be met by the spiritual force of *dan* (cutting). Personally *dan* means self-denial, and collectively, it is 'to cut the vicious circle of revenge'.[11] Kim Chi-ha writes in his 'Declaration of Conscience':

> People's *han* and rage ought to be liberated from its masochistic exercise to be a great and fervent clamour asking for God's justice. If needed, it ought to be developed into a decisive and organized explosion. This

miraculous transition lies in religious commitment and in internal and spiritual transformation.[12]

Accumulated *han* must be met by continuous *dan*! Is not this a profound expression that comes from Korean Christians which points to the prayer of Stephan; 'Lord, do not hold this sin against them'? Did not Stephen overcome *han* with *dan*? How difficult it is, however, to *cut* the accumulation of *han* of the last 5000 years! The 'unification of *han* and *dan*' suggested by the Korean Christians challenges the concept of *onryo*.[13]

The spirit of Jesus, at his own instruction, is not seen as an unpacified spirit (*onryo*) but as the Holy Spirit, the Comforter (John 14.26). Biblical language rejects the language of necromancer, or communication between the living and the dead. It has no programme for the pacification of the spirits of the dead. The language of religions that speak to the dead tends to become esoteric whereas biblical language is open and historical rather than closed and a-historical. It speaks a concrete ethical language. Rejecting communication with the dead, the biblical faith is not esoteric. 'Leave the dead to bury their own dead; but as for you, go and proclaim the kingdom of God' (Luke 9.60). The subject of the unpacified spirits is one of the most remarkable contrasts between the traditions of Mount Fuji and Mount Sinai.

I have pointed out that the *goryo-ye* (the ritual of the pacification of the unpacified spirits) developed from Shinto-Buddhist *shugō* in the eighth and ninth centuries. The art of communication with the dead became more sophisticated as these two strands of thoughts amalgamated. The biblical position that condemns necromancy and discourages any programme for appeasing the unpacified spirits of the dead freed Christianity from the vast area of discussions on the spirits of the dead, and from the tendency to be amalgamated with the religious positions that espouse positive programmes for the pacification of the departed spirits.

Fourthly, Hirata's amalgamation between Shinto and Christianity was essentially a primitive use of Christian images to strengthen shinto deities. There was no serious theological exploration, probably because of his limited access to information. This *shugō* does show that Christianity can be used (misused) to bolster certain aspects of other religious traditions. Christian concepts were used by him towards the theoretical formulation of shinto absolutism. When the form of monotheism was grafted into the polytheistic cultural context which included the concept of the imperial line of Japan, it created a dangerous possibility. Adopting the form without the historical experience and materials to substantiate that form, the host culture was not challenged. A certain aspect of polytheism was strengthened by the monotheistic emphasis so that it was able to draw to itself such concentration of attention that the emperor cult of this century became a possibility. Japan became 'monotheistic' in her devotion to the emperor during the war years. That monotheism was far more dangerous than her former polytheism because it did not contain the critical contents of monotheism which are so important a part of the Mount Sinai tradition.

Finally, I must comment briefly upon the concepts of amalgamation and syncretism. The Japanese *shugō* is syncretic. The word 'syncretism', meaning a mixing of religions, has been given a negative connotation in the history of Christian theology. Yet, whether we like it or not, there is an inevitable process of one religion interacting with another and appropriating certain aspects of other religion into its own system. Religions come with cultures, and *vice versa*. When cultures meet religions meet, and when religions meet cultures meet. It is difficult to draw a clear line of demarcation between religion and culture. Missionaries from the West working in Asia have always warned their Asian converts of the serious evil of mixing the Christian faith with Asian religious and cultural heritages, apparently quite unaware that the Christianity they preached has been defined by the Western way of thinking and living. Any attempt to 'asianize' Christianity was vigorously suppressed as 'syncretic' though Christianity in the United States certainly influenced and is influenced by American culture. It would not be possible to be otherwise. The question is whether such interaction of the gospel with any religion or culture produces an enrichment or a distortion of the gospel. The distortion of the gospel occurs when a culture or religion is placed in an equal position with the name of Jesus Christ. Such 'equal placing' is the manifestation of the spirit of syncretism so far as a Christian viewpoint is concerned. Probably, Buddhists may make a similar observation that if Mohammad is placed in an equal standing with the Buddha then Buddhism is threatened by syncretism. In the Christian perspective, as long as cultural expressions are examined in the light of the gospel and subordinated to the value of the gospel the influence is one of enrichment rather than syncretism.

Thus the encounter of religions must be appreciated with a mind that is able to understand the complexity and richness of cultures and religions in general. The words 'culture' or 'religion' are simple, but what they imply is an enormous reality, a reality far more dynamic than the concept of syncretism itself. Religious amalgamation is an extremely complex phenomenon which can produce all sorts of unexpected results. No religion is, as I have said, 'pure' and 'intact' in itself. Religion has its identifiable message in spite of the complex reality of interactions and appropriation from different sources. It is possible, I think, through *shugō* that a certain religion may become less idolatrous than it was previously. It may also become more idolatrous. Idolatry is idolatry in the perspective of Christian faith. But in the concrete historical conditions in which we live everyday life, religion (or culture or ideology) less idolatrous is preferred to the one which is more idolatrous. The complex *shugō* phenomena are constantly producing new religious situations before our eyes. Our criticism of idolatry must be done in this dynamic flux of human spiritual commitment and fascination. The *goryo-ye* motif is distinctively expressed in the national cult of the shrine for the war dead up to the end of the war in 1945. This cult which is associated with the name of the Yasukuni Shrine in Tokyo is fast regaining its war-time prestige and influence today. Christianity's critique of the cult of pacification of the departed souls is met by strong opposition which can draw its spiritual and philosophical energy from Japan's ancient tradition. The *goryo-ye* outlook expressed by the national cult of Yasukuni Shrine is far more idolatrous than *goryo-ye* engaged in the ancient time. In the perspective of Christian faith naive shintoism of nature is less idolatrous than the shintoism of the emperor cult. As it is impossible, in my view, to eradicate idolatry completely from our history, it is important for us to endeavour to make idolatry less idolatrous and less harmful to human life. For this reason, the study of the history of *shugō* has its importance in our theological reflection. To all 'swampy' religious situations of Japan the commandment is directed; 'You shall not take the name of the Lord your God in vain'.

15
Wealthy Nation Strong Army

Totalitarian violence comes when the concepts of
'heaven' and 'people' are not related.

Within a span of one hundred years, beginning in the late seventeenth
century, the Confucian political philosophy became prominent in Japan.
The philosopher and social critic, Ogyu Sorai (1666–1728) said that there is
no better way to govern the nation than the way of the ancient sage. In
another context he observed, 'The origin of the way is in heaven. The
ancient sage kings found the heavenly law and established the way'. This is
the fundamental Confucian concept of the 'Mutuality between Heaven and
People'. Another political philosopher, Yamaga Soko (1622–85) wrote,
'The courtiers follow the example of the son of heaven. People under
heaven follow the example of the courtiers. The rulers must practise
according to the principle of heaven and earth. The ruler must follow the
example of the rulers before him'. Dazai Shundai (1680–1747), a disciple of
Sorai, taught that 'in the way of government, first comes the *Rei Gaku*. *Rei
Gaku* is the creation of the ancient sages'. *Rei* is the sense of morality by
which our deeds become noble while *gaku* is the music which makes our
mind peaceful. Prominent in all of this is the Confucian political
philosophy of Rule by Virtue.

Honda Toshiaki (1744–1821) philosophized, 'Are not the people the
people of heaven and do they not belong to the ruler? Every one of them is
important since each one is a person of heaven. There is no reason to allow
a person to suffer or to be killed. The government must protect them. Is this
not the work of government?' According to Kumazawa Banzan (1619–91)
people are 'loaned to the rulers' (*azukari mono*) by heaven. Rulers are
answerable to heaven for whatever they do to the people. Ikeda Mitsumasa
(1609–82) said, 'The shogun is responsible for all people placed under his
care by heaven, the lords are responsible for the people loaned from the
shogun'. Thus the shogun was seen as morally and politically responsible to

heaven. Shibano Ritsuzan (1736–1807) said, 'All people under heaven, from the high lords to the beggars and outcasts, the shogun must be heaven and earth, father and mother to them'. The shogun, says Ritsuzan, is the 'Vicar of Heaven'.

A central idea here is that the people are loaned or trusted to the ruler by heaven. The movement from heaven to shogun to feudal lords corresponds to the line from ancestor to self to descendants. In fact Uesugi Yozan (1746–1822) says that the feudal house continues just as we transmit from the ancestors to the descendants. Therefore it must not be looked upon as private property. Uesugi looks upon any particular feudal lord as a passing functionary. Yamaga Soko says that 'Lords may change according to the passage of time, but people and state are one and they do not pass away'. The shogun has a duty to oversee that the feudal lords are 'ruling people with benevolence (*Jin Sei*)'.

Both Yamaga Soko and Kumazawa Banzan held that the emperors had lost their real political power since the time of the Kamakura Shogunate because of their lack of virtue. Ogyu Sorai held that the virtuous Tokugawa line, having destroyed the less virtuous line of Toyotomi Hideyoshi, now properly enjoys the heavenly mandate.[1]

Throughout the period of the Tokugawa Shogunate (1603–1867) the Confucian political and social theories played an important role. The principle of heaven, the relationship between the rulers and the ruled, and even the value of the individual person were emphasized. This was the period of the Closed Nation. The Confucian political philosophy was geared to maintaining peace within the closed nation. In the middle of the nineteenth century, however, a fundamental change was forced upon Japan from outside. Within a hundred years Japan would undergo the most turbulent and violent period of its history in which all religious traditions would be forced to submit to the national ideology of 'Wealthy Nation Strong Army' under a system of imperial absolutism.

In July 1852 a naval expedition under the charge of Matthew C. Perry, commissioned by the American President, Millard Fillmore, to open Japanese ports to United States ships, arrived at Uraga with four battleships. He pressured the Japanese to receive a letter from President Fillmore. After surveying Tokyo Bay, Perry left for Okinawa, promising to return the following year to receive the reply to the presidential letter. He sailed into the harbour again on 16 January 1854 and was able to force the shogunate to sign a treaty of commerce on 3 March 1954. In December of the same year the Kyoto Imperial Court issued an order to make temple bells into cannons in order to defend the nation. It was the first administrative order to come from the imperial court in the modern era.

The Shimoda Trade Treaty between the United States and Japan was signed on 21 July 1857.

After over two hundred years of isolation Japan was suddenly brought into direct confrontation with the powerful nations of the world. Frightened by what she saw, she decided to imitate the powerful nations, to modernize and to achieve in the shortest time possible the status of a strong nation. Under the slogan, 'Wealthy Nation Strong Army', she was soon able to effect total mobilization, but not without serious social strain. People were coerced to make incredible sacrifice, even to the sacrifice of life itself. Two military victories, over China in 1895 and Russia in 1905, established Japan as a military nation.

The year 1868 was the first year of the Meiji emperor, grandfather of the present emperor. Japan, as a unified nation under the direct rule of the emperor was established with what is called the Meiji Constitutional System. The System comprised the Constitution of the Empire, the Peerage, the Cabinet System, the Judicial System, the Rescript on Education, the Military System, the District Bureaucracy, and local governments. Fundamentally it was a centralized political system under a divine right emperor. All power was concentrated in the Imperial Court. Motoda Eifu (1818–91) and Ito Hirobumi (1841–1909), influential among the architects of the System, agreed on the imperial ideology, with Motoda emphasizing a Confucianism of personal virtue in government while Ito's interest was in fashioning a rational legal system of government.[2]

In 1886 work was begun on the Constitution and on the codification of Imperial Household Law. A draft of the Constitution prepared by Ito, Inoue, and Herman Roesler from Germany was submitted to the emperor in April 1888. It was then examined in the Privy Council, the emperor's inner circle. The Imperial Household Law was submitted to the Privy Council in May 1888. These two documents insured the inviolability of the Imperial household from any incursion by the Diet or the people.

The Constitution was accompanied on the day of its Promulgation by the Emperor's Personal Sentences and also his Rescript (1889). These became a part of the Constitution itself. The point was emphasized that the Constitution was based on the teaching of the imperial ancestors and was in keeping with the 'Prestige of the Nation' doctrine. By giving the Constitution the emperor was fulfilling the wish of the imperial ancestor of 'loving the people'. In this Constitution the emperor is the substance of all rights, and the land and the people are objects to be governed. Imperial authority, which is supreme, is based on divine decree from ancient times and the throne continues by blood succession. The vision of humanity expressed in this Constitution is inferior to that of the Constitution associated with the name of Prince Shotoku in the early seventh century. There the guiding principles were taken from the central message of

Buddhism and Confucianism, instead of an ideological definition of imperial ancestors.

In his commentary on Article III of the Constitution, ('The Personage of the Emperor is Sacred and Inviolable') Herman Roesler writes:

> ... the Emperor holds His power from heaven through the medium of His glorious ancestors, but not from any human authorization or concession; consequently He cannot be held responsible to His subjects, but to Heaven alone.
>
> This article is found in most European constitutions. In the Belgian Constitution the person of the King is declared inviolable, but the declaration of his sacredness has been omitted, probably on account of that constitution declaring all powers of the state to emanate from the people, and the King being entitled only to the exercise of the special powers expressly conceded to him. Thus there is in the Belgian Constitution a mixture of monarchical and democratic principles which is quite inadmissible in Japan.
>
> In a more legal sense, the Emperor is declared sacred because He is the most exalted person in the Empire, invested with a power of divine nature the reflection of which on His august person must be acknowledged by the laws of the country....
>
> In virtue of His inviolability, the Emperor is subject to no human force on the part of His subjects.[3]

Thus Article III was destined to play a fateful role in the years up to 1945. In it is stated that the emperor is subject to no human force and judgment. He is responsible to Heaven alone. But what is the meaning of Heaven here? How do the people relate to Heaven? In this Constitution the Imperial Prerogative did not originate from the Constitution. Rather the Imperial Prerogative defined the Constitution. The duty of the people was to be obedient to the emperor. The veneration of the emperor is understood not as the religion but the duty of the people. 'Japanese subjects shall, within limit not prejudicial to peace and order, and not antagonistic to their duties as subjects, enjoy religious freedom' (Article xxviii). The Diet only 'supports' the decision of the emperor. The Privy Council is all powerful. With this Meiji Constitution imperial absolutism was imposed upon the people of Japan.

The Meiji Constitutional system generated artificial and coerced dedication to the emperor. The people lived with minimal rights under the powerful Imperial Prerogative. They were pressed into the dangerous fanaticism of the emperor cult and militarism. Feeling smaller and smaller within Japan they began to behave bigger and bigger towards their neighbours. China was spoken of as the 'great decaying tree' of Asia and Korea as 'a nation of unprincipled, shameless people'. Japan herself was 'the bright master of Asia'. The nation that came under the ideology of imperial absolutism began to speak destructive language which the traditions of Prince Shotoku or the Tokugawa Confucian scholars would not condone. The concept of heaven lost its universality, and it was monopolized by the rulers of Japan.

The Meiji army was an Imperial Army controlled by the Imperial Prerogative. The Imperial Rescript Addressed to Soldiers, issued in January, 1882 (*Gunjin Chokuyu*) begins with the affirmation that, since the time of the emperor Jimmu (a mythological figure), the army of Japan is the emperor's army. It urges military personnel not to be concerned about public opinion and politics. They are only to execute the order that comes ultimately from the emperor himself. The Constitution stipulates that the emperor commands the army and decides its size. It was in the light of this Meiji Constitutional system and in particular in the doctrine expounded in the Imperial Rescript Addressed to Soldiers that the emperor was rightly held, after the war, to be responsible for the war.

The Japanese did not accept conscription without resistance. The government had to instigate trouble outside the country to justify its conscription programme, though the major assignment of the imperial army was the suppression of civil insurrection. During the ten year period from 1868 to 1877 there were 674 social disturbances reported. Of these 499 were insurrections of farm population, 24 were urban disturbances and 151 were other rural disturbances. There were 16 demonstrations against conscription itself.[4]

Thus the imperial system of armed force moved Japan toward aggression at the same time it was used to suppress the local population. From the time of the declaration of war against Russia in February, 1904, such expressions as 'National Benefit of the Empire', 'Maintaining the Glory of the Empire' and 'Military Might of the Empire' were frequently used in documents related to international affairs. The emperor expressed his approval of the performance of the Japanese soldiers in Manchuria saying, in May 1907, that their success enabled him to perform the heaven trusted duty of protecting the nation's interest.

In 1872 a system of universal schooling was established. Education was controlled to advance the national goal of 'Wealthy Nation Strong Army'. The cost of education was paid directly by the people. Tuition for primary school was 50 sen a month when a *koku* of rice could be purchased for 400 sen[5]. The content of education was also strictly controlled. In August and September, 1880, government agents examined the books and textbooks written by progressive authors such as Fukuzawa Yukichi (1834–1901) and Kato Hiroyuki (1836–1916) and even those published by the Ministry of Education itself. Wherever there was found an inference to political consciousness or the rights of the people the book was banned. The

Confucian orientation of morality, with its hierarchical emphasis on the supremacy of the emperor and the eternal imperial succession, was promoted by the government. 'Instruction to the Primary Teachers', inspired by Motoda and issued in 1881, prohibited teachers from discussing political concerns but encouraged them to teach the virtue of submission to the emperor and the glory of the empire. The separation of the teachers from politics and the use of them for government political ends continued to the end of the Pacific War.

In 1880 Ueki Emori (1857–92) objected to the totalitarian aims of education. Calling for variety and independence of mind, he insisted that education should be free from political pressure so that the citizen would be able to participate in politics with a mature and independent mind. Political thought is important, he held, and political pressure is not desirable in the schools. Ueki was ahead of his time. The idea that the citizen could have rights and responsibilities had not yet developed in nineteenth-century Japan. The Meiji government was pushing the Confucian ideology in education. Motoda emphasized that the emperor had authority over the education of the whole nation.

From the beginning there was a vigorous promotion of the imperial cult. On 17 January 1868, the government established *Shingika*, Department of Religion, and Shintoism became an official state religion. The leaders of the nation were confident that the ideology of the divine emperor would give the nation the concentration needed to achieve its goal of Wealthy Nation Strong Army. In 1869 the spirits of the imperial ancestors which in the past had been pacified through the Buddhist ritual were repacified through the Shinto ritual by government Shinto priests. The Meiji emperor himself was actively involved in this ideological orientation. The *kami* pacified, and thus given a new status were those mentioned in the *Kojiki, Nihon Shoki* and the *Engi Shiki* (Engi Period Regulations of the tenth century) and the souls of those who died for the glory of the emperor. Local gods and gods of ancestral spirits of the people were placed at a lower level in religious classification. Thus the traditional understanding of the *kami* was redefined in the light of the imperial ideology. The result was the separation and eventual isolation of Shintoism from Buddhism.

The separation could not be accomplished without a great disturbance in the whole religious life of the Japanese people. Immediately there were strong objections to this policy but official Buddhism did not have enough courage to stand against the pressure of the government. On 17 October 1871, *Honganji* (Shinran school of Buddhism) issued a statement indicating that their Buddhism venerates the Buddha called Amida. He is identical with the heavenly ancestor of the imperial family, though called differently. When looked upon in his respect of wisdom he is called *Amenominaka nushi no kami*, Heavenly Centre Deity of Shintoism, but viewed in his aspect of mercy he is Amida! But the compromise was an awkward one. Yanagida Kunio, dean of the study of folk religion in Japan, has pointed out that the Meiji government had no understanding of the religion of the people and tried artificially to create a comprehensive system of religious life by force.

The ferment within Buddhist circles during this time has been well documented. Shimachi Mokurai (1838–1911) of the Shinran school, believing that Buddhism could serve the interest of the national ideology, tried to reorganize it to conform to the national goal of Wealthy Nation Strong Army. On the other side, Fukuda Gyokai (1809–88) of the Honen school argued that as Buddhism believes in the non-self and the value of nirvana it could not be integrated into the ideology of militarism. Progressive Buddhists, who criticized the degeneration of Buddhism and expressed a strong interest in social reform, were particularly critical of the invasion of the emperor ideology into Buddhist spiritual life and sought to establish a working relationship with the socialists. The government took repressive measures against them.

Religions of the people, such as Konko-kyo, Tenri-kyo and Omoto-kyo which had sprung up during the nineteenth century, were most able to stand up against the power of the government's religious policy. These people's religions, of which the three mentioned are only the most renowned, share certain characteristics. They all believe in some kind of benevolent 'high god'. They emphasize the importance of this present life. Personal and social healing are goals. They have revelational oracles from their gods. They called for a change of mind and for discipline in life.

In general these groups had a difficult time with the government until 1945. In 1873 the government demanded that Konko-kyo destroy its altar. The founder Kawate Bunjiro (1814–83), a farmer, is reported to have said, 'Do not be dismayed, the world is always changing. Wait five hard years'. But in 1883 the pressure was still on. The government suggested an approved god for Konko-kyo which the leaders of the group rejected saying, 'That god is different from ours'. Nakayama Miki (1798–1888), a housewife, foundress of Tenri-kyo, was jailed eighteen times in her life time. Strong pressures were placed upon the Tenri-kyo movement by the government. At that time Nakayama is reported to have said, 'Do you fear the government or our god? Make a choice!' Omoto-kyo, whose foundress was also a housewife, Deguchi Nao (1836–1919) saw this world as evil and her god as the one who saved us from this evil world. All these religions have an eschatological outlook and are strongly messianic. Konko-kyo announced the coming of a new world, a world of equality. Some of their devotees walked with lanterns in the daylight to signify the darkness of this world.

The Westernization of Japan, achieved in the span of several decades, was accompanied by a great deal of human suffering. It was, in my view, a Westernization and not a modernization. The structure in which the ideology of the imperial cult was at the centre cannot be called modernization. It was not until the post-war Constitution of 1947 that true modernization began. Westernization, for Japan, was militarization, preparation to defend herself and eventually to carry out massive aggression. Japanese leaders saw that their armaments must be Westernized if they were to stand up to the challenge of the West. All the people and the resources of the nation were mobilized to achieve the national aim of 'Wealthy Nation Strong Army'. Hijacked by a powerful government, at the centre of which stood a human who was beyond human, the nation was exploited brutally and suffered immensely. Wealthy Nation was for the few, Strong Army was to suppress her own people. The success of war against China and Russia, in historical perspective, harmed the nation and brought it no good. Taiwan was colonized in 1896 and Korea in 1910. These events convinced the militarists that they were now master of Asia and that the way to national greatness through military might was confirmed.

The spirit of harmony and peace (*wa*) which Prince Shotoku gave the nation was gone. The profound humanity that came to expression in the religious experiences of Honen and Shinran was ignored. Christianity, both Catholic and Protestant traditions, was looked upon as a religion that is not fitted to the fundamental principle of Japan. Shintoism became State Shintoism. Buddhism was unable to criticize effectively the new totalitarianism. The concept of *jinsei* (rule by virtue) of Confucianism was distorted to support a policy of absolute heaven in the person of the emperor. A section of the Christian church, some popular religions and socialists demonstrated sharp criticism but massive government power was able to crush them. 'Wealthy Nation Strong Army' was a nightmare into which the people of Japan entered immediately upon the opening of Japan to the world after her period of closure. Perhaps there was no other way for nineteenth-century Japan, suddenly brought into the reality of world trade and political pressure, to avoid colonization. It would seem that her slogan meant 'colonize or be colonized'. Were there other alternatives? Could the way of imperial absolutism have been avoided? If there were other ways, Japan's leaders did not see them and took the tragic path of national totalitarian mobilization.

Our observation of the rise and fall of nations seems to teach us that any nation, aware of becoming great, will become progressively self-centred and imperialistic, a development which leads to self-destruction. No moral teaching, spiritual heritage or rational arguments have been found to stop the accelerated movement towards such destruction. Since 1930 Japan and Germany, with their great differences in culture, religion and history, had taken the similar course of self-destruction until 1945.

Perhaps the element that brought the ruination of Japan in 1945 was the exploitation of its own people. 'Wealthy Nation Strong Army' by itself may not destroy a nation, but the enslavement of the people by framing a political and social system designed to hinder the people's participation in political power sharing, that is, totalitarianism, destroyed the nation. I have come to see that the use of the Strong Army to suppress the people is not an unusual tactic of leaders who are ambitious to create a Strong Nation. I perceive that the policy meets with apparent success in the short term but eventual disaster. Isaiah's picturesque description of the production of an idol (Isa. 44.9–20) can be used as a metaphor here. A piece of wood is taken, measured, cut and chiselled and made into an idol. The idol does not appear suddenly. It is produced by a plan. The idol of the Wealthy Nation Strong Army was carefully planned and executed. It was our creation, we worshipped it and we came to disaster. The time that the Japanese experienced with the idol, a period of fifty years, (1895–1945) was a demonic time, it must not be forgotten.

After Hiroshima the people moved into a different experience of time. They passed from the time of idolatry to the time of repentance. These two periods make up one important experience for the Japanese people. In a theological sense, they are in a spiritual search to speak the name of God in the right way, even though their culture does not know the name of God explicitly. An intriguing theological question is how to interpret the criticism of Konko-kyo levelled against the shinto absolute state Shintoism ('That god is different from ours') in the light of the commandment: 'You shall not take the name of the Lord your God in vain'.

16

The Post-War Constitution

'The right of belligerency of the state will not be
recognized'– An act of faith.

The Meiji Constitution, declaring the person of the emperor to be divine
and absolute, continued to be effective to the date that Japan accepted the
stipulation of the Potsdam Declaration, 14 August 1945. It is important to
know that the Pacific War was executed under the Meiji Constitution.
Under its authority the emperor had the full prerogative in all fundamental
military decisions, including the declaration of war and capitulation.

The postwar Constitution came into effect on 3 May 1947 while Japan
was under the occupation of the Allied Powers. The shadow of the critical
moment of defeat lay over the nation. Legally the new constitution was
promulgated as a revision of the Meiji Constitution, as provided in Article
73 of the old document. This was done because of the wish of General
Douglas MacArthur, Supreme Commander for the Allied Powers and the
Japanese government to guarantee 'complete legal continuity' (Instructions
of General D. MacArthur, 23 June 1946). The draft was prepared in less
than ten days by the staff of General Headquarters of the Supreme
Commander for the Allied Powers. It was not, of course, written 'from
scratch'. Constitutions from European and American nations were used as
models. Japanese critics of the constitution called it the 'MacArthur
Constitution' or the 'Translation Constitution'. It should, they said have
been written 'according to the free will of the people', and there is no
freedom under occupation.

Nevertheless, the Japanese people recognized the significance of their
emancipation from the tyranny of the imperial cult by the occupational
forces and they accepted the new constitution. They took the spirit of the
constitution as their own. Perhaps only so drastic a historical situation as
the defeat of a nation could make possible such a remarkable spiritual
coincidence.

The preambles of the two constitutions make a striking contrast.
The 1889 Constitution, The Preamble:

Having, by virtue of the glories of Our Ancestors, ascended the Throne
of a lineal succession unbroken for ages eternal; desiring to promote the
welfare of, and to give development to the moral and intellectual
faculties of Our beloved subjects, the very same that have been favoured
with the benevolent care and affectionate vigilance of Our Ancestors;
and hoping to maintain the prosperity of the State, in concert with Our
people and with their support, We hereby promulgate in pursuance of
Our Imperial Rescript of the 12th day of the 10th month of the 14th year
of Meiji, a fundamental law of State, to exhibit the principles, by which
We are to be guided in Our conduct, and to point out to what Our
descendants and Our subjects and their descendants are forever to
conform.

The rights of sovereignty of the State, We have inherited from Our
Ancestors, and We shall bequeath them to Our descendants. Neither We
nor they shall in future fail to wield them, in accordance with the
provisions of the Constitution hereby granted.

The 1947 Constitution, The Preamble:

We, the Japanese people, acting through our duly elected representatives
in the National Diet, determined that we shall secure for ourselves and
our posterity the fruits of peaceful cooperation with all nations and the
blessings of liberty throughout this land, and resolved that never again
shall we be visited with the horrors of war through the action of
government, do proclaim that sovereign power resides with the people
and do firmly establish this Constitution. Government is a sacred trust of
the people, the authority for which is derived from the people, the
powers of which are exercised by the representatives of the people, and
the benefits of which are enjoyed by the people. This is a universal
principle of mankind upon which this Constitution is founded. We reject
and revoke all constitutions, laws, ordinances and rescripts in conflict
herewith.

We, the Japanese people, desire peace for all time and are deeply
conscious of the high ideals controlling human relationship, and we have
determined to preserve our security and existence, trusting in the justice
and faith of the peace-loving peoples of the world. We desire to occupy
an honoured place in an international society striving for the
preservation of peace, and the banishment of tyranny and slavery,
oppression and intolerance for all time from the earth. We recognize that
all peoples of the world have the right to live in peace, free from fear and
want.

We believe that no nation is responsible to itself alone, but that laws of political morality are universal; and that obedience to such laws is incumbent upon all nations who would sustain their own sovereignty and justify their sovereign relationship with other nations.

We, the Japanese people, pledge our national honour to accomplish these high ideals and purposes with all our resources.

The contrast between the authority 'inherited from Our Ancestors' invoked in the earlier constitution and the political philosophy that 'government is a sacred trust of the people' which expressed a 'universal principle of mankind' addressed in the new constitution is a radical one. I believe the sentence, 'no nation is responsible to itself alone, but that laws of political morality are universal' represents a break through from the narrow vista of tribalism to the emancipating space of universalism. The 1889 preamble is mythological, while the 1947 preamble is rational and enlightened.

Three principles are presented in the preamble of the new constitution. There is, first, the basic principle that sovereign power resides with the people. This is the democratic principle of government based on the modern concept of natural law. Second, there is the dedication of the Japanese people to the ideal of peace for all time. Rejecting the nation's egoism, the preamble expresses, thirdly, Japan's adherence to the principle of international harmony. Then the preamble ends with the pledge of the national honour to accomplish these high ideals.

The importance of this preamble is that it states clearly the determination of the people to establish a nation dedicated to peace and democracy. '... never again shall we be visited with the horrors of war through the action of government.' The preamble echoes the words of the Charter of the United Nations:

Determined to save succeeding generations from the scourge of war, which twice in our lifetime has brought untold sorrow to mankind, ...

Out of the deep wounds of history important words were born in this constitution. In the war she initiated, Japan perpetrated untold damage upon others and upon herself. She suffered defeat. Out of that history these words came. Thus the new constitution, in the most dramatic sense, combined the basic theological ingredients, words and history. Special words and special history! The coming together of these two is a rare and costly event. Although we must not overlook the fact that not a word is said in the constitution about the suffering of the peoples, in particular, of Asian nations, caused by Japan!

'Never again shall we be visited with the horrors of war through the action of government.' These are the words of 'confession of faith' by the

Japanese people in 1947. There is a parallelism between what these words mean to the constitution and what Exodus 20.2 is to the Ten Commandments.

I am the Lord your God, who brought you out of the land of Egypt, out of the house of bondage.

The Ten Commandments can only be fully appreciated in the light of the fundamental truth about the people of God, that they were 'saved out of the house of bondage'. This preamble is the proclamation of the initiative of grace taken by God. The preamble to Japan's new constitution is the sincere human reflection upon the horrors of war for which they themselves are responsible. Both preambles signify historical experiences so complex that they are not easily described. Their significance is in their position in relation to what follows. The laws follow the preamble. They must be read in the light of the preamble. The laws are not unrelated to history but arise out of the concrete historical situation.

There is, however, a significant difference between these two preambles. The Exodus preamble speaks about 'God'. It is theological. The Japanese preamble is not theological in this sense. It speaks about the concrete historical experience. The horrors of the war were experienced directly by all Japanese people. 'God' cannot be experienced with any such directness. It takes faith to experience God in history. In this sense the Japanese preamble is more straightforward than that of Exodus.

Yet, when I reflect upon the more than three decades of Japanese politics in the postwar years, the meaning of the preamble has proved to be not so simple as we might think. It invokes not one, but two possibilities; the decision to move towards disarmament, to avoid involvement in war; and the decision to move in the direction of armament, in order not to repeat the horrors of war. In effect, the simple historical determination – 'Never again shall we be visited with the horrors of war through the action of government' – has produced two convictions about history; peace by way of disarmament and peace by way of armament. Two gods? Perhaps? There are the false god and the true God, the false prophet and the true prophet. I find, then, that the straightforward preamble of the Japanese constitution is not unrelated to the discussion of 'God'.

The God who declares 'I am the Lord your God, who brought you out of the land of Egypt, out of the house of bondage' is the 'true' God. This is not a scientific truth, but a truth to which faith commits itself. Does this true God identify himself with the position of realization of peace through disarmament? Or through armament? Or through a mixture of these two positions? What is precisely God's position on war and peace? When does the true God become a false god? The Japanese people, totally unaware of the theological implications, decided to commit themselves to the principle of renunciation of war, the position of complete disarmament. Article Nine of the postwar constitution takes the name of 'God' *not* in vain.

> Aspiring sincerely to an international peace based on justice and order, the Japanese people forever renounce war as a sovereign right of the nation and the threat or use of force as means of settling international disputes.
>   In order to accomplish the aim of the preceding paragraph, land, sea, and air forces, as well as other war potential, will never be maintained. The right of belligerency of the state will not be recognized.

I would like to make some comments on this well-known article before I come back to the question of 'God' expressed in these words of the fundamental law of Japan. Now what does it mean to 'renounce war as a sovereign right of the nation'? Since no war begins unless a nation takes it as a 'sovereign right' this would seem to renounce all war. The problem arises with the conditional phrase, 'as a means of settling international disputes'. In general this has been interpreted in two ways. What may be seen as a strict interpretation is that all war, including war of self-defence, is renounced. This position argues that no war is unrelated to the 'settling (of) international disputes'. It is, morover, very difficult to draw a line between aggressive and defensive war. Even aggressive wars are justified, by their perpetrators, as being defensive in some sense.

In opposition to this view are those who would interpret the constitution more flexibly in order to allow for some kind of rearmament. They hold that 'war as the means of settling international disputes' means only aggressive war and does not include war of self-defence. Wars which are not a 'means of settling international disputes' are not renounced. This would mean that war for self-defence, and therefore preparation for self-defence, is permissible. The discussion must be seen in the light of the historical experience of the war. Just as no nation would admit to engaging in aggressive war, Japan did not. With the memory of the war and the political struggles that accompanied it so fresh, no political figures in 1947 would have thought that this article would permit Japan to have a self-defence force. They all knew that such an exception would nullify the substance of the article immediately.[1]

How, then, are the people of Japan to find security in terms of Article Nine? Ultimately, the constitution suggests, all nations in the world will realize the ideal of Article Nine and the force of arms will not be needed. More immediately, the postwar constitution depends upon the security provided by the United Nations for disarmament and neutrality. '... we have determined to preserve our security and existence, trusting in the justice and faith of the peace loving peoples of the world', says the preamble in its second paragraph. The Japanese peace constitution depends virtually on Article One (1) of the Charter of the United Nations:

> The purposes of the United Nations are:
> (1) To maintain international peace and security, and to that end: to take effective collective measures for the prevention and removal of threats to the peace and for the suppression of acts of aggression or other breaches of the peace, and to bring about by peaceful means, and in conformity with the principles of justice and international law, adjustment or settlement of international disputes or situations which might lead to a breach of the peace.

Again, the Second Article (3) of the Charter is echoed in the Japanese peace constitution. The words of the Charter are:

> All members shall settle their international disputes by peaceful means in such a manner that international peace, and security, and justice, are not endangered.

Article Nine, then, is an act of faith. It will remain a meaningful historical force as long as Japanese people 'trust in the justice and faith of the peace loving peoples of the world'.

But what happened historically was the conclusion of the United States Japan Mutual Security Pact (1951) which took a far different position from that of neutrality and disarmament. Was the Security Pact in conflict with the Constitution? On 16 December 1959 the Supreme Court of Japan decided that the issue of the Security Pact is beyond the limit of Judiciary, and that the presence of the United States army in Japan was constitutional. The Supreme Court put forth the argument: The constitution stipulates the renunciation of war and non-possession of war potential. It does not, however, deny the nation's proper right to defend itself as a sovereign nation. The constitution does not define non-resistance and non-defence. Taking measures to ensure the security and peace of the nation belongs to the very concept of nation. Therefore, to supplement the lack of defence power in order to maintain the peace and security of Japan is constitutional. The Supreme Court judged that the military presence of another nation within Japan is not Japanese war potential, therefore it is not in conflict with the second paragraph of Article Nine.[2]

The dangerous part of the disscussion was the upholding of the presence of a foreign military force, according to the view critical of the Supreme Court decision, to supplement the lack of defence capability as constitutional. This kind of interpretation would undercut the fundamental spirit of the constitution and opens the way to move again toward rearmament and militarism.

Japanese philosophy of war and peace has been distanced from the kind of thought expressed in the Book of Psalms (20.7).

> Some boast of chariots, and some of horses; But we boast of the name of the Lord Our God.

Or in the Book of Isaiah (2.4):

> He shall judge between the nations, and shall decide for many peoples; and they shall beat their swords into plowshares, and their spears into pruning hooks; nation shall not lift up sword against nation, neither shall they learn war any more.

Yet it is this country that accepted renunciation of war as a fundamental law of the nation. The *kichi* oriented continuity people have been trying to uphold this ideal of the universal principle of humanity. I feel like lodging a complaint with Almighty God for giving such a difficult assignment to a country which has had no Judaeo-Christian training and which is without the biblical way of looking at history. Article Nine should have been given to a nation with centuries of Christian philosophy and nurture, such as Great Britain or Italy or Sweden. It came to the *ashi kabi* people, of all peoples. Is it possible that the Japanese people proclaimed this article because they are a basically optimistic people? Have they accepted this article in the spirit of the Shinto prayer; 'Day by day ever more flourishing/Until myriads of years hence/The pleasure will not cease'?

I do not think so. The experience of utter desolation which changed the nation was shocking for them. In the wilderness they felt that their swords must be 'beaten into plowshares'. I believe that momentarily the Japanese people experienced something other than the alternate movement of the *kyo* and *kichi*. They must have experienced discontinuity and negation stronger than the ones they knew previously. This time the end has come to the nation! They were brought to their knees. Not in a confident standing posture, but on their knees, as one vanquished, the people embraced Article Nine and it became the expression of their own will and their understanding of the history of Japan.[3] In it there is the sincerity of the returning prodigal son. 'I have sinned against heaven and before you' (Luke 15.18) and therefore 'I have decided to be disarmed'. On 3 November 1946, the then president of Tokyo University, Nambara Shigeru, gave a public address on the new constitution then waiting to be promulgated, in which he said that the ideal of renunciation of war and a peaceful nation is the lesson Japanese people learned by going through the destruction of war. What the people learned through the war experience was that 'all who take the sword will perish by the sword'.

Do we hear the word of God in Article Nine? Does it express the mind of God who comes to us through the words of the Bible? Is it correct to say that Article Nine did not take the name of God in vain? Do we see God coming to us, the God who said 'I am the Lord your God, who brought you out of the land of Egypt, out of the house of bondage'?

I find the spirit of Article Nine and that of the God of Exodus congruent. That is to say, I do not find it particularly difficult to locate the spirit of the biblical God in the words of Article Nine. Article Nine is not simply an ideal. It is more than that. It is a realistic ideal. It is realistic because it is only in this way of Article Nine that humanity can survive and prosper upon this earth. The concept of 'realistic ideal' is theological since God is the unity of the real and the ideal. God who is responsible and concerned about history cannot but be 'real and ideal'. The biblical salvation is real and ideal at the same time. To respond to the call of such a God produces discipleship on our side. Christian discipleship is based on the real – the present – and the ideal – the future as these two are combined in the image of Jesus Christ. Article Nine demands the spirit of discipleship from us. It demands religious commitment of self-discipline from us. This observation can be made to the whole section of the preamble of the postwar constitution. 'We, the Japanese people, pledge our national honour to accomplish these high ideals and purposes with all our resources.' It is only through the mind of discipleship we can respond to such high determination. 'God' means to take risk for peace rather than to take risk for war. '. . . and the weakness of God is stronger than men' (I Cor.1.25).

A study of post war Japan shows that Japan did remain unarmed for five years, from 1945–50. In January 1950 General Douglas MacArthur himself affirmed and emphasized the Japanese right of self-defence. When the Korean War broke out in June he demanded that the Japanese government establish a National Police Reserve of 75,000 men. The National Police Reserve was renamed the Self-Defence Force in 1954 and came to number 140,000 by the late 1970s. Already in the early 1950s, then, Japan was being openly urged by the United States government to rearm herself. In spite of this sad erosion of the initial commitment to the high ideal, the fact that the Japanese people were truly shaken and committed in 1947 to Article Nine cannot be questioned. This moment must be looked upon as a new experience for this nation. It was an 'eschatological' moment which in spite of so many solemn expressions and words the Meiji Constitution failed to produce.

The new constitution has effectively changed the relationship between the emperor and the people. Article One of the constitution reads:

> The Emperor shall be the symbol of the State and of the unity of the people, deriving his position from the will of the people with whom resides sovereign power.

The new symbolic nature of the emperor's role is decisively different from the role he held under the 1889 constitution under which the emperor was a supreme entity and the people owed him unquestioning obedience. Fundamental to the nature of symbol is that it receives its meaning from outside itself. Therefore it is impossible for the emperor to grasp ultimate power to himself if his entity is defined as a symbol. There is now a shield between the emperor and the kind of idolatrous position he had under the 1889 constitution.

Significantly the emperor is defined not as a symbol of the cosmic totality and vitality, but as a symbol of 'the State and the unity of the people'. With these words Japanese perception of symbolism has made a delicate move from the cosmological to the historical. No symbol is purely historical as long as symbol requires some mental image which comes from our experience of the cosmos. But in Article One we notice a subtle and important shift from the cosmo-mythological to the historical. Through the use of the concept of symbolism in Article One, Japan has been awakened from the world of cosmological politics to the historical ethical practices for 'the unity of the people'. That when the highest position in the state is symbolic, we are protected from imperial idolatry must be understood with this significant shift from the cosmological to the historical in mind.

Sovereign power, according to Article One, resides with the people. It is not possessed by any one person. The people must use that power together, democratically. In order to insure the welfare of the people, the will of the people must be expressed and must effect the maintenance of government. The emperor's symbolic position derives from this sovereign power exercised by the people. The emperor is now a derived entity. This is the political and human meaning of the symbolic emperor.

Article One speaks words of emancipation. It releases the people of Japan from the fascist doctrine of the divine emperor. Indirectly and yet significantly, this Article One speaks the language congruent with the commandment; 'You shall not take the name of the Lord your God in vain'.

Article Ninety-Seven of the constitution states a principle of human rights that is new to Japan:

> The fundamental human rights by this Constitution guaranteed to the people of Japan are fruits of the age-old struggle of man to be free; they have survived the many exacting tests for durability and are conferred upon this and future generations in trust, to be held for all time inviolate.

In the 1889 constitution any rights the people had were derived from the centre where the emperor held absolute prerogatives. It was a completely paternalistic system. In the new constitution the foundation for human rights is derived not from the parochial tradition of Japan but from the far greater experiments and experience of human history.

The concept of the right of the individual person has been established through a long and painful history. Abolition of slavery, rights of suffrage and the right to dissent are positions that have been hard won and remain tenuous in certain places and situations today. The rights of women and of minorities continue to be at issue. What we are likely to forget is that one of the most subtle and dangerous threats to the rights of people arises from what might be called the 'tyranny of God' which arises when the name of God is taken 'in vain' by persons in power to strengthen their own position and build their own honour and glory.

The dignity of the human individual is expressed, as we have seen, in the motto of the Jesuit mission.

For what will it profit a man, if he gains the whole world and forfeits his life? Or what shall a man give in return for his life? (Matt. 16.26)

These words have a history of 'the age-long struggle of man to be free'. Article Ninety-Seven is positively participating in Matthew 16.26. If so, Article Ninety-Seven is congruent in spirit with the observance of the commandment; 'you shall not take the name of the Lord your God in vain'.

'The name of the Lord your God' does not come to any one or any group of people all of a sudden, as it were, 'out of the blue'. The reason for this is that the name of God is a historical concept. That is to say, 'the name of the Lord your God' means 'the history of the name of the Lord your God'. The name has past and future. It is constantly revealing itself to us in our histories, no matter how diversified they may be. The decisive revelation of the name has taken place. We come to that revelation in scripture. But the name of the living God cannot be confined among the people who produced scripture. The name of God is continuously making itself salvific and meaningful to us through historical events. It invites us to come to itself. It comes to us as it urges us to participate in the events of revelation of the meaning of the name today in the twentieth-century context. We learn to see the saving message of the name of God in the light of scripture as we live through history today. Thus the name of the Lord your God is a historical and participatory concept. It is therefore emancipating to hear this name.

Part III is a brief description of the coming of this name of God to Japan. When the name of God comes we all begin to say, each in our own language, the words of the blind man; 'I see men; but they look like trees, walking'. This confession expresses the hope of obtaining the clear vision in the future. Then as soon as we say this with the blind man, we find ourselves in an 'eschatological' tension. We are moving towards the clear vision of salvation! And this movement is again not a matter of speculation, but a concrete historical experience. We are to see the glory of the name of God in and through the events that take place in our history.

In Part IV we explore one of the outstanding meanings of the name of God, that is, the agitated mind of God. If the mind of God is agitated, it must be made so because of God's love towards the creation and humanity. God is agitated. Then history is agitated. When God is agitated, history cannot be tranquil. The tradition of Mount Sinai speaks about this agitated mind of God. The theme of Part IV is 'My mind is turning over in me. My emotions are agitated all together'. This agitated mind of God reaches its great intensity in the event of Jesus Christ. How then do I see the interactions between two traditions of Mount Fuji and Mount Sinai in the light of the event of Jesus Christ? What do they look like if placed in the perspective of the theology of the cross (*theologia crucis*)? In what way does the theology of the cross expose and condemn the idolatry that is destroying humanity? What is its message to both Mount Fuji and Mount Sinai traditions? It is in this perspective and with these questions in mind that we now move on to Part IV.

PART IV

My Mind is Turning Over Inside Me. My Emotions are Agitated All Together

(Hosea 11.8)

17
Limping Dance between God and Baal

No history as we know it is free from God *and* Baal.

The ancient Chinese, observing the sunlit and shadow sides of the mountain, saw in nature a symbol of the opposing realities that make up totality. Their perception of totality was cosmological. The ancient Japanese, observing the alternation of good and bad times, expressed a similar concern for totality in their philosophy of *kichi* and *kyo*. It was as though they saw a sunlit and shadow side of time. It is an attractive thought that, viewing history from some superhistorical position, we could see a totality which encompasses reality in a comprehensive whole, symbolizing salvation. In truth, however, history is a far more complex subject than the cosmological image can convey. It is, as it were, a 'problematic time' in which we have continually to struggle to know what is good or bad, which God is the true God and which God is not. The themes of the three preceding parts point fearlessly to such soul-searching complexity and ambiguity of history. 'All its cities were laid in ruins before his fierce anger.' How do we know that the cities were destroyed by 'his fierce anger'? Very likely they were simply ruined by the Babylonian or American armies! 'My help comes from the Lord, who made heaven and earth.' How can we draw a line between the help we receive from 'the Lord who made heaven and earth' and the help we receive from 'heaven and earth'? Why is this delicate distinction so important? Does this distinction intensify complexity of history or does it eliminate ambiguity of history? 'You shall not take the name of the Lord your God in vain'. If this commandment has universal validity to all peoples of all cultures and religions, then, what does it mean to the people who live in a pantheistic nature-oriented culture? What does this say to the people of Buddhist culture? What kind of light does it throw on this or on that particular culture in which people live? How does this commandment make itself significant in the polytheistic culture?

Or shall we hear these three biblical themes only as the world parochially addressed to the Jews or Christians, and decide that they have really nothing to do with the 'gentiles'? My view is that if we take this easy option, then, their original meaning in the given historical contexts would eventually be lost. They will remain fresh and meaningful as they keep speaking to the world outside their original home. This is, as it were, the destiny of these great words of the Bible. They have come to a particular people in a particular historical moment. Yet they address themselves to all peoples upon the earth. They are not parochial but universal words. The parochial words are less complex and ambiguous. They are correspondingly less creative and healing. The universal words are more complex and ambiguous. But they are more creative and healing.

The theme of this part is taken from the Book of Hosea; 'My mind is turning over inside me. My emotions are agitated all together' (Anchor Commentary translation). This is one of the most disturbing pieces of information on the 'psychology of God'. In the language of the Book of Exodus this God is called 'an impassioned God' as we have seen (20.5). This is the God of *pathos* in the words of Abraham Heschel. The God, however, whose 'emotions are agitated all together' is not an ideal God for the people of the *nirvana* oriented culture. Such a God, I was once told by a Thai Buddhist monk, must discipline himself in the Buddhist monastery! Agitation of mind is an anti-nirvanic value. It must be overcome. What is the religious and cultural value of an agitated mind? What is this agitated mind? From where does it come? Why should we be agitated if we see sunlit and shadow side in one mountain? Does this imply that the God of the Bible cannot see this plain cosmological truth? Is this why God is agitated? Is the God of the Bible unable to see the totality of heaven and earth? Is this why God is agitated?

The complexity and ambiguity of history is far more intense and profound than the cosmological image of sunlit and shadow mountain can solve. History again does not run according to the attractive alternation of *kichi* and *kyo*. Our theories of history break down before the reality of history. The famous choice of Deuteronomy expresses the awesome mystery of history concisely and powerfully:

I have set before you life and death, blessing and curse; therefore choose life, that you and your descendants may live (Deut. 30.19).

What is said here is simple straightforward advice to all humanity that it should choose life and blessing, not death and curse. But then, why is it so hard for us to choose life and blessing over death and curse? Why do we do something we do not want to do (Rom. 7.15–21)? Why cannot we settle down with the idea that life and blessing represent the sunlit side of the mountain and death and curse, the shadow side? If we do not do what we want to do, and if cosmological totality does not help us, where shall we go? But ...to begin with why has God not set only life and blessing before us?

Why has God set before us life and death, blessing and curse? Was this not the question that tormented the sixteenth-century Japanese people when they heard the gospel of Francis Xavier? Why must we choose between life and death? Is it possible that what the English word 'God' means is 'therefore choose life'?

Why do we find ourselves in the situation as described by these words of Deuteronomy and why do we hear 'therefore choose life' and try to do so in this confusing history... This is a mystery beyond our understanding, yet is is this mystery that makes history as we know it. History as we know it always has life and death, blessing and curse. If either life or death could be destroyed, history would disappear. This means that in history as we experience it, we are always confronted with the question of 'choosing'. The promise of Revelation, then, does not speak of history.

> Behold, the dwelling of God is with man. He will dwell with them, and they shall be his people, and God himself will be with them, he will wipe away every tear from their eyes, and death shall be no more, neither shall there be mourning nor crying nor pain any more, for the former things have passed away (Rev. 21.3,4).

In the history that we know tears, death, mourning and pain are always present. When these things disappear and 'the former things have passed away' history has disappeared too. These words of Revelation speak about the marvellous work of God (*maya* in the Hindu terminology) but they do not speak about history as we know it. To believe in the midst of all the confusing pains of the world that the reign of God is among us is the biblical awareness of history. 'The kingdom of God is in the midst of you' (Luke 17.21). It is this difficult theme to which we turn our attention now. The kingdom of God is the kingdom of God whose 'emotions are agitated all together'.

The prophet Elijah, a man of Gilead in the ninth century BC northern kingdom of Israel, confronts the people of Israel and the prophets of Baal.

> How long will you go limping with two different opionions? If the Lord is God, follow him; but if Baal, then follow him (I Kings 18.21).

The occasion for the story is a severe drought. A Chinese emperor might have lost his heavenly mandate over such a circumstance. Ahab, culturally sophisticated and broadminded, will seek whatever assistance he can to end the drought. The rain may come from the Lord, or it may come for Baal. He is prepared to pursue both possibilities. Elijah rejects this attitude out of hand. Therefore Elijah is a problem to Ahab, who calls him a 'troubler of Israel'. Elijah's talk of a 'limping dance' between Baal and the Lord opens a theological debate which is potentially explosive. The prophet has disturbed the spiritual and cultural peace of the people. The word 'troubler' used here, in its Arabic linguistic background, denotes the pollution of water by mud. The King is suggesting that Elijah has polluted the water of public tranquillity by stirring up the mud.

In the eyes of the uncompromising Elijah it is the God of Israel, Yahweh, who gives rain. The people know this God to be very much involved in their history, but now Elijah is extending his role by insisting that he also takes care of the rain. Baal (literally, lord or owner) is the fertility god of Canaan. He, particularly, has been regarded as the giver of rain and of growth to vegetation. Baal sends rain (semen) to the earth and insures the harvest. He also supervises the procreation of animals. Related to the cult is the practice of sacred prostitution (I Kings 15.12 and Deut. 23.18). The prostitutes live at the temple. Through 'sympathetic magic' fertility rites between priests and the prostitutes Baal is believed to influence the cosmic fertility between heaven and earth. As long as the people believe in this sympathetic magic the fertility cult prospers.

Elijah sees that the Baal is not another god who takes care of particular functions, but he also sees that Baal can in no way be confused with the Yahweh that Israel worships. Yahweh, the Lord, God of Israel, gives the people the grain, the wine and the oil and refuses to be worshipped as a fertility god.

> Since the Baal cult was synchronized with the cyclical events of nature, which had great significance for the agricultural population of Canaan, its fertility rites (sacral prostitution) appeared obscene to the worshippers of Yahweh and their myths deifications of nature. ... The Canaanites could explain the change from one season to another and differences between good and bad years only by believing that sometimes Baal was weak, sick, or even dead. This was a basic assumption of their religion. But such ideas were foreign to monotheistic Yahwism.[1]

According to the fertility cult the whole cosmos is viewed as a manifestation of vitality. The deities of procreative pairs are, par excellence, expressions of this vitality. In the Hindu University of Benares in India the symbols of *lingam* (male organ) and *yoni* (female organ) are placed in the most sacred area of the Shiva Temple. Water from the Ganges drops on them from a brass container hung above them. Devotees come to venerate these symbols of procreative forces working between the male and female principles. In the Japanese *Kojiki* the procreation by Izanagi and Izanami is expressly related:

> Then let us, you and me, walk in a circle around this heavenly pillar and meet and have conjugal intercourse.[2]

Yasuda Naomichi, the Japanese scholar in folk culture, collected fifteen examples in Japan to show that the *Kojiki* line is originally a part of agricultural rite which was practised until only several decades ago. As a part of an the agricultural rite, husband and wife, both naked in privacy crawl on hands and knees around the family fire-place. As they do this the husband first says the auspicious words of fertility and the wife responds by saying that abundant harvest is coming.[3]

The God of Israel refuses to be identified with such ritual of crawling on hands and knees around the family fire-place. God is not a manifestation of cosmic vitality. This God creates rather than procreates. God creates sexuality but does not engage in the sexual act. God's relation to the activity of nature is ·one of transcendence. The biblical insight is that the fertility god is an idol while the creator is the true God. Increase of productivity is to have no absolute place in human community. It must remain under the judgment of the true God. Elijah insists that this God who is concerned about the life (history) of the people is also the creator and is ruler over all things in nature. There is no need to have a 'specialist' god for the forest, the sea or the field. One God, the creator of all things, takes care of all concerns. In its form Elijah's monotheistic theology is much simpler than polytheistic nature religion which involves many gods.

Elijah rejects Baal. Yet Baal persists in human history. One way to look at history is to see it as the story of confrontation between Yahweh and Baal. The experience of fertility is primordial, enveloped in the sense of the mystery and joy of increase. Nature is the manifestation of the power of the cosmos to rejuvenate itself. Images and thoughts of god arising out of the experience of nature are understandable. Hosea's description of the confusion arising around the provisions of nature is as applicable today as it was in the eighth century BC.

> And she did not know it was I who gave her the grain, the wine, and the oil, and who lavished upon her silver and gold which they used for Baal (Hos. 2.8).

In history we will always have Yahweh and Baal. We are engaged in a ritual of limping dance between the two. Elijah confronts us and tells us that we must stop this dancing! Yet, we continue. History as we know it always contains this possibility and reality of idolatry. Complete elimination of idolatry then comes only when history as we know it comes to an end.

Fascination with the power of vitality needs guidance and orientation. The fertility cult must be described and criticized so that it does not become demonic and destroy humanity. History and nature must be viewed under one sovereign God, creator of both and in whose name is hidden the truth about history and nature as one reality. To describe and make critical comments on this reality is the task of theology. 'And she did not know that it was I.....' From one perspective the Baal cult may seem relatively harmless. There can be great joy in the worship of nature. The problem is that Baal's rain does not just stay within the realm of nature. It eventually challenges Yahweh's sovereignty over other situations as well. It will encroach upon history, influencing our view of history and politics. The politics of Baal is directed towards the idea of 'increase'; economic, political, psycholgical, cultural and religious self-centred gain. The increase of self is the most fascinating of all human experience. 'My' increase makes me feel more secure, more righteous, more authentic, more religious, more divine. Thus the words of Deuteronomy come as a criticism of the Baal spirituality of increase:

> Beware lest you say in your heart, 'My power and the might of my hand have gotten me this wealth, you shall remember the Lord your God for it is he who gives you power to get wealth; that he may confirm his covenant which he swore to your fathers, as at this day' (Deut. 8.17,18).

The theology of the covenant, central to the very existence of the people of Israel, pronounces the danger of 'My power and the might of my hand'. This is the description of the Baal spirituality. Jeremiah describes the terrifying reality of destruction which eventually came to be associated with the fertility god, Baal:

> ...and have built the high places of Baal to burn their sons in the fire as burnt offerings of Baal, which I did not command or decree, nor did it come into my mind (Jer. 19.5).

This passage from the later prophet indicates that human sacrifices were made on the altar to Baal, as they had been made to Molok (Lev. 20.2–5; II Kings 23.10; Jer. 32.35). Baal was no longer just a rain god. He was a demonic idol that could be used to fan religious fanaticism to the extent of promoting human sacrifice. Religious fanaticism of this nature can be translated, in a moment, to political fanaticism. 'My power....', the increase of self, is behind it.

That there is a connection between the Baal fertility cult and the Molok imperial cult, was well demonstrated by Japan in this century. The mythological name for Japan used in *Kojiki, Toyoashihara no chiakino nakaihoakino mizuhonokuni* or Rich Reed Plain of Eternity with Rice Harvest, is a vivid agricultural name. This agricultural mythology was expressed politically in the *Kojiki*. The fertility cult and the imperial cult share the increase orientation. The *Kojiki* may be seen as planting the seed of increase which fed the power hunger of the imperial cult.

The God of the Bible does not condemn increase as such. Increase becomes idolatrous when it is achieved by the suppression or oppression of parts of the community. In its extreme form it demands human sacrifice. All versions of the imperial cult demand some kind of human sacrifice. It is not always necessary to have the person of an emperor for an imperial cult to develop. The obsession of the nations today with military armaments is a clear example of the relation between fertility and idolatry. The phallic shapes of the bombs and missiles are reminders of this development. Our dedication to armament and the excitment of war have long ago reached the point of irrationality. The words that described the prophets of Baal in the context of Mount Carmel can be applied to our own frenzy with armament.

... [they] called on the name of Baal from morning until noon, saying 'O Baal, answer us!' ...And they limped about the altar which they had made. ...And they cried aloud, and cut themselves after their custom with swords and lances, until the blood gushed out upon them (I Kings 18.26–28).

These ancient words must be read together with the following words of George F. Kennan:

Look at the record. Over all these years the competition in the development of nuclear weaponry has proceeded steadily, relentlessly, without the faintest regard for all these warning voices. We have gone on piling weapon upon weapon, missile upon missile, new levels of destructiveness upon old ones. We have done this helplessly, almost involuntarily: like the victims of some sort of hypnotism, like men in a dream, like lemmings heading for the sea, like the children of Hamlin marching blindly along behind their Pied Piper. And the result is that today we have achieved, we and the Russians together, in the creation of these devices and their means of delivery, levels of redundancy of such grotesque dimensions as to defy rational understanding.[4]

The doctrine of national glory made the Japanese people irrational, blind and fanatical. Are the leaders of the nations becoming, again, irrational and fanatical? Yet, though Baal's doctrine of glory commands a great following, Yahweh has not disappeared from history. Hitler's Molok doctrine of glory kept the Third Reich going for only twelve years in comparison to his own 'conservative estimate' of one thousand years. Japan's glory lasted only fifty years. We are fascinated by the glory of Baal but at the same time we are inspired by Yahweh. This does not mean that the inspiration of Yahweh comes to everyone. That Yahweh has not disappeared from history is a confession of faith rather than an objective observation of history. Indeed the demonic grip of Hitler continued for only twelve years. But oppression by one sector of humanity over another has continued from the beginning of civilization to our own day. There is something within us which tells us that any system which demands human sacrifice must be rejected.

We live between Yahweh and Baal. Indecisively we limp between Yahweh and Baal.

The limping between Yahweh and Baal is a kind of picture of the movement of history as I have come to see it. Deep in our souls we have this indecision. For some deep reason, hidden in the mystery of the human spirit, we cannot stop limping between Yahweh and Baal. 'I have set before you life and death, blessing and curse; therefore choose life'. ...we limp. Before the words of the Gospel of Mark, 'I have come not to call the righteous, but sinners'. ...we limp. We feel spiritual hesitation and confusion. In spite of Elijah's challenge, strangely our dignity – our being human – expresses itself in the tragic necessity to engage in a limping dance before Yahweh and Baal. Do we all have 'some Yahweh' and 'some Baal' within us?

We cannot come to know Yahweh without knowing Baal. The knowledge of God comes to us through what happens in situations represented dramatically on Mount Carmel. The possibilities of idol worship and the worship of the true God are mysteriously related within human souls. To come to Yahweh we must observe within ourselves and around us those who 'cry aloud and cut themselves after their custom with swords and lances'. While the history we know continues there will be idolatry. Elijah and the prophets of Baal are always with us. How, then, do we understand the kingdom of God? Is the kingdom of God realized when all the prophets of Baal are eliminated?

> And when all the people saw it, they fell on their faces; and they said, 'The Lord , he is God; the Lord, he is God'. And Elijah said to them, 'Seize the prophets of Baal; let not one of them escape'. And they seized them; and Elijah brought them down to the brook Kishon, and killed them there (I Kings 18.39,40).

Elijah seemed to think that the elimination of the prophets of Baal is what he was called to bring about. My feeling is that this was 'overkill'. I am reminded, when he says, 'Let not one of them escape', of the fire-bombing of Tokyo on the night of 10 March 1945. To my twentieth-century mind what Elijah did is repugnant to both reason and morality if I use the expression of Gandhi. His overkill is not a good political model for human civilization, though unfortunately it has become such a model. The 'holy war' employs Elijah's destructive surgical approach. The nation which thinks of itself as chosen of God may be tempted to such a solution. The Ten Commandments says 'You shall not kill' (Ex. 20.13). In a later development we see Jesus speaking with Moses and Elijah on the mountain of transfiguration. The subject of this conversation is, however, not the purification of history by the destruction of the prophets of Baal, but rather

Jesus's own 'departure' (death) to heal history (Luke 9.31). Has the model of the jealous Elijah played a more dominant influence upon us than that of Jesus of whom it is said, 'he saved others, he cannot save himself' (Mark 15.31)? When we pray the Lord's Prayer,

> Our Father who art in heaven,
> Hallowed be thy name
> Thy kingdom come ....

are we praying for the coming of the kingdom by purifying our history from the prophets of Baal by destroying them with our own hands?

After the slaying of the prophets of Baal a curious story emerges. Jezebel, the wife of king Ahab, confronts Elijah vowing to kill him. The great prophet, we read, 'was afraid, and he arose and went for his life' (I Kings 19.3). After an extended drama in which Yahweh and Elijah are the only participants, the word of Yahweh comes to Elijah out of a profound stillness.

> Yet I will leave seven thousand in Israel, all the knees that have not bowed to Baal, and every mouth that has not kissed him (I Kings 19.18).

This must have been a shocking anticlimax for Elijah who had been very jealous for the Lord. Is it possible that Elijah misappropriated the 'jealousy' (impassionedness) of God, becoming himself 'very impassioned for the Lord' (I Kings 19.10–14)? Unfaithful, wayward people make God jealous. But our jealousy *for* the Lord, particularly if we are *very* jealous for the Lord, may be of another kind. The Buddha would undoubtedly have suspected that Elijah's jealousy was more of the nature of *tanha*, a hidden greed for conquering others, rather than *karuna*, mercy and concern for others. The very jealous Elijah became confrontational.

The impassioned God is broken-hearted when faced by the faithless people. This divine broken-heartedness is different from our everyday language about broken-hearted persons. It does not mean a dejected, hopeless and tearful situation. It is a divine reaction to the faithlessness of the people. It is a picturesque way to describe the pain of God. Divine broken-heartedness is not simply confrontational. The concept of confrontation is a linear notion. The divine compassion which seeks the healing of the broken convenant over and over again has a strangely circular emotion and image. In contrast, how many 'overkills' have been motivated in the history of humankind by confrontational theology! Are we not more linear and confrontational than the Lord the 'Judge of all the earth' (Gen.18.25)?

It is customary to associate a linear interpretation of history with purposefulness while the circular concept of history suggests blindness. The linear symbol has also been appropriated by psychology to represent confrontation and self-assertion. The study of Buddhism has made me aware of a subtle inner connection between purposefulness and greediness. I am not saying that purposefulness always means greediness, but I am suggesting that purposefulness can be an expression of our greediness. Is not there a subtle linkage between purposefulness and imperialism? Just briefly, we can cite the Crusades, the White Man's Burden of the British and the doctrine of Manifest Destiny of the United States.

In contrast, the Ark of Noah, in which the purpose of history was symbolically placed, had no rudder. The fire on the mountain prevents us from ascending to the top of Mount Sinai to 'view history'. 'You cannot see my face; for man shall not see me and live' (Ex. 33.20). The hands of Elijah that destroyed the prophets of Baal, and the mouth of Elijah which said, 'how long will you go limping with two different opinions' indeed reveal the depth of our history as we live in it, yet perhaps in the quiet voice which gave instructions to Elijah we hear an even more penetrating comment about history. It is an image of history that is seen in the coming of the broken-hearted God.

> They departed from me. They sacrificed to Baals. ...
> They did not acknowledge that I had healed them, ...
> My people are bent on turning from me. ...
> How can I give you up, Ephraim? How can I relinquish
> you, Israel? ...My mind is turning over inside me.
> My emotions are agitated all together (Hos. 11.2,3,7,8).

These words of Hosea come closer to the heart of the Christian hope, I believe, than the words from Revelation promising that there shall be no more death. This inner battle of God, this profound divine agitation, this depth of God's passion towards us and our history is the dynamic of the reign of God. Christian theology in general has not seen human history under the light of God whose mind is 'turning over inside'. There is here a sense of divine helplessness which heightens the passion of God's broken-heartedness. God feels 'broken' not by defeat but by the unfaithfulness of the people and because of the intense love God has for the people.

Elijah demands of the people that they make a specific decision. It is this decision which stands at the centre of Elijah's faith. The world is divided into two groups; the followers of Yahweh and the followers of Baal. This is a fundamental image for the reign of God in history. But this image must be subordinated to the profound passion of God, 'my mind is turning over inside me. My emotions are agitated all together'. In the light of this profound agitation the demand for decision must be made. Unless this is so we will tend to 'overkill', a zeal which is not congruent to the mind of God who rules history.

At the depth of history there is the 'agitated mind of God' which judges all forms of idolatries. The one who judges history is the one who is most involved in history. This God whose emotions are agitated all together is salvation to us who engage in dancing between God and Baal in this historical hour.

18

Why Do All Who are Treacherous Thrive?

Cool Karman and the agitated mind of God.
Invitation to experience history as God experiences it.

The Sanskrit word *karman* means 'deeds'. It refers to human actions, whether by movement of the body, by word of mouth or by thought conceived and expressed in will. Human deeds are believed to generate an invisible force which creates a reaction or retribution. This fundamental insight, pervasive in Indian thought and religion, has become a part of Japanese religious outlook of life through Buddhism.

The *karman* works impersonally, precisely and objectively. Paul's words, 'whatever a man sows, that he will also reap' (Gal. 6.7) have a sound of the doctrine of *karman*. Buddhist scholar in Bangkok, Wasin Indasara writes of *karman*.

> There is no reason why everyone should put the blame on the Law, which is natural, neutral and infallible in its function of meting out justice impersonally to everybody. ... Patience and the resultant courage are other benefits to be derived from belief in the Law of Karma. ... Such is an effect coming from causes, he reminds himself, and to suffer such an experience is but a payment of an outstanding debt, lessening the amount of debt he owed somebody or something in the past. It is like unloading a shop of its waste or unwanted products. This is lightening the ship of his life, making it reach the shore of security sooner. In another sense, what evil should there be in the settlement of a bill or an overdrawn account of our own? It is the settlement we have to do anyway.[1]

In its complicated and sophisticated development, the *karman* thought seeks to interpret complex and confusing human situations through addition and substraction of the karmic force in an individual's life. The good karman can neutralize the evil karman.

This may be comparable to a poisonous acid with killing effects on life. If it is steadily neutralised by adding to it more and more alkali, it will be diluted and finally neutralised, with its killing effect lost. This is a comparison to show how the poisonous effect can be diluted and then dissolved or neutralised.[2]

This accounting of the karman extends beyond the span of the individual's life to his or her previous existences as well as into future existences. The standard understanding among the people of Thailand to account for the present happiness and glory of their king is that the king must have accumulated a vast amoung of merit in his previous existences. That something done in previous lives may cause fortune or misfortune in this present life opens up an ever extending horizon on life. The *Jataka*, an impressive collection of stories of the past lives of the Buddha in which he was progressing towards Buddhahood, is well known by the Buddhist people at large and has become the foundation for popular piety.[3]

'The Story of the King of the Sibis' in the *Jataka* begins with these words:

> The Buddha was once a king of the Sibis in one of his pre-existences. The king was noble-hearted, full of compassion and wealthy. Sakra, the Lord of the Devas, assumed the shape of an old, blind Brahman and came to the king. ...'A blind, old man, I have come hither from afar begging thy eye, O highest of kings. For the purpose of ruling the world's regular course one eye may be sufficient, O lotus-eyed monarch'.

The story goes on to tell that the king of Sibis gave both his eyes to the old Brahman.

> Then the king ordered one eye of his, the lovely brightness of which appeared like a petal of a blue lotus, to be extirpated after the precepts of the physicians gradually and intact, and with the greatest gladness he had it handed over to the beggar, who asked it. ...When the king beheld the eye-asker in the possession of one unclosed eye, his heart expanded with the utmost delight, and he presented him with the other eye too. The eyes being given away, the king's visage looked like a lotus-pond without lotuses, yet it bore the expression of satisfaction, not shared however by the citizens.[4]

What a selfless king! In this and many similar stories the *Jataka* tells of how the Buddha in his previous existences accumulated, through acts of self-sacrifice, the good karman which made it possible for him to attain Buddhahood. Personal *karman*, and not social conscience, is the subject of these stories. The king exhibits profound compassion but not a reforming zeal directed toward social welfare of the people. He does not ask how this old man became a beggar or became blind. What was it that reduced him to such a sorry state of health? In that sense the *Jataka* is one dimensional and does not have concrete social and ethical implications for life in an ambiguous world. Yet it describes emotional contents of the karman doctrine.

The karman conception of life is that good can be accumulated and death does not wipe away the count but preserves it from life to life. Conversely, evil deeds have a negative count which will be substracted from the positive accumulated as I have indicated. There is an implacable mathematics involved which has strong personal and moral implications. The distinction, however, between good and bad is not a fundamental concept for karman. The thought of the objective meting out of the consequence of all our actions is central to it. That 'those whose conduct here has been good will quickly attain a good birth' does not address itself to the theme of morality, but to the objective functioning of the karman.[5] Can the shape and meaning of human life be formed in this kind of mathematics? Does this kind of figuring contribute to a concept of history? One night the northern capital of Thailand, Chiengmai, had a great fire in its main market. The force of the fire was beyond the control of the city fire department. At about midnight the direction of the wind changed suddenly saving a certain section of the city. The change of the wind came, people said, because the people who lived in that particular section obviously had more good karman than the people whose properties were destroyed by fire. What does this say to our experience of history?

If we apply the doctrine of karman to the nuclear bombing of Hiroshima we would say that Hiroshima was bombed rather than the city of Kokura which was targetted that morning because there was more bad karman in Hiroshima than in Kokura. According to the United States Air Command, the attack on Kokura was cancelled because of the overcast meteorological situation. Karman would then see that the good accumulation of karman of the citizens of Kokura brought them the protection of the clouds. Karman is a comprehensive view which takes in all accidents and contingencies. Oddly, this is simultaneously a full explanation and no explanation. That the direction of the wind changed at midnight in the Chiengmai fire by the good and bad karman of the people there is also both a full explanation and no explanation, but it is a comforting thought to those who were spared.

Jeremiah asked the painful question that arises in the observation of human community: 'Why do all who are treacherous thrive?' (12.1). From the viewpoint of the karman this is both a difficult and easy question to answer. It is difficult because the treacherous person should receive the fruit of his or her own treacherousness. To be thriving then contradicts the basic principle of karman. How then is the confusing accumulation of karman in that person's past working itself out? No investigation into past lives can be comprehensive and objective. It is simply beyond human ability to do so.

How could any one estimate all the accumulation and substractions of any person's karman? There the karman doctrine would say simply that it is due to the work of the karman which is beyond our understanding that the person who is treacherous is thriving. Perhaps the person has more good karman than bad karman at this point. The karman doctrine then destroys the sense of ethical urgency and responsibility in human community. It has consistently inspired people towards fatalism.

In contrast to the *Jataka* Buddhism, we have a more critical Buddhism which provides with us these words of the Buddha:

> Through many diverse births I passed
> Seeking in vain the builder of the house,
> But O framer of houses, thou art found –
> Never again shall thou fashion a house for me!
> Broken are all thy beams,
> The kingpost shattered!
> My mind has passed into the stillness of Nibbana
> The ending of desire has been attained at last![6]

The 'house' in the quotation refers to individual existence and the 'builder' of the house is 'greed' (*tanha*). Through many existences the Buddha struggled against the power of greed which ensnared him. Finally he overcame it. 'Never again shall thou fashion a house for me!' His 'mind has passed into the stillness of Nibbana (*nirvana*)', the stillness of the 'ending of greed', The kingpost of greed has been shattered! To propagate the message that the kingpost of greed can be shattered, the Buddhist mission was begun.

> Fare ye forth, brethren, on the mission that is for the good of the many, for the happiness of the many, to take compassion on the world, to work profit and good and happiness to gods and men. Go not singly; go in pairs; teach ye, brethren, the Truth, lovely in its origin, lovely in its progress, lovely in its consummation, both in the spirit and in the letter, proclaim ye the higher life in all its fullness and in all its purity. Beings there are whose eyes are hardly dimmed with dust, perishing because they hear not the Truth.[7]

This lovely truth is the shattering of the kingpost of greed. All other Buddhist doctrines and practices must derive from this shattering. This shattering occurred in the historical person, Gotama Siddhartha. And this historical example demonstrates to us that when our greed is destroyed we will be free from suffering. At this point, Buddhism must be understood to be a 'historical' faith. Fantastic speculation we encountered in the Jataka has meaning only so far as it points to this 'shattering of the kingpost of greed', which is 'historical'.

What does this shattering of the kingpost of greed, or 'no more house built' mean to the doctrine of karman? Professor Ui Hakuju, the great Japanese Buddhist scholar, says that in the earliest tradition we can discern the image of the Buddha who has transcended all the workings of karman. this appeared in the understanding that he of his own free accord, not by the karman, went into nirvana (died) after accomplishing all his preaching.[8]

Thought of the karman is not absent from the teachings of Conditional Arising and Four Noble Truths. It is, however, not at all prominent. These two primary expressions of the Buddhist position express a stronger truth than that of karman. I am tempted to say that in the gospel of the Buddha the karman is seen in the light of the shattering of the kingpost of greed rather than the other way round. In this critical moment existential religious experience takes the lead over the metaphysical deterministic karman outlook of life. If we look at the karman thought in the light of the shattering of the kingpost of greed, we would see a new meaning of the karman doctrine. Then we are subjecting the impersonal objective workings of the karman to the ethical responsibility in our human community here and now. That we are ethically responsible becomes the first concern in our life. Karman under the influence of ethics cannot maintain impersonality and the precision of objectivity. If the question of Jeremiah. 'Why do all who are treacherous thrive?' were put to the Buddha, he would no doubt utter the words of judgment upon such people; 'Treacherous people's kingpost of greed must be shattered'! The call to them would be immediate and clear; 'Destroy your greed'!

Sometimes Paul sounds much like he is speaking of the doctrine of karman.

> There will be tribulation and distress for every human being who does evil, the Jew first and also the Greek, but glory and honour and peace for every one who does good, and the Jew first and also the Greek. For God shows no partiality (Rom. 2.9–11).

Japan experienced 'tribulation and distress' in 1945 because she did evil. This may be a simple application of what is said here. But, as I have indicated in the earlier chapters of this book, the situation was not that simple. The view that Japanese people were victims of the Japanese military clique cannot be ignored. We cannot simply say that Japan suffered 'tribulation and distress' because she did evil. It is rather Japan suffered because a small band of mad people hijacked the nation in blind and irrational arrogance. In the post war years those who destroyed the nation fared well, and people suffered!

In the situation of the African people under the rule of the destructive apartheid race policy of South Africa, we cannot say that they are suffering because they did evil. The regime is doing evil against them. Black people's 'tribulation and distress' does not come from their own evil-doing. The oppressive rulers in the land are free from 'tribulation and distress', at least they are not subjected to the kind of suffering that the black population is undergoing. By oppressing others the oppressors are dehumanized. But this type of dehumanization is understood to be 'blessed life' that comes from God by the oppressors since they do not see it, in fact, as dehumanization.

I find what is said here by Paul can be potentially dangerous if we make direct application to the ambiguous, conflicting situations of human history. This passage may be used to justify what Hitler did to the Jewish people during the war. The Jewish people suffered 'tribulation and distress' (of final degree) in Auschwitz because they did evil! Such superficial application of Paul would be extremely harmful. History is tragically full of suffering of the innocents. It is hard to say 'God shows no partiality' on the basis of our observation of historical human situations.

Yet, the biblical faith holds that 'God is not partial and takes no bribe' (Deut. 10.17). And Paul says; 'Do not be deceived; God is not mocked, for whatever a man sows, that he will also reap' (Gal. 6.7). In the East, it is said that 'karman shows no partiality', and in the biblical tradition 'God shows no partiality'. When we profess our faith in saying 'God shows no partiality' we are not solving the problem of terrible ambiguity in our human history. Indeed, the position to say that 'karman shows no partiality' is less troublesome than this biblical viewpoint. The depth of Jeremiah's pain has to do with God's own integrity.

Righteous art thou, O Lord, when I complain to thee; yet I would plead my case before thee. Why does the way of the wicked prosper? Why do all who are treacherous thrive? (Jer.12.1)

Jeremiah does not speak about karman in the Hindu style. His thought world is different from that of the Hindu world. In this pleading the prophet is questioning the integrity and justice of God. He is in a theological battle. He is plainly faced by the reality of the injustice in this world which is ruled by God. That Jeremiah's complaints are directed to God and not to karman, or variation of the karman principle, touches deeply the mystery of evil in human history and personal life. As long as the history as we know it continues, This question of Jeremiah will not disappear.

The important difference, however, is that Jeremiah can plead his case before God, but it would be nonsensical to do so before the karman. Karman remains to be karman by not being influenced by any human pleading. On the contrary God can change his mind. There is a remarkable intimation of this following the idolatrous incident of the golden calf of Aaron. God's anger against the people was averted by the pleading of Moses.

But Moses besought the Lord his God, and said, 'O Lord, why does thy wrath burn hot against thy poeple, whom thou hast brought forth out of the land of Egypt with great power and with a mighty hand? .... Turn from they fierce wrath, and repent of this evil against thy people. Remember Abraham, Isaac, and Israel, thy servants, to whom thou didst swear by thine own self, and didst say to them, "I will multiply your descendants as the stars of heaven, and all this land that I have promised I will give to your descendants, and they shall inherit if for ever."' And the Lord repented of the evil which he thought to do to his people (Ex. 32.11–14).

God is impartial. But God is not under impartiality. Impartiality is not God. God is not a principle. God listens to our interpretation of history as we try to understand the words of God spoken to our history. God's impartiality is not mechanical. It is not a separate concept from the relationship between God and people. It is an impartiality within this living relationship. According to Buddha pleading to God (or gods) is of no use whatsoever. It is harmful delusion. If we have time to complain to the supernatural being, then we should use that time and energy to destroy our own greed! The issue is not 'theological'. It is to do with 'the complete cessation of the thirst, with the abandoning of the thirst, with the doing away with it'. With the biblical God impartiality is not an impersonal and objective concept. With the Buddha that the karman is impartial is subjected to the far more crucial event, i.e., the destruction of greed. Do you live in relationship with God? This is the decisive question according to the Bible. Do you try to eliminate your greed? This is the decisive question according to the Buddha. Impartiality is judged respectively under these lights.

Jeremiah's query represents the complaint of the Korean people against Japan. Of the relationship between Korea (and China) and Japan Irokawa Daikichi writes:

That Japan has never been conquered by the strong nations of the Continent cannot be ascribed to the geographical accidents or the bravery of the Japanese warrior class. It is largely due to the grace of the climactic environment of the monsoon Asia which has nurtured patient and peaceful people and created also a peaceful international environment. In particular, the Chinese and the Koreans have been a huge bulwark that for more than a millennium protected Japan from the attacks of the warlike nomadics. Japan has never been invaded by those exceptionally peace loving neighbours. ... The Japanese, though they have been benefited for so long by the friendly attitude of the neighbouring countries, came out with sword in hand to repay their friendship. It was an act of betrayal to the teaching of Mercy by the

Buddha and Reciprocal Friendship by Confucius which have supposedly influenced Japanese spirit deeply. The one hundred years since the Meiji period is particularly a history of Japanese aggression and atrocity against her Asian neighbours. Among the leaders of the nation today we cannot notice a reflection upon this history of evil.[9]

The cultural history of Japan indicates her substantial indebtedness of China and Korea. Through the help of these two friendly countries ancient Japan achieved the transition from primitive gathering to an agricultural society. From Korea, for instance, Japan learned the flooded paddy field technique for the cultivation of rice in the third and second centuries BC. In 1910 Japan annexed Korea and for thirty-six years Korea was brutally exploited while Japan prospered. In those short thirty-six years the suffering inflicted upon the Korean people by the hand of the Japanese far exceeded the human scheme of oppression. People were murdered. Enormous evil was done. 'Why does the way of the wicked prosper?' Why does not the karman catch up the wicked? Why does God allow the wicked to prosper? Why is greed having prosperous days?

Then came 1945. The events of this fateful year can be interpreted in three ways; first, it was the work of karman. At last Japan's karman caught up with her. 'Karman shows no partiality.' And it worked. Secondly, it can be interpreted in the manner of Jeremiah: 'All its cities were laid in ruins before the Lord, before his fierce anger' (4.26). The God, the Lord of history, judged Japan. And thirdly, Japan was destroyed because she had not destroyed the kingpost of their greed. Her greed ruined her. I find all these three views acceptable. I do have reservations about the working of karman but in a general sense, that judgment will eventually come to the doers of evil seems to be true, even though in the 'meantime' great harm can be done. I accept the view of Jeremiah that it is not blind fate or military accidents that destroyed Japan but some serious 'theological' dimension, even though I cannot quite describe it. Most directly and with least trouble in terms of my understanding, I can accept the Buddha's view, which is that it is greed that destroyed Japan. Although in closer reflection, why greed brings forth destruction is not self-evident. These three interpretations are not unrelated in my mind. I see the first and the third in the light of the second. And that gives me richer meaning to the second and at the same time to the first and the third.

Jeremiah pleaded the case before God. He lived in this personal relationship with God. God does not stand for the mechanical objective functioning of justice. God creates justice. The prophet Isaiah speaks thus:

I, I am He who blots out your transgressions for my own sake, and I will not remember your sins (Isa.43.25).

For my name's sake I defer my anger, for the sake of my praise I restrain it for you, that I may not cut you off (Isa. 48.9).

God who is involved in history not as a principle but as a Person, makes a free and responsible decision for his own sake. This free decision of God may not be identical with our ethical decision.

It is this primary decision of God, however, that gives life and meaning to human ethical decision. This is the living message of the biblical tradition to which we must listen today. These biblical passages of Isaiah are not to be treated as unrelated to our domestic and international politics. The ethical meaning of God's primary decision must be brought into thinking about our 'real' political situations to give us a much needed perspective in which we can judge ourselves and all our doings. It can illuminate, in a profound way, our understanding of ourselves and the world (John.1.9). It could then have a critical effect on our conduct in the areas of politics, economics and government. I do not mean to say that any given nation in history would realize and practise the politics of God's primary decision. I am simply pointing out the possibility of a deeply spiritual and practical leadership given to humanity by such a person as Martin Luther King Jr. His movement of civil rights was theologically informed. He was inspired by the primary decision of the impassioned God. It is the intention of this God that the human world will not be left without witness to the mind of God which is expressed in the words; 'I, I am He who blots out your transgressions for my own sake,...'. Without such a primary decision of God, which theology calls the 'grace of God', history could not continue meaningfully. The primary decision of God, primary also for human ethical decision, represents a different perception and understanding of history than the principle of karman. The perspective of the primary decision of God also has its own way of dealing with human greed.

These words of Isaiah must not be taken as an answer to the question of Jeremiah. There is no easy answer in the Bible to that question. The primary decision comes to Christians as 'the word of the cross' (I Cor.1.18). The word of the cross does not give a simple answer to the question of Jeremiah, but it does give us a new orientation to look at the question, 'Why do all who are treacherous thrive?'. The word of the cross gives us hints about how to explore the depths of the mind of God expressed in the words quoted above from Isaiah.

'For my name's sake I defer my anger.' This must be appreciated in the light of I Corinthians 1.25: 'for the foolishness of God is wiser than men, and the weaknessof God is stronger than men'. God's name is not an ordinary name. It is the name that demonstrates its real authority and power in its 'foolishness and weakness' which are 'wiser and stronger' than men! When this name is mentioned history is seen neither as a karman-field nor as a chain of accidents. Karman and accidents are controlled by God whose sovereignty expresses itself 'foolishly and weakly' in the crucified Christ. We are led to see and experience history as God experiences it, through the agitated mind of God, not through cool operation of karman nor through an image of a chain of blind accidents.

If God is directly and immediately 'wise and strong' we may have a quick answer to the question of Jeremiah. But God is not so, since God's mind is agitated about our history, and God comes to us through the word of the cross, thus Jeremiah's question remains with us whenever we mention the name of God. When we stop saying 'Righteous art Thou, O Lord', then Jeremiah's question will disappear. As long as we confess our faith in God in saying 'Righteous art Thou, O Lord' – by the power of the Holy Spirit – we are to imitate the *pathos* (passion) and *ethos* (ethical involvement) of God whose attention is directed to our history.[10]

19

Vanity of Vanities, Says the Preacher

Christian meaning of the image of 'a fast spinning top'.

A strange voice that comes from within the tradition of Mount Sinai attracts the attention of the people of Mount Fuji. It is that of Ecclesiastes (*Qoheleth*). The mode of thinking and the message itself of this piece of literature are very different from that of the Torah and the Prophets. It begins with this striking statement:

Vanity of vanities, says the Preacher, vanity of vanities! All is vanity.

The word translated 'vanity' in the Revised Standard Version appears as 'emptiness' in the New English Bible and 'futility' in the Jewish translation of *Kethubim* (The Writings).[1] The word in the Hebrew text is *hebhel* which originally meant breath, vapour, mist, smoke and wind. The prophets used the word. Isaiah 30.7 carries the fundamental meaning of the word.[2]

For Egypt's help is worthless (*hebhel*) and empty (*riq*).

The word indicates transience and impermanence.[3] The Preacher in Ecclesiastes uses the word *hebhel* in a persistent refrain to express a profound cynicism.

All is vanity and striving after wind (1.14).

Then I said to myself 'What befalls the fool will befall me also; why then have I been so very wise?' And I said to myself that this also is vanity (2.15).

He who loves money will not be satisfied with money; nor he who loves wealth, with gain; this also is vanity (5.10).

There is a vanity which takes place on earth, that there are righteous men to whom it happens according to the deeds of the wicked, and there are wicked men to whom it happens according to the deeds of the righteous. I said that this also is vanity (8.14).

This sense of vanity is strengthened by an awareness of mortality.

All go to one place; all are from the dust and all turn to dust again. Who knows whether the spirit of man goes upward and the spirit of the beast goes down to the earth? (3.20,21)

The Preacher concludes that we should therefore make the most of life while we are alive.

And I commend enjoyment, for man has no good thing under the sun but to eat and drink and enjoy himself (8.15).

Go, eat your bread with enjoyment, and drink your wine with a merry heart (9.7, also see 3.12,22).

In this connection a comment from Von Rad's study of Ecclesiastes is suggestive.

But Ecclesiastes thinks entirely without any reference to history – with him the Wisdom literature lost its last contact with Israel's old way of thinking in terms of saving history and, quite consistently, fell back on the cyclical way of thinking common to the East, the only difference being that in Ecclesiastes this way of thinking is expressed in an utterly secular form. But – and this tragedy is the book's theme – in this world devoid of all action of Jahweh in history, Ecclesiastes seeks for God.[4]

The God of the Preacher does not involve himself in history in order to give meaning to it. There is no sense of social responsibility in the outlook of the Preacher. Von Rad relates Ecclesiastes to the thinking of the East. There is an obvious similarity, but I would like to quote the Buddhist *Sutta-Nipata* to indicate that the relation of Buddhism to the ordinary Eastern concept of the cyclical is more complex. the quotation begins with the tone of the Preacher.

How short indeed is life!
Within a hundred years
One dies; who longer lives
Dies surely of decay.

Folk grieve o'er thoughts of 'mine',
For wealth lasts not for aye
And fortune veers about;
See this and homeless dwell!

'Tis left behind in death,
Yet man thinks 'It is mine!'
the wise know this; and not
To 'mine' should stoop my friend.

As one awake sees not
The things he met in sleep,
So too he seeth not
The dear friend dead and gone.

Greedy for 'mine', they quit
Not envy, grief, laments;
Hence sages fare claim-free,
Seers in security.

In naught the sage puts trust,
Makes none a friend or foe;
As water soils no leaf,
Envy, laments, not him.[5]

Here is expressed the view of human life by the Buddha. 'How short indeed is life'! But he does not suggest that we may as well enjoy it as much as we can within this short period of life. Instead he asks us to discard the idea of 'mine'. The source of human problem is in regarding that something is mine (*mamayita*). We may have 'dear friends' but once they are dead, we will not see them any more. We must free ourselves from such thoughts of 'mine', then 'As water soils no leaf, Envy, laments, not him'. In the words of *Sutta-Nipata* there is no God mentioned. The world of the Buddha is in this sense fundamentally different from that of Israel. Buddha never thought about 'God' who creates a saving history for all humanity. The Buddha emphasized; 'Greedy for "mine", they quit/ Not envy, grief, laments; /Hence sages fare claim-free,/ Seers in security'. Here is a quotation from the *Dhammapada*:

'Sons have I; wealth have I': Thus is the fool worried; Verily, he himself is not his own. Whence sons? Whence wealth? (62)[6]

This makes a contrast to the words of the Preacher; 'And I commend enjoyment, for man has no good thing under the sun but to eat and drink and enjoy himself'.

The greatness of the Buddhist message is that it placed the cyclical view of life under the light of the renunciation of *mamayita*. The cyclical view of life has been challenged throughout centuries by the thought of renunciation of 'mine'. The words of *Sutta-Nipata* indicate the fundamental message of Buddhism. They correspond to the words of Jesus recorded in the Gospel of Matthew;

If any man would come after me, let him deny himself and take up his cross and follow me. For whoever would save his life will lose it, and whoever loses his life for my sake will find it (Matt. 16.24,25).

I am not suggesting that Christian discipleship and the Buddhist renunciation of 'mine' are identical. They appear in different religious and cultural contexts. Yet they are closer to each other than either is to the saying of the Preacher; 'I commend enjoyment....'

The *Sutta-Nipata* speaks about the need for the destruction of *mamayita*. The destruction of *mamayita* is fundamental to the important Mahayana Buddhist concept of *sunya*, which is usually translated as 'emptiness', 'void' or 'nothingness'. In the Japanese Zen tradition it is translated as '*mu*'. Originally the word *sunya* means something which is swelled up and hollow inside. It carries a suggestion, also, of being absent or lacking. The word *sunya* does share the meaning of futility and meaninglessness with the biblical word *hebhel* but this is a peripheral connotation for *sunya*. In Mahayana Buddhism the concept of *sunya* is more dynamic and paradoxical.

The *sunya* points to the fullness or the powerfulness of a person who has renounced the 'mine' and thus has become zero '*mu*' person. It is the fullness that comes from nothingness! Hisamatsu Shinichi expresses this concisely; 'Because I died, all things have become alive to me. Because I threw away all things, all things have come back to me'.[7] Izutsu Toshihiko, the Japanese orientalist, sees the inner connection between spiritual qualities depicted in *Bhagavadgita* and the psychological description of the Zen mind. The *Bhagavadgita* speaks about *sattva* (goodness), *rajas* (passion) and *tamas* (dullness) (XVIII,20–22). These three correspond to Zen's *mu-shin* (no-mind), *yu-shin* (be-mind) and *shitsu-shin* (possessive mind).[8] The *mu-shin* is most free while the *yu-shin*, which is the mind which has not completely 'died', is unfree and tends to become the mind that is possessive. There is, then, a correspondence between the goodness(*sattva*) of the Bhagavadgita and no-mind (*mu-shin*) of the Zen. The important point is the freedom of no-mind.

It is understood that out of this freedom comes the spirituality of mercy which is the source of Buddhist ethics. The Sanskrit word for 'mercy' is *karuna*. Originally this word signifies 'groaning with those who suffer'. *Karuna* is a strong social concept. Only those who follow the way of emancipation from personal greed can groan with those who are suffering. In *karuna* the emancipated soul (*mu-shin*) expresses itself.

Sunya is thus an emptiness which is creative and not at all futile and meaningless. It is not nihilistic. According to D.T. Suzuki it is the stillness of the fast spinning top. *Sunya* has a strong historical and salvific meaning when it expresses itself through mercy, 'groaning with those who suffer'. Even the image of the fast spinning top, quiet yet most active, may portray the image of Christian discipleship, taking up the cross and following Jesus.

I find, then, a sharp contrast between the *hebhel* in Ecclesiastes and the *sunya* of Mahayana Buddhism. Ecclesiastes speaks in an 'utterly secular' language (Von Rad) while Mahayana Buddhism speaks of the creativity of self-denial; 'because I died, all things have become alive to me'.

The philosophy of the Preacher has undeniable universal appeal. Speaking of the finality of death, the Preacher says:

> Their love and their hate and their envy have already perished, and they have no more forever any share in all that is done under the sun (Eccles. 9.6).

Whether we agree or disagree with the sentiment, there is here an honest observation we cannot ignore. The sense of futility is a part of the truth about human life. There is no meaningfulness of life which is unrelated to the question of the futility of life. Yet there is a difference between the Preacher and the Buddha. Compared to the Buddha who taught destruction of *mamayita* as a creative religious existence of human life, the Preacher is nihilistic. There is something in the message of the Buddha which says that the finality of death can be challenged. He suggests that it can be challenged by the power of eradication of self and selfishness.

I am not suggesting that the Buddha stands for the East and the Preacher for the West. Such a suggestion is too simplistic. What I am saying is that the Buddhist emphasis on the destruction of *mamayita* is closer to the tradition of Mount Sinai than the Preacher's teaching, 'I commend enjoyment,...'. Therefore, the bridge between Mount Fuji and Mount Sinai would be better built from the Fuji side on the basis of *sunya* than from the Sinai side if the Preacher's understanding of *hebhel* were to be the foundation.

A second word from the religio-philosophical world of Asia which comes to my mind as I read Ecclesiastes is the Sanskrit word *maya*. *Maya* is derived from the root *ma* which means 'to measure, form, build'. The word means 'art, marvellous power, device, trick, deceit, fraud, illusory image, phantom, illusion'. A parable of the Buddha suggests the meaning of this concept.[9]

Kosa Gotami was despised by her husband's family because of her poor birth. At last she bore a son and they respected her. When her son was old enough to play with other children he fell ill and died. Gotami, fearing the loss of her honour, went from door to door with the child asking for medicine for him. Everyone laughed at her, saying, 'Who can give medicine

for the dead?'. At last Gotami met the Buddha who said to her, 'Go make
the rounds of the city, and in whatever house no one has ever died, from
that house fetch tiny grains of mustard seed'. Gotami went to the city and
could not find one house in which no one had ever died. She went outside of
the city, carried her son to the burning-ground, and holding him in her
arms, said, 'Dear son, I thought that you alone had been overtaken by
death. But you are not alone. This is a law common to all mankind'. In this
parable the Buddha awakens Kisa Gotami from her illusion. She must
accept the universality of death. In attaining enlightenment she does not
say, 'All is vanity'. On the contrary, she realized that all things are
impermanent.[10]

In a Hindu *Purana*, ancient story, we have a story of Vishnu and Narada,
crossing a strip of desert under the scorching sun. They became very thirsty
and seeing a small hamlet in the distance Vishnu asked Narada, his disciple,
to fetch him some water. Narada went off to the huts while Vishnu rested
under the shadow of a cliff. When Narada knocked on the first door he was
greeted by the beautiful daughter of the house who welcomed him. He
stayed with the family and married her. Twelve years passed. One night a
storm came, and he lost everything, house, wife and children in the torrent
of flood. 'Child!' he heard a familiar voice. 'Where is the water you went to
fetch for me?'[11]

Water, in Hindu thought, signifies the essence of the divine. Vishnu
showed Narada how he was caught in unreality, forgetting the reality which
is beyond this phenomenal, transient world. This story does not, in the
manner of the Preacher of Ecclesiates, say, 'This also is vanity'. Rather, we
are urged to see the transience of this world and to 'fetch the water' which
endures. We must be on guard to distinguish reality from unreality. And
this distinction is not 'vain' according to Hinduism.

The depth of the despair in Ecclesiastes is felt when the Preacher, in his
great wisdom, observes the world and comes to pronounce the vanity even
of life itself.

> And I thought the dead who are already dead more fortunate than the
> living who are still alive; but better than both is he who has not yet been,
> and has not seen the evil deeds that are done under the sun (Eccles.
> 4.2,3).

The nihilistic resignation presented here does not, in my mind, represent the
main biblical message. Kisa Gotami realized that all are transient (*anicca*).
And through this realization she achieved enlightenment. Achieving
enlightenment is not a nihilistic exercise. It is a very meaningful spiritual
attainment. The historical meaning of this enlightenment is elimination of
personal greed. Narada must learn the distinction between reality and
unreality. Vishnu has a divine power to frame such a fantasy context, *maya*

through which Vishnu can teach Narada this distinction. Constant movement from unreality to reality gives meaning to human life. If this is true, then the end result of human life cannot be summarized in 'vanity of vanities'.

Our reflection on Ecclesiastes reminds us of the words of Paul addressed to the Christian community in Rome:

> I consider that the sufferings of this present time are not worth comparing with the glory that is to be revealed to us. For the creation waits with eager longing for the revealing of the sons of God; for the creation was subjected to futility not of its own will but by the will of him who subjected it in hope, because the creation itself will be set free from its bondage to decay and obtain the glorious liberty of the children of God. We know that the whole creation has been groaning in travail together until now; and not only the creation, but we ourselves, who have the first fruits of the Spirit, groan inwardly as we wait for adoption as sons, the redemption of our bodies (Rom. 8.18–23).

Ecclesiastes begins with the words, 'all is vanity'. Here Paul says the 'creation was subjected to futility' (*mataiotes*). Paul then seems to be supporting the view of Ecclesiastes. In closer study, however, this *mataiotes* of Paul and *hebhel* of Ecclesiastes appear in different theological contexts. The futility that appears in Romans is not hopeless, as is that of Ecclesiastes. Paul's futility has a beginning and an end. It is eschatologically limited. It will eventually bring the fulfilment of the promise. All creation 'sighs together' (*sustenazo* because it has been subjected to 'bondage to decay' through the fall of Adam. Christians who have 'the first fruits of the Spirit' groan also because their bodies are still subject to corruption. The *mataiotes* that covers creation does not have the final word since the world is subjected to it 'by the will of him who subjected it in hope'.

The word 'groaning' (*stenazo*), which Paul uses, is a strong word.

> I hear a voice as of one in travail,
> Anguish as of a woman bearing her first child (Jer. 4.31).[12]

These are the words by which Jeremiah describes his vision of destruction of Jerusalem. 'Anguish' here means 'screaming' or 'groaning'.

> Thus says the Lord God to Tyre; Will not the coastlands shake at the sound of your fall, when the wounded groan, when slaughter is made in the midst of you? (Ezek. 26.15)

These are the words that speak about the destruction of Tyre by Nebuchadnezzar.

We all growl like bears and moan like doves. We hope for redress, and there is none; For victory, and it is far from us (Isa. 59.11).[13]

Judah will find herself like this because of her own sin and unfaithfulness to the God of covenant.

The image that 'groaning' carries is different from the image of 'commending enjoyment'. The former suggests a serious involvement in history while the latter does not. Indeed there is 'futility' in the world. But futility is not absolute. It is controlled by God. Human groaning in history is not blind happening. Where there is groaning humanity, the biblical faith insists, there is the God who hears groaning. History is not understood to be a tranquil time and space. It is a critical time and space in which we must battle against the power of futility. The Buddha says that we must fight against our own greed. Even though now creation is subjected to futility that futility is not the final word. The mind of our God is agitated because of love towards us and to the whole creation. We catch a glimpse of this agitated mind of God through the Mahayana doctrine of groaning (showing mercy). When we say that all is *not* vanity, then we begin to have a theologically agitated mind. The ordinary distinction between East and West must be re-examined in terms of the presence of this agitated mind. For God all is not vanity. All is full of promise. Therefore the mind of God is agitated.

20
Theology of the Cross

The broken Christ heals the world broken by idolatry.

In the world of nauture-oriented religions we have innumerable 'instant gods', some being more harmful to human welfare than others. One such instant god, the Japanese imperial cult, was ruinous to Japanese people. In comparison, the worship of a cereal god may not be so destructive to anyone. However, many 'harmless' gods may be used by a strong ideological god to produce a system of destructive idolatry. This seems to me to be what happened in the recent history of Japan. When a demonic ideological god appeared on the horizon of Japan, there were only a few gods who were ready to fight against that demonic state power. These gods, indeed few in number, are the gods of popular religious movements concerned about social justice which as we have seen appeared since the early nineteenth century.

The contrast between Mount Fuji spirituality and Mount Sinai spirituality is the contrast between a cosmological and an eschatological orientation.

If the world of nature-oriented religions produces 'instant gods' then the world that speaks of the 'maker of heaven and earth' often 'takes the name of God in vain'. When the name of God is taken in vain, the scourge of idolatrous tyranny will eventually visit humanity. It is because 'taking the name of God in vain' means deification of the people who take the name of God in vain. That is to say, the name of God is used by the people to enhance their prestige and power. This is a destructive 'theological' operation. Often the failure of eschatological religion brings more dread upon humanity than the activity of the people dedicated to the cosmological instant gods. When I say this I am aware that in the concrete historical situation the 'instant gods' and 'taking the name of God in vain' are emotionally and philosophically mixed up. The cosmological Shinto Japan and the eschatological Christian Germany were on one side against the

Allied Powers during World War II. History as we know it is not free from the power of this destructive combination of the 'two theologies'; theology of instant gods, and theology of taking the name of God in vain.

The 'two theologies' can destroy humanity. I see these two theologies at work actively in our history today. Theology which addresses itself of 'the true light that enlightens every man' (John1.9) is in conflict with these 'two theologies' which take the whole humanity into darkness. Our problem is then deeply 'theological'. It is human idolatry that threatens the survival of the human race upon this planet.

The name, Jesus Christ, is not a magic name which transforms the broken world into an instant paradise. Has not the true dimension of the glory of this name suffered since the faith associated with this name became the state religion of the Roman Empire? Has it not been difficult to maintain the quality of the stumbling block of this name when the church became the powerful social group? How could the prestigious church proclaim the crucified Christ? The name of Jesus Christ is not a powerful name in the manner of the imperial power. It is a 'foolish and weak' name (I Cor. 1.21–25)! His name does not solve the problem of idolatry in human history with a magic touch. Jesus Christ is not a quick answer. If Jesus Christ is the answer he is the answer in the way portrayed in crucifixion! He remains to be a stumbling block (Matt.13 57).

I am not proposing in this last chapter, 'Theology of the Cross', an immediate and quick solution to the problem of idolatry in our world. Hosea describes the painful inner life of God; 'My mind is turning over in me. My emotions are agitated all together'. I have no precise theological formulations by which I would connect the words of Hosea about God and 'the word of the cross' (I Cor. 1.18). But I find that the image of the agitated mind of God, given by Hosea, illuminates the 'word of the cross' for me 'from inside God', if we are allowed to say such a thing at all in our theology. The word of the cross points to God's agitated emotions because of God's love towards us. The word of the cross heals our history by giving it hope and life. It is this word of the cross that exposes the deception of the 'two theologies' – theology of instant gods, and theology of taking the name of God in vain – in the most profound fashion.

> On that cross he discarded the cosmic powers and authorities like a garment; he made a public spectacle of them and led them as captives in his triumphal procession (Col. 2.15, NEB).

1. 'He saved others; he cannot save himself' (Mark 15.31)

Jesus Christ is the centre of the biblical message for Christians. The wealth of materials in the New Testament inspire us with the variety of images which symbolize the person and work of Jesus Christ.

I will focus on one image which seems particularly meaningful to me. It is the image of the broken Christ healing the broken world. In the words of Paul:

> The Lord Jesus on the night when he was betrayed took bread and when he had given thanks, he broke it, and said, 'This is my body which is (broken) for you. ...' (I Cor. 11.23,24).

In this last night with his disciples he indicated that his body would be broken just as the bread was broken. He kept this solemn and sacred symbolism for the night in which he was betrayed as though that were the best possible time! To our modern military minds that would seem to have been the time for resistance, the time to demolish his enemy by force, if possible. Instead, Jesus Christ left the strong symbol of love. The moment of the breaking of bread became a most sacred moment for the Christian church. This broken Christ – the torn and mutilated Christ – is the one who heals the broken world! The New Testament does not speak about a beautiful, unbroken, unmutilated Christ. What a strange faith, that focusses itself upon the broken crucified Christ! 'For I decided to know nothing among you except Jesus Christ and him crucified' (I Cor. 2.2).

In our modern context we are tempted to speak more positively about an unbroken Christ, a powerful, conquering Christ. Christian theology, under the influence of the Greek philosophical mind and the Latin administrative mind, has become largely a theology of the unbroken Christ. The theological meaning of the brokenness in the depth of the work and person of Jesus Christ has been ignored. Both philosophical and administrative minds are attracted to the concept of 'perfection' and they dislike 'brokenness'. Indeed, we question whether we can find hope in the broken Christ. How can we trust in such a 'weak', even repelling, image of Christ? A strong Western civilization and the 'weak' Christ cannot be reconciled harmoniously. Christ must become 'strong'. A strong United States and a strong Christ!

The word 'broken' is a negative word. It is used in such expressions as 'broken family', 'broken human relationship', 'broken heart'. Yet in speaking about the broken Christ, we are speaking about creation, construction, integration, reconciliation and healing. We are listening now to the ancient words of the Bible, 'he was bruised for our iniquities; upon him was the chastisement that made us whole' (Isa. 53.5). The image of the broken Christ comes to us every time we approach the Lord's Supper. And it is this broken Christ who exposes human idolatry.

In the last night with his disciples, he broke the bread. He created the space between one piece of bread and another as he held up the broken bread. New space is created at the cost of the life of Christ. This is not an ordinary space like our living room, our kitchen or our athletic field. This special space is charged with the suffering love of Christ. This is the space in which the church is built. It is a sacred space. All other space must receive its meaning from this sacred goes back, thus, to the image of the broken bread at the Last Supper. And it was not only sacred space that was created there, but also sacred time. As it has been pointed out, the event of love took place in the night in which he was betrayed. Did not time receive a new sacred meaning from such an event? When this had taken place has not time become sacred?

In the Last Supper holiness and brokenness are brought together and made into one. This unity of holiness and brokenness is called 'sacramental'.

May I invite you to consider two images that come to my mind as I think of the sacrament of the Holy Supper. Jesus Christ who gives himself in the sacrament is the person of utter self-denial. Yet he is in truth, the centre of all things according to the New Testament. 'All things were made through him' (John 1.3), 'For no other foundation can anyone lay than that which is laid, which is Jesus Christ' (I Cor. 3.11) and 'In him all things hold together' (Col. 1.17). But about this centre person we learn of his advent that when the time came for his mother to be delivered she gave birth to her first-born son and wrapped him in swaddling cloths, and laid him in a manger, because there was no place for them in the inn (Luke 2.6,7). The person 'through whom all things were made' was placed in a manger. During his active ministry, he, the foundation of the church and the world, told one of his ardent followers; 'Foxes have holes, and birds of the air have nests; but the son of man has nowhere to lay his head' (Luke 9.58). He was said to be 'a friend of tax collectors and sinners' (Luke 7.34). He was crucified outside the city gate of Jerusalem (Heb. 13.12). This centre person lived on the periphery. No! He established his centrality by going to the periphery. He became the Lord by being crucified. What a contradiction! The apostle Paul says about this most strange story; 'God's weakness is stronger than men, and god's foolishness is wiser than men' (I Cor. 1.25). Christ's 'weak' activity at the periphery is more creative than the 'strong' activity at human centres. Christ's 'foolish' death on the cross is more life-giving than all the 'wise' human contrivances for giving meaning to life! It is this contradiction of Christ that can expose idolatry.

Therefore I can now say his whole life was sacramental. When holiness and brokenness come together for the sake of the salvation of others, we have Christian sacrament. Christian theology then is fundamentally sacramental theology since Jesus Christ is the central sacrament of our faith. In him the holiness of God is expressed through the brokenness of Jesus Christ. Do we have many theologies? Black theology, feminist theology, Asian theology, classic theology, traditional theology, ... All theologies must express the creativity of Jesus Christ who is 'broken and holy', 'holy and broken' for our salvation. Conflicts among theologies must be examined in the light of what happened in the night in which Jesus was betrayed. Theological positions are asked to go to the periphery in order to witness for Jesus Christ the centre-person who has gone to the periphery.

Let me move on to the second related image. This image that expands our imagination to the sacramental Christ is taken from the Sermon on the Mount.

> If you are offering your gift at the altar and there remember that your brother has something against you, leave your gift there before the altar and go; first be reconciled to your brother, and then come and offer your gift (Matt. 5.23,24).

This saying of Jesus is sacramental. It gives us the sacramental meaning of the altar. Christian understanding of the altar must be guided by the two motifs; holiness and brokenness. 'If you are offering your gift at the altar and there remember....' suggests the appearance of holiness and brokenness. In the most holy moment at the altar we are to remember our broken relationship with our neighbours. At the altar you will remember that your brothers and sisters – hungry, poverty stricken, 'widows, orphans, aliens' and marginalized, have something against you. It is not that you remember that *you* have complaints against others! That would be a moment of egocentric imagination, instead of the moment inspired by the holy and broken Jesus Christ.

But why should such an embarrassing thing happen at the altar? Why can we not just proceed to the offering of our gift? It is because the meaning of the altar is to remind us of the necessity for reconciliation. Jesus says, take a *side trip* to our brothers and sisters and first be reconciled with them. This trip may take two days, two weeks, two centuries,...Leave your gift there before the altar! How we deal with our fellow human being is very important to God whose symbol the altar is. The altar at the centre inspires us to go to the periphery of difficult reconciliation. There the symbol of the altar finds its sacramental character. Where there is no 'side trip' there is no sacrament. In our day liberation theologies emphasize this Christian teaching of 'side trip'. Liberation theologies are not something completely new. They are an expression of sacramental theology. When this side trip is taken in the name of the holy and broken Jesus Christ, this trip itself will become sacramental, and this trip itself will become the altar.

The New Testament speaks about 'the fullness of God dwelling in Jesus Christ' (Col. 1.19). We are told by John that we receive, not just grace, but 'grace upon grace' from the fullness of Jesus Christ. The fullness of God is not a 'cool' fullness of God. It is the fullness of an 'impassioned God'. The grace of an impassioned God is an impassioned grace. This impassioned grace comes to us through the symbolism of the Last Supper. God in Jesus Christ comes to us in holiness and brokenness.

Such is the spirituality portrayed in the Last Supper. The unity of holiness and brokenness in Jesus Christ is the energy that inspires the church to reform itself from time to time. In spite of all disappointing realities within the church, there is something in the gospel of Christ that inspires us to engage in self-criticism. 'You are the salt of the earth' (Matt. 5.13) if you demonstrate, even fragmentally, the holiness and brokenness of the sacramental Jesus Christ to the world.

In this sacramental theology of Jesus Christ there is no room for a 'Christian superiority complex' over the people of other faiths. If we understand the name of Jesus Christ to be the unity of holiness and brokenness, we Christians must be freed from 'teachers' complex'. This will give us a new possibility in our encounter with the people of other faiths and ideologies. We can be critical about them because we are critical about ourselves. We judge ourselves before we judge others in the theology of the Last Supper in which Jesus washed his disciples' feet (John 13.5). The Christian faith has given humanity a new concept of centre symbolism. The centre becomes the real saving centre by moving to the periphery! 'For whoever would save his life will lose it, and whoever loses his life for my sake will find it' (Matt. 16.25). Or, in the words of the Gospel of Mark, the sacramental spirituality is expressed in the mocking words that were hurled against the crucified Christ; 'He saved others, he cannot save himself'! (15.31). The holiness and brokenness of Christ are sharply attested to in these words of taunting. It is true that he saved others and he did not save himself!

2. Theology of the cross

The expression 'theology of the cross' (*theologia crucis*) was coined by Luther in 1518 in the course of his dispute over indulgences. The basic text for his theology of the cross is I Corinthians 1.18–25:

> For the word of the cross is folly to those who are perishing, but to us who are being saved it is the power of God. For it is written, 'I will destroy the wisdom of the wise, and the cleverness of the clever I will thwart'. Where is the wise man? Where is the scribe? Where is the debater of this age? Has not God made foolish the wisdom of the world? For since, in the wisdom of God, the world did not know God through wisdom, it pleased God through the folly of what we preach to save those who believe. For Jews demand signs and Greeks seek wisdom, but we preach Christ crucified, a stumbling block to Jews and folly to Gentiles, but to those who are called, both Jews and Greeks, Christ the power of

God and the wisdom of God. For the foolishness of God is wiser than
men, and the weakness of God is stronger than men.

The word of the cross is folly, yet it is the expression of the hidden wisdom
of God and the centre of the Christian proclamation. I would like to
highlight the key theological thought of Luther from his Commentary on
the First Twenty-two Psalms written in 1519–21.[1]

The Commentary declares the clear distinction between the Law of God
and the law of man. 'He is like a tree planted by streams of water' (1.1)
means that delight in the Law of God is not found in the nature of man but
is only planted by God. Faith must be planted in us if we are able to see God
and his work.[2] These are simple words. But behind them is Luther's
conviction that the Church Council and the Popes can err as well as his
criticism of medieval Aristotelian scholasticism, which was the very
character of the accepted theology itself.

The God who is revealed through the word of the cross is the hidden God
(*deus absconditus*), hidden in contradictions. Thus Luther asserts that when
God visits us in his secret operation 'man is savingly killed (*salubiterque
occiduntur*). God kills man (strange work – opus alienum) in order to save
him (proper work – opus proprium).' Luther quotes Isaiah 28.21: '...
strange is his deed! and to work his work – alien is his work!'. He writes:

> ...though God is the God of life and salvation, and these are his proper
> works; yet, in order to accomplish these, he kills and destroys, that he
> may thereby come unto his proper work. For he kills our will, that he
> may establish his own in us. He mortifies the flesh and its desires, that he
> may implant the Spirit and his desires.[3]

We cannot come to the saving God without meeting the killing God. God
hides himself *sub contraria specie*. The strange and proper works of God
are symbolized by the right and left hands of God. The right hand of God
signifies the favour of God. The left hand, on the contrary, throws us into
tribulation.

The First Commandment teaches the faith in the one true God. It is the
exclusive principle that commends the intense concentration of faith in one
God. To believe in, to hope in, to love and to fear God (*credere, sperare,
diligere, timere deum*) at all times is the message of the First
Commandment. [4] God alone and no one else brings us out of the 'straits'
(*angustia*) of affliction into the broad of consolation.[5] The one who is blind
to the saving God of the First Commandment will flee to man (*ad hominem
confugitis*) and put his trust in created things (*fiducia rerum incumbitis*).[6]

The Commentary then comes to Jesus Christ who believed in God. On
the cross he was forsaken by God, ('My God, my God, why hast thou
forsaken me?' Mark 15.34) yet at that very moment Jesus firmly trusted in
God.

A strong faith! which can speak to an angry God, call to him when persecuting you, flee unto him when driving you back, praise him as your helper, your glory, and the lifter up of your head, when you feel him deserting, confounding and oppressing you:[7]

Here Jesus demonstrated the ultimate faith in God. Faith is 'to flee to God against God' (*ad deum contra deum confugere*).[8] This is the key message of the Commentary on the Psalms. Jesus trusted in the forsaking God on the cross. He looked 'for all good' in God in this time of utmost need! His faith was right, then likewise his God is the true God!

Ad deum contra deum confugere. This is the character of Christian faith. Faith in God is not an easy-going experience. It involves radical self-denial. To God alone we are to flee, not to someone or something else. If we flee to someone or something else we are engaged in idolatry. Only God is 'absolute'. Then all other 'absolutes' must be dethroned as we have seen in the words of H. Richard Neibuhr in chapter 13 above. In this thread of thought the words of Isaiah come to me:

Your new moons and your appointed feasts my soul hates; they have become a burden to me, I am weary of bearing them. When you spread forth your hands, I will hide my eyes from you; even though you make prayers, I will not listen; your hands are full of blood (Isa.1.14.15).

In the time of Luther, and perhaps today too, the church was busy in conducting all sorts of 'appointed feasts' with 'authoritative theology and prayer'. Theology has often become an ideology. Theology that has become an ideology is far more pernicious than an ideology which is simply ideology. 'Taking the name of god in vain' is less harmful to the welfare of humanity than 'taking the name of the Lord your God in vain'. But unfortunately ideology often has a 'religious quality' or 'theological basis'. Luther attacks the gigantic ideological theological system of the church with the language of the theology of the cross. It was a battle between theology and theology; a theology which is not ideologized and a theology which is ideologized.

God hates 'appointed feasts with self-authorized theology and prayer'. This is the ultimate principle for revolution. God rejects ideologized theology, that is, the theology in which humanity, not God, is at the centre, in which the freedom of God is ignored and God is programmed to do what we ask God to do, in which the appearance of the sacred is scheduled according to our convenience to enhance our own social and religious prestige. In Luther such dethronement took place.

But while I sat still and drank beer with Philip and Amsdorf, God dealt the papacy a mighty blow.[9]

The Reformation was a theological battle. It was a battle in which both sides spoke 'theologically'. In the depth of Luther's theology is 'fleeing to God against God'. Luther's *theologia crucis* tells us that it is not 'fleeing to God', but 'fleeing to God against God' that we affirm our faith in God. 'Fleeing to God' is an easy theology which will eventually end up in an ideological system of 'appointed feasts' that will take 'the name of the Lord your God in vain'. Those who 'flee to God against God' dethrone the idols. Critique of idols in Luther's theology has come from the image of Jesus who trusted in the forsaking God! It points to Jesus Christ who saved others and did not save himself.

3. Confrontation of embrace

Why is it that God intends to heal the broken world through the broken Christ? This is a question that is beyond human thought and imagination to answer. This will remain to us either a stumbling block or folly. Yet the apostolic proclamation affirms that this is the way that God comes to us. How can the broken Christ heal the broken world? 'He was bruised for our iniquities; upon him was the chastisement that made us whole.' But how? How is this possible? This is beyond our understanding. Nevertheless, once again, this is the content of the gospel preached by the apostles. They bore witness to this message by becoming 'fools for Christ's sake'.

There are two images when we think of the relationship between the broken Christ and the broken world; confrontation and embrace. Truth makes itself clear by confrontation. Truth *aletheia*, means 'unconcealedness'. In order to 'unconceal' the falsehood of false prophets, one way or another, true prophets must confront them. Truth may make itself clear by confrontation. The story of Elijah gives a classic image of confrontation. 'How long will you go limping with two different opinions? If the Lord is God, follow him; but if Baal, then follow him' (I Kings 18.21). On Mount Carmel Elijah confronts the prophets of Baal. The Lord responds to the request of Elijah:

> Then the fire of the Lord fell, and consumed the burnt offering, and the wood, and the stones, and the dust, and licked up the water that was in the trench. And when all the people saw it, they fell on their faces; and they said, 'the Lord, he is God; the Lord, he is God'.

Elijah then seizes the prophets of Baal and kills them (I Kings 18.17–40). The truth has been established and the false prophets are eliminated. Confrontation did work!

Was it not, however, an overkill? Should we adopt the way of Elijah towards the false gods and their prophets? Take all of them to 'the brook

Kishon and kill them there'? After Elijah has destroyed the prophets of the Baal, Jezebel confronts Elijah and vows to kill him. The great prophet, we read, 'was afraid, and he arose and went for his life' (I Kings 19.3). God comes to Elijah in 'a soft murmuring sound' (The Jewish Publication Society of America translation), a voice which is not confrontational but carefully pastoral. In soft speech God discharges Elijah and gives him the task of employing his own successor. Elijah is also given instructions for the nation concluding with these words;

> Yet I will leave seven thousand in Israel, all the knees that have not bowed to Baal, and every mouth that has not kissed him (I Kings 19.18).

It is possible that Elijah misappropriated the jealousy of God by becoming himself 'very jealous of the Lord' (I Kings 19.10–14). The very jealous Elijah became confrontational. Confrontational is linear. The image of broken Christ is not linear. It is more circular. It points to the mind that comes back again and again to seek the healing of the broken relationship. That which is linear cannot come back. That which cannot come back cannot really suffer. How often the linear mentality has been responsible for 'overkills' in the history of humankind!

The relationship, at a profound level, between truth and confrontation is complex. I believe that truth expresses and affirms itself in order to remain true. In affirming itself truth will necessarily confront and expose falsehood. Thus truth as it functions involves confrontation. But confrontation is not the only manner of expressing the truth. 'To do truth' (*ten aletheian poiein* John 3.21) may confront the falsehood but it does more than confronting. The Bible is not just a confrontation book.

In confrontation we oppose someone externally. The word 'confrontation' means 'to adjoin with a mutual frontier'. When we say that the United States confronts the Soviet Union it means the former 'stands or comes in front of' the Soviet Union (*Oxford Dictionary*). Confrontation implies criticism applied from outside. This is the limitation of confrontation. It is difficult to place the words of Isaiah 'He was bruised for our iniquities; upon him was the chastisement that made us whole' in this confrontational mood. The one at whom the mocking words were hurled; 'He saved others, he cannot save himself' hardly gives us an image of confrontation. The one who establishes his centrality by going to the periphery and the one who gives his life in search of us cannot be presented as the confronting one.

Jesus Christ, in his words and actions, is far more educational than confrontational. If he confronts he confronts us through inner persuasion. He speaks to us from inside. If we speak about confrontation in relation to the name of Jesus Christ we must speak in this sense. This is confrontation understood in the light of the theology of the cross. Direct confrontation characterizes the spirit of militarism. Confrontation through inner persuasion is the spirit of community building. Militarism is run by the spirit of efficiency. It confronts the opponent with naked force. Community building cannot be achieved by such efficient confrontation. It must be guided by the patient spirituality which is ready to accept inefficiency as it deals with human being not as a 'target'. This sense of living with inefficiency opposes the spirit of imperialism. To illuminate where we are in the dangerous tension between the two superpowers, the Soviet Union and the United States, Anthony Lewis quotes some words of President Eisenhower who speaks about the self-defeating limitation of militarism.

> I have spent my life in the study of military strength as a deterrent to war, and in the character of military armaments necessary to win a war. The study of the first of these questions is still profitable, but we are rapidly getting to the point that no war can be *won*. War implies a contest; when you get to the point that contest is no longer involved and the outlook comes close to destruction of the enemy and suicide for ourselves – an outlook that neither side can ignore – then arguments as to the exact amount of available strength as compared to somebody else's are no longer the vital issues.[10]

This style of thinking hints at the direction of the theology of the cross. It rejects military philosophy of confrontation. President Eisenhower asks American people to ponder about a situation in which no wars can be won. He approaches people by way of 'inner persuasion'. By 'inner persuasion' I refer not to a psychological but to a historical process. 'Inner' to, that is not distanced from, historical reality, In fact, 'inner' here means, in a more explicitly theological language, 'through historical suffering', in the words of the Apostles' Creed; '…suffered under Pontius Pilate'. Jesus comes to us as he is suffering in history under Pontius Pilate. This is the theological meaning of 'inner' persuasion. The concept of 'inner' and 'suffering' are inseparable. Then 'inner' is not just a spacial concept, but a historical concept. It refers to someone through whose suffering history is renewed. Such 'inner persuasion' is not individualistic. It has a decisive community orientation. 'Believe in the Lord Jesus, and you will be saved, you and your household' (Acts 16.31). This 'inner' theology is to be contrasted with the self-righteous prayer: 'God, I thank thee that I am not like other men, extortioners, unjust, adulterers, or even like this tax collector….' (Luke 18.11).

Confrontation by the one who saved others and cannot save himself is the content of theology of the cross. In order to describe, however, such unusual confrontation through Jesus Christ who suffered under Pontius Pilate we should use the image of embracing. It is in this image the theology of the cross comes to a proper expression according to Kitamori Kazoh, the Japanese theologian. He defines the love of God revealed through Jesus Christ as the love that embraces us who are 'not worthy to be embraced'. This is the focus of his work *Theology of the Pain of God*.

The Asian cosmological mind tends to embrace often indiscriminately, while the Western eschatological mind tends to confront. What is important here is that Christianity teaches a new combination of the eschatological embracing us. This is the surprise! God who is not supposed to embrace sinner is embracing sinner! This is the paradox of the grace of God. This must be the source from which we obtain the needed perspective and sensitivity to judge the idols. When the cosmological embraces us there would be no judgment implied. But when the eschatological embraces, there is judgment.

> For judgment I came into this world, that those who do not see may see, and that those who see may become blind (John 9.39).

4. An unemployed God who meets us at the periphery

The visual symbol of Christ's brokenness is the bread at the Last Supper. He is broken to embrace sinners. As he is broken he allows his identity to be bound up with the identity of sinners. 'Why do you eat and drink with tax collectors and sinners?' (Luke 5.30). These words, in the form of a simple question point to the meaning of the weighty theological definition of the Fourth Ecumenical Council at Chalcedon AD 451); 'We declare that he is perfect both in his divinity and in his humanity, truly God and truly man, ...'[11] These theologically laboured words cannot compete with the simplicity of the gospel words.

'Why do you eat and drink with tax collectors and sinners?' So Jesus Christ demonstrates his centrality by going to the periphery. Where is the periphery? The periphery is the place without honour, prestige and power. In Jeremiah the periphery is the place of widows, orphans and aliens (7.6) The place where people are dying from starvation is the periphery. At the centre, in the place of honour, prestige and power, people are nicely salaried and caloried. This understanding of periphery is important. The theology of the cross is fundamentally different from a theology of honour, prestige and power. Honour, prestige and power must be examined in the light of the 'refuse of the world, the offscouring of all things'. That is to say, honour, prestige and power must be assessed in the light of discipleship. 'If any man would come after me, let him deny himself and take up his cross and follow me' (Matt 16.24). The periphery is the place of discipleship. If we follow Jesus we will come to the periphery with him.

The periphery is the place of the cross. It is the place where we are asked to save others and not ourselves. This description of periphery itself is a description of the gospel of Christ. Jesus Christ is the centre, therefore, wherever he is becomes the centre. If he goes to the periphery, the periphery, because of his presence, becomes the centre. But this centre is not an ordinary centre. It is a centre which affirms that 'God's weakness is stronger than men, and God's foolishness is wiser than men'. This strange centre, then, is the cross. And the cross is the point of denial of self-centredness. The message of the cross is that when God in Christ embraces the self-centred humanity, and out of this divine embrace, through the mystery of grace, healing will flow into human history.

'God's foolishness is wiser than men.' These are the key words of the theology of the cross. Then theology of the cross must be a kind of theology which expresses 'God's foolishness'. All theological thinkings are, then, challenged by the 'God's foolishness'. This is the remarkable quality of all Christian theologies. If Jesus Christ has gone to the periphery, theology itself must go there following Jesus Christ. Liberation theology of Latin America – perhaps we should call it 'periphery theology' – must not be dealt lightly since in it is the theology of the cross. Often theologies which are not shaken by 'God's foolishness' speak arrogantly about the periphery theology of Asia, Africa, Latin America and the Pacific. 'God's foolishness' is the moment of judgment upon all theologies. 'Not reading books or speculating, but living, dying and being damned make a theologian.'[12]

Once again, what does it mean that Christ affirmed his centrality by going to the periphery? The well known passage from the Book of Exodus comes to me;

God said to Moses, 'I am who I am' (Ex.3.14).

The passage which can be translated as 'I will be what I will be' speaks the language of promise. God will be with the people wherever they go. This is the promise declaring God's intention that God will not forsake his people even though they may stray away from God into disobedience and unbelief. God will come and seek them in that periphery. This, as we have seen, is the centre of the Sinai Tradition. Moses will come down twice from the mountain carrying the commandments of God! There is a story in the first Book of Samuel in which the honour of God is impugned and God makes a characteristic response. The people of Israel are clamouring for a king. 'Now appoint for us a king to govern us like all the nations.'

And the Lord said to Samuel, 'hearken to the voice of the people in all that they say to you, for they have not rejected you, but they have rejected me from being king over them' (I Sam. 8.6,7).

The people are asking God to resign from being king over them. They are 'firing' God. God is to be unemployed! Yet it is at this point that a deeper engagement between God and the people begins. The people will learn that God, whom they rejected, is with them still, loving them, seeking them in the periphery made up of the power of darkness. The relationship between God and the people is a 'post-rejection' relationship. So we do not say simply that God loves us. We must say that God loves us in spite of our rejection. Even though 'the whole world should tear the garment of His honour into rags' God still comes to us and calls us to return to God. [13] In spite of all human sinfulness, God has goodwill towards them (Luke 2.14). This is what we learn about the periphery. The periphery is not a forsaken place. It is the place where salvation takes place. The biblical God comes to the periphery in search of us. And this going to the periphery becomes a part of God's own identity. Let me quote from Amos' litany of 'yet you did not return to me'.

> 'I smote you with blight and mildew. I laid waste your gardens and your vineyards; your fig trees and your olive trees the locust devoured; yet you did not return to me' says the Lord.
> 'I sent among you a pestilence after the manner of Egypt; I slew your young men with the sword; I carried away your horses; and I made the stench of your camp go up into your nostrils; yet you did not return to me' says the Lord.
> 'I overthrew some of you, as when God overthrew Sodom and Gomorrah, and you were as a brand plucked out of the burning; yet you did not return to me', says the Lord (4.9,10; see also vv. 6–8).

The painful refrain, 'yet you did not return to me' points to the 'agitated mind of God' because of the unfaithfulness of the people. Salvation is to return to God. *Teshuva* (from *shuv*, turning the whole person) is a critically important word in the Hebrew Bible.

> Let the wicked forsake his way, and the unrighteous man his thoughts; let him return to the Lord, that he may have mercy on him, and to our God, for he will abundantly pardon (Isa. 55.7).

> If you return, I will restore you and you shall stand before me (Jer. 15.19).

> Let us test and examine our ways, and return to the Lord (Lam. 3.40).

What I am suggesting is that the call to 'return to the Lord' comes from God who brings his people to himself 'on eagles' wings' (Ex. 19.4). This call comes from God who, in the parable of Jesus portrayed as father running out to meet his returning son:

But while he was yet at a distance, his father saw him and had
compassion and ran and embraced him and kissed him (Luke 15.20).

The God who 'ran and embraced him' and declared that 'I will restore you
and you shall stand before me' is the God who is not an Unmoved Mover,
The First Cause and The Eternal Contemplation of Aristotle who stands at
the centre unmoved. On the contrary, Hosea tells us the inner turmoil of
this impassioned God. 'My mind is turning over in me. My emotions are
agitated all together.' The 'trouble' with this God is that he cannot stay
quietly at the centre. His mind is turning over in him and pouring itself out
towards the direction of the periphery. What is happening in the periphery
is very much in the mind of God.

The story of Jesus Christ (christology) is nothing but an exposition of this
'trouble'. If I place Jesus Christ in the context of Amos's refrain, it would
read like this; 'Christ died for your sins, yet you did not return to me'. Far
more than smiting with blight and mildew, God has taken the ultimate step
of letting Christ die for our sins. That is to say, Christ came to the extreme
periphery of crucifixion.

Have this mind among yourselves, which you have in Christ Jesus, who,
though he was in the form of God, did not count equality with God a
thing to be grasped, but emptied himself, taking the form of a servant,
being born in the likeness of men. And being found in human form he
humbled himself and became obedient unto death, even death on a cross
(Phil. 2.5–8).

The New Testament proclamation about Jesus Christ does not suffer from
placing Jesus Christ in the refrain of Amos. 'Christ died for you sins, yet
you did not return to me' is fully meaningful to Christians. Such *teshuvah*
christology, if I may call it so, invites us to think carefully about the
'trouble' of God who is at the centre yet his mind is turning over towards
the periphery. The *teshuvah* christology does not 'demote' Jesus Christ.
The creativity of the Christian gospel is that the name of Jesus Christ can
appear in the refrain of Amos, and at the same time, this name signifies a
new possibility that the 'returning to the Lord' *and* 'returning to Christ' is
identical. This Christian development of the *teshuvah* christology is, I
believe, not acceptable to the Jewish faith, and indeed it creates a complex
set of theological issues. Since, in the New Testament, Jesus Christ is
presented as someone more than 'one of the prophets' Christianity must
work out the relationship between these two images of returning.

At this moment I would like to make only one observation on this. It is to
do with the image of Christ who affirms his centrality by going to the
periphery. Because of this going – even to death on a cross – Christ fully
revealed the mind of God which says 'If you return, I will restore you and

you shall stand before me'. In his life he presented this saving truth to humanity.

> Therefore God has highly exalted him and bestowed on him the name which is above every name, that at the name of Jesus every knee should bow, in heaven and on earth and under the earth, and every tongue confess that Jesus Christ is Lord, to the glory of God the Father (Phil. 2.9–11).

Jesus Christ deepens the prophetic call to return to the Lord. The depth that Christ reached is the depth of the 'death on a cross'. And in this context the word *therefore* appears. It is God who exalts Christ who has gone to the extreme periphery. And *in this* salvation takes place. 'The atonement in the New Testament is a mystery, not a problem.'[14] The unity between the 'returning to the Lord' and 'returning to Christ' is found in 'the glory of God the Father'. The glory of God is revealed when the broken Christ embraces the broken world.

Once more I would like to take up Amos' refrain. What if we put the name of the Buddha in the refrain? 'I have sent the Buddha who taught you to battle against your own greed, yet you did not return to me'?

First of all, I think the Buddhists would not appreciate the thought that God has sent the Buddha. Such an idea is fundamentally contrary to the spirit of Buddhism. We would be accused as religious imperialists, then, if we say 'I have sent the Buddha....'. But the question posed here is the one unavoidable to all Christians who seek after theological illumination upon their own relationship with the people of other faiths. Theology must engage itself in a task of relating the Buddha's teaching on battle against human greed and the agitated mind of the God of Israel who says, 'yet you did not return to me'. I am suggesting *theological* bridging between the two.

A quick answer to this problem would be found in the view that Buddhists are 'anonymous Christians'. Those who fight against their own greed according to the doctrine of the Buddha are, even though they may not know, anonymously already Christians. They have then anonymously returned to God. This may sound acceptable to Christians but arrogant and imperialistic to the ears of the Buddhists. They would object to this 'extension' programme of Christianity.

But then, how do we go about it? This is not the place to develop an extensive discussion on this. I think this bridging is not an easy task and involves extensive doctrinal and historical studies. In the context of the present discussion I would like to make only one remark on this. Theology must go, as I have said before, to the periphery following Christ who has gone there. That is to say, theology must walk into the overwhelming territory of ambiguity courageously following Christ. The zone of ambiguity is one type of periphery. At the centre all concepts are nicely defined, methodology established, authoritative books published and teachers available. On the periphery – in the place of cross and discipleship – ambiguity overwhelms us. Theology must say in the midst of ambiguity that the atonement is a mystery, not a problem. And it takes a theological mind which is informed by the broken Christ, the Christ who goes to the periphery, the Christ who is passionately involved in salvation of humanity, to come to study Amos' refrain which contains the name of Buddha. Theology of the cross which is inspired and maintained by the words; 'the foolishness of God is wiser than men, and the weakness of God is stronger than men' is a theology which is able to meet the claim that other faiths make. The Christ who affirms his centrality by going to the periphery is the Christ who can establish a healing tie with the other faiths. He has been to the extreme periphery, and therefore no situation can paralyse him. The theology of the cross suggests to us that interreligious discussion must be seen from the perspective of the 'refuse of the world' which defines an apostolic quality of life and message.

5. Criticism of idolatry by the theology of the 'scars of Jesus' (Gal. 6.17)

The cross is not a tranquil situation. It is a passionate event of God in search of humanity. Christians are committed to this impassioned event of God. It is not concerned with speculation but with commitment. Luther called speculative theology a theology of glory. It is 'glorious' since there our own power of speculation domesticates God. Reason is playing a masterly role over God. In contrast

> the concealment of the crucified God, which is an offence to reason, becomes for the believer the abrogation of all his own wisdom and righteousness, so that God can do his work.[15]

In this way, according to Luther, we learn the theology of the cross. Otherwise we will be learning a theology of glory, a theology that controls God by reason which is not crucified with Christ. Luther was thinking about the scholastic theology of his day as theology of glory. The theology of the cross meditates and speaks about the broken Christ embracing the broken world. This is the image of reconciliation. And Christ does it with the passion of God; '...go after the one which is lost, until he finds it'! Without manipulation and distortion Christ gives himself in order to heal the demonic in human history. The divine sincerity painfully embraces human insincerity and creates sincerity in the place of insincerity. This is the way that theology describes human salvation in history.

In the light of the theology of the cross there are four important implications to be drawn for our Christian life as we live it in this world today.

First of all, in the light of the crucified Christ who staked all the fullness of God (Col. 1.19) for the salvation of humanity we must say that we stand for creation and not for destruction; for the inhabited world, not for bombed wilderness; for life and not for death; for hospitality and not for hostility; for mercy and not for cruelty. Jesus said, 'Be merciful, even as your Father is merciful' (Luke 6.36). Believers in God in terms of the theology of the cross must live a life of commitment and must reject any justification for cruelty or callousness. This decision to walk towards mercy and not towards cruelty is fundamental to our Christian life, ministry, mission, politics and ethics. For the Christian the famous words of Micah must come through the perspective of the theology of the cross;

> He has showed you, O man, what is good; and what does the Lord require of you but to do justice, and to love kindness, and to walk humbly with your God? (Micah 6.8)

These words are not just words of command or injunction. Jesus Christ has done justice, and loved kindness and walked humbly with his God. Therefore he is the Lamb of God who takes away the sin of the world (John 1.29). That is to say, he did justice, loved kindness and walked humbly with God by doing so he became himself a broken Christ. Justice is not just a sociological but a christological concept. The justice of Christ embraces unjust humanity – on the cross – and doing so creates a new possibility for justice in the world. The same thing must be said about human cruelty and arrogance. Christian ethics must be studied in the perspective of theology of the cross. This may be a 'foolish' proposal. It is to seek meaningful connections between the 'marks of Jesus' Paul bore on his body (Gal. 6.17; 'marks' – *stigmata* – were brands stamped on slaves) and social ethics. In this theological meditation we seek to see the mind of Christ which relates the assassination of Martin Luther King with the unjust American society. In this 'foolish' proposal we try to see the impact of the crucified Christ upon social injustice. What is the ethical impact of the ancient event symbolized by the episode of 'eagles' wings'? How is the Creator God, 'who gives life to the dead and calls into existence the things that do not exist' (Rom. 4.17), changing injustice to justice in the human community? The theology of the cross is deeply concerned about social ethics.

Secondly, the theology of the cross teaches us that we do not have the last word about the world and our destiny. What we say and do is subject to 'the word of the cross'. If we have the last word then we are followers of the theology of glory. If we speak the last word about ourselves and the world, making a complete circle without a break, as it were, we produce tyranny. Tyranny as totalitarianism claims the possession of the last word.

Believers in God renounce such an arrogant position. That 'God is spirit and those who worship him must worship in spirit and truth' (John 4.24) means that God cannot be grasped in our hands, as we hold an egg or a fish. 'God is spirit.' To 'worship in spirit and truth' means to profess with humility that the complete truth does not belong to us, but to God. '...Now we see only puzzling reflections in a mirror...' (I Cor. 13.12). God has the full last word about us and the world. This is the meaning of Christian worship. In Christian worship and ministry, we do not attempt to complete the circle with our own words. The circle is left broken by the presence of the broken Christ.

But if God speaks the last word about the world and humanity, is God totalitarian? This is a serious question which theology cannot evade. God, seen in the perspective of the theology of the cross, cannot be a totalitarian God. How can a God who revealed himself in Jesus Christ who is crucified, who walks towards the periphery, and who is passionately concerned about the welfare of people – Christ who saves others and does not save himself – be a totalitarian God in the secular parlance? God is concerned about our wholeness. God still asks the question; 'Where are you?' (Gen. 3.9). This God is a theological, not an ideological God. There is a delicate distinction between theology and ideology. Theology lives on the basis of a broken circle as it reflects the broken Christ. It is through this brokenness that it exerts its influence upon history. 'Brokenness' is the essential *stigmata* of theology.

Ideology is different. It is not essential for ideology to have a 'broken circle'. Brokenness can be viewed as weakness in ideology. A strong ideology cannot accept the uncertainity of brokenness. Ideology then does not share with theology 'marks of Christ'. Having said this we immediately notice that the relationship between ideology and theology is far more complex than we may readily accept. First of all we must face the problem of interactions between, or even a mixing of, the two. I find , for instance, the comprehensive race policy of South Africa is a strong ideology which does not admit any brokenness. A theological document entitled 'Human Relations and the South African Scene in the Light of Scripture' approved and accepted by the General Synod of the Dutch Reformed Church in South Africa in October 1974 presents a curious example of a substantial theological work to which ideology is granted the concluding word. In all it is a tragically deceptive piece of theological work. Deception comes from quoting the name of Jesus Christ apart from the perspective of the theology of the cross.

I also sense this error in the American President Reagan's speech before the National Association of Evangelicals on 8 March 1983, in which he said:

> So in your dicussions of the nuclear freeze proposals, I urge you to
> beware the temptation of pride – the temptation blithely to declare

yourselves above it all and label both sides equally at fault, to ignore the facts of history and the aggressive impulses of an evil empire, to simply call the arms race a giant misunderstanding and thereby remove yourself from the struggle between right and wrong, good and evil.[16]

There is an obvious lack of self-criticism in these words. In this scheme the world is divided into two neat portions. We are to understand America to be a good empire which stands in righteous indignation against an evil empire, the Soviet Union. This division is ideological. It is too efficient to be theological. There is no sense of brokenness in this quick division. Theology demands a more critical assessment of the historical situation, particularly when it is guided by the word of the cross. The word of the cross brings us to a realization that the American empire is not that free from the manifestation of evil. Theology, to be genuine, must contain the moment of sharp self-criticism.

Often the ideological and the theological cannot be neatly separated. They sit together and create a confusing picture of historical reality. This implies that none of us is free from ideology. The question is then focussed upon what kind of ideology it is that is influencing us. Is that an ideology of racism? cold war? welfare state? nuclear freeze? human rights? A report of the Asian theologians' conference on 'Towards an Ideology and Theology of People' (1981) concludes with these words; 'Ideology without theology – that leaves little room for hope; theology without theology – that leaves little scope for action'.[17] God who speaks the last word about the world and humanity is not a totalitarian ruler. This is an insight we receive from the theology of the cross. It is the crucified Christ who exposes the idolatry of totalitarianism (Col. 2.15).

Thirdly, the theology of the cross makes us aware of the presence of many gods. Some gods – gods of colour of skin, intellectual capacity, good income, guns and missiles – are very fascinating to us. These gods are fascinating because they claim to give us our identity and security more directly and quickly than can the crucified Lord. Identity? Yes. Quickly, by the power of increase, 'have more'! Security? Yes. Quickly, by making more bombs! The selling point of these gods is directness and quickness. They give us instant service. This is the fundamental reason for the fascination of these gods. But directness and quickness are principal ingredients of magic. The theology of the cross is strongly critical of magic. In the light of the theology of the cross, the truth about human salvation is neither 'directly' graspable nor 'instant'. An instant truth, free from the constraints of long suffering love is not truth. The God of the theology of the cross is a hidden God, who refuses to be grasped by us directly and quickly.

Magic is direct and quick. Militarism is a magic because it is direct and quick in all its thoughts and actions. So it racism. Directly and quickly everything is decided by the colour of skin. Totalitarianism is magic. It is direct and quick when all values relating to human life are decided by one human being, called a dictator. Religion, too, can degenerate to magic when the value it espouses is promised directly and quickly. Magic is efficient. Theology of the cross involves extremely 'inefficient' and 'painful' processes before it speaks about the possibility of the salvation of humanity.

Fourthly, the theology of the cross gives us a criterion by which we can make a distinction between the true God and the false gods, and true prophets and false prophets. Strangely the criterion the theology of the cross proposes is given us in the mocking words, 'He saved others; he cannot save himself'. This Christ who saved others did not save himself, reveals the fundmental character of the true God. False gods save themselves; they do not save others.

Our God is a jealous God. That is our God is an impassioned God who comes to us not to destroy us but to save us. God has unconditional goodwill towards us. This goodwill expresses itself through the suffering of Jesus Christ,...'even to death on a cross'.

The cosmological embraces us. The eschatological confronts us. But what the theology of the cross says is that the eschatological is embracing us. This is not 'natural'. This is unusual and extraordinary.

What no eye has seen, nor ear heard, nor the heart of man conceived, what God has prepared for those who love him (I Cor. 2.9).

'He saved others. He cannot save himself.' These are mocking words. 'He' is Jesus Christ. He is the eschatological person since he has a decisive meaning to humanity. It is this decisive eschatological person who embraces us. How does Jesus Christ embrace us? By not saving himself! The apostolic proclamation says that this is the way God experiences history.

Jesus Christ who comes to us through the word of the cross stands against the 'boosting of the finite to infinite', idolatry. He is personally the truth. In his truth, the finite is finite, and infinite is infinite. Humanity is humanity. God is God. Yet this God in Jesus Christ comes to the periphery to reveal the truth about human life with God, the truth of *immanuel*, 'God with us' (Matt. 1. 23). If this is the way God experiences history, then this must be the way by which God empowers us as we live towards the coming of the reign of God. Christ who established his centrality by going to the periphery is the source of Christian social perception and ethics. It is not an esoteric doctrine. It belongs to the heart of Christian theology. Human idolatry

must be judged under the light of this Christ of whom it is said tauntingly
'He saved others. He cannot save himself'! It is the crucified Christ who
exposes the subtle essence and manifestation of idolatry.

Notes

1. Let Us go up to the Mountain of the Lord

1. Paul Tillich, *Systematic Theology*, James Nisbet 1953, Vol. 1, p. 16.
2. Abraham J. Heschel, *The Prophets*, Harper & Row 1962, p. 172.
3. *The New York Times*, 22 May 1983.
4. Ruth Leger Sivard, *World Military and Social Expenditures, 1982* World Priorities 1982, p. 5.
5. Martin Buber, *Collected Works* (4 vols), *Der Jude und sein Judentum*, 1963, p. 569. Quoted in *Disputation and Dialogue: Readings in the Jewish–Christian Encounter*, ed. F. E. Talmage, KTAV, New York 1975, p. 246.
6. The Nippon Gakujitsu Shinkokai Translation, *The Manyoshu*, Columbia University Press 1965, p. 188.
7. Miyata Noburu (ed.), *Sangaku Shukyo* (Mountain Religion), Shunju-Sha 1980, p. 3.
8. Heschel, op. cit., p. 225.

2. Parochial god – Attractive yet Destructive

1. H. Byron Earhart, *Religion in the Japanese Experience*, Dickenson Publishing Company, Inc. 1974, p.207.
2. Ibid., p. 209.
3. Tomura Masahiro (ed.), *Jinja Mondai to Kiristokyo* (Shinto Shrine and Christianity, Conflict) Shinkyo Shuppansha 1976, p. 340.
4. A significant number of Japanese scholars, some of them Christian, joined the government's efforts to legitimize shinto worship. The extent to which this mystification took hold in Japan and the confusion it produced may be illustrated by a conversation recorded of the Committee on the Constitution in the Japanese Diet as late as 9 March 1960, fifteen years after the end of the war.

   Mr Takayanagi: May I ask you a simplistic question. This is in relation to the discussion whether Shinto is a religion or not. If, for instance, the emperor were to decide to convert to Christianity, would it not have a shocking effect on Shintoists? Would they not be alarmed? But if Shinto is not a religion, why should not the emperor become a Christian?

   Mr Kishimoto (scholar in history of religions): I suppose such an eventuality must be quite shocking to the Shintoists.

   Mr T: Does that not tell that Shinto is a religion?

   Mr K: In my understanding, Shinto is a religion in at least 70 per cent of its practice. Such a reaction on the part of Shinto is then quite understandable.

Mr T: If the conversion of the emperor to Christianity were to take place, could the Shinto people welcome it? Or would they feel some resistance?

Mr Iimuma (Shinto priest): Of whom are you speaking among the Shinto people?

Mr T: Yes. For the instance the leaders and priests.

Mr I: The reaction would be far more than resistance.
It would be a great shock.

Mr T: Then how can you say that Shinto is not a religion?
It would be difficult to say that.

Mr I: You mean shrines?

Mr T: We have freedom of religion. The emperor can become a Christian. Because shinto is not a religion. . . .

Mr I: Yes, in the light of the legal discussion.

Mr T: No, in terms of social phenomenon.

Mr I: If such a thing happened as a social phenomenon, I believe there would be a strong resistance. . . .

Mr T: Then priests of the Shinto must have a strong feeling that the Shinto is religion.

Taken from Tomura Masahiro, ibid., p. 20.

5. Ike Nobutaka (ed.), *Japan's Decision for War: Records of the 1941 Policy Conferences*, Stanford University Press 1967, p. 283.
6. Ibid.
7. Arnold J. Toynbee (ed.), *Survey of International Affairs*, published under the auspices of the British Institute of International Affairs, Oxford University Press, p. 489. (*The Times*, 9 December 1941)
8. Fujiwara Akira, 'Haisen' (Defeat of War), *Nihon Rekishi Koza* (Japanese History Lecture Series), Iwanami Shoten 1977, Vol. 21, p. 330.
9. In June 1945 the Ministry of Public Welfare reported to the government that people were dying from lack of calory intake. The report said that while a Japanese person needs 2400 calories a day, the average person was now getting only 1200 to 1400 calories a day. The implication was that the war could not continue for this reason. During the war years rice production in Japan decreased rapidly from 66,780,000 koku (1 koku = 150 kg, or 5 bushels) in 1942 to 62,890,000 koku in 1943, 58,560,000 koku in 1944 and 39,150,000 koku in 1945. It had decreased more than forty per cent in three years. Tooyama Shigeki, *Showa Shi* (History of the Showa Era), Iwanami Shoten 1959, p. 223.
10. Fujiwara Akira, ibid., p. 361.

3. Wilderness Tokyo

1. David J. Lu (ed.), *Sources of Japanese History*, McGraw-Hill 1974, Vol. II, p. 176.
2. From the *Engi* Period Law (*Engi-Shiki*) of AD 907.

3. *Hidaka Rokuro (ed.)*, *Sengo Shiso no Shuppatsu* (Beginning of the Post War Thought), Chikuma Shobo 1976, p. 54.
4. Arnold J. Toynbee (ed.), op. cit., p. 507.
5. Fujii Shinichi, *The Constitution of Japan, A Historical Survey*, Kokushikan University 1965, p. 322. The English text of the constitutions, both of 1889 and 1947, is taken from this book.
6. According to Information Center of the United Church of Christ in Japan (Bulletin issued on 20 June 1979) the officials of Yasukuni Shrine for the War Dead revealed that 1,005 war criminals have been added to the list of *kami* (gods) at the Shrine during a decade between 1969–79. These new names include Tojo Hideki and other A Class war criminals. This was done secretly and only made public in 1979.

4. The Holy God Repudiates Idolatry

1. Tertullian, 'On Idolatry', *Early Latin Theology*, The Library of Christian Classics, Vol. V, tr. and ed., S. L. Greenslade, SCM Press, London 1956, p. 83.
2. Yehezkel Kaufmann, *The Religion of Israel*, Schocken Books 1972, p. 13.
3. Waldo Beach and H. Richard Niebuhr (ed.) *Christian Ethics, Sources of the Living Tradition*, The Ronald Press Company 1955, p. 245.
4. Whitfield Foy (ed.), *Man's Religious Quest,* Croom Helm, London 1978, p. 153.
5. Timothy Ware, *The Orthodox Church*, Penguin Books 1963, p. 40.
6. Tertullian, op. cit., p. 85.
7. John Philips, *The Reformation of Images*, University of California Press, Berkeley 1973, p. 201.
8. Richard D. Heffner, *A Documentary History of the United States*, A Mentor Book 1976, p. 162.
9. James Mays, *Hosea*, SCM Press and The Westminster Press 1969. p. 117.
10. ibid.
11. The draft of the Imperial Rescript of the Emperor's Disavowal of His Divinity was in the hand of Principal Yamanashi of the Tokyo Peer School in December 1945. There is a dispute whether the initial motivation to issue the Rescript originated in the Ministry of the Imperial Household or in the Allied Occupational Forces. It is known that Dr R. H. Blyth, Professor in English literature at Peer School was a liaison between the Japanese authority and the Allied Forces. In 1945 world opinion was strongly against the emperor and there was a real possibility that he would be indicated as a war criminal. Against this background of world opinion a proclamation denying his divinity was thought to be helpful to put an end to the divinity mythology. According to Mrs Blyth, the emperor, upon studying the draft, was in agreement with it, but he had a question whether he could deny divinity which from the beginning he had never had. The advice given the emperor was that as the people had been forced to accept mythical divinity the perception of the world is that the emperor thinks of himself as divine. The Rescript was in order to clarify the situation. It was finally written in both English and Japanese by Prime Minister Shinohara and Minister of Education, Maeda. What is important is that the Rescript expresses the mind of the emperor himself.

   For this I am indebted to Takeda Kiyoko, *Tenno Kan no Sokoku* (Conflicts in Imperial System), Iwanami Shoten 1978, pp. 258-261. The text is taken from *Political Reorientation of Japan, from September 1945 to September 1948,*

Report by Supreme Commander for the Allied Powers, Washington, US Govt.
Print. Office 1949, Appendix B:3b, p. 470.
12. Gerhard Kittel (ed.), *Theological Dictionary of the New Testament*, Eerdmans
Publishing Company 1964, Vol. I, article 'aeon'.
13. Earhart, *Religion in the Japanese Experience*, p. 204.
14. *The Torah*, Jewish Publication Society of America, Philadelphia 1962.

5. Before the Fierce Anger of God

1. Bernhard W. Anderson, *Creation Versus Chaos*, Association Press 1967, p. 12.
2. Jonathan Schell, *The Fate of the Earth*, Picador 1982, p. 23.
3. Abraham Heschel, *The Prophets*, p. 224.

6. Reed-Shoot Culture

1. The *Kojiki*, ed. Kurano Kenji, Iwanami Shoten 1974, p. 18.
2. Shibata Minoru, 'Sosen Suhai no Genryu' (Sources of Ancestor Veneration) in
Nihon Shukyo Shi Koza, San Itsu Shobo 1971, vol. 3, pp. 26-28. According to
Shibata the Japanese deities can be classified into two groups; *musubi* group
and *hi* (solar) group. But these two concepts are closely interrelated.
3. Maruyama Masao, 'Rekishi Ishiki no Koso' (Ancient Layer of Japanese History
Awareness) in *Rekishi Shiso Shu* (Works on Historical Thoughts), Chikuma
Shobo 1974, p. 12. and pp. 3–46.
4. Muraoka Tsunetsugu, *Nihon Shiso Shi Kenkyu* (Studies in History of Japanese
Thoughts) Iwanami Shoten 1975, vol. 3, pp. 53f.
5. Donald L. Philippi (tr.), *Norito* (Ancient Japanese Ritual Prayers), Kokugakuin
University 1959, p. 82.
6. Kurano Kenji, op. cit, p. 28.
7. Takeuchi Yoshio, *Chugoku Shiso Shi* (History of Chinese Thought), Iwanami
Shoten 1973, pp. 5f.
8. S. Radhakrishnan (ed. tr.), *The Principal Upanisads*, Allen & Unwin 1953, pp.
314ff. and p. 433. Brihad-aranyaka Upanisad VI.2,16 and Chandogya
Upanisad, V.10,7).
9. R. C. Zaehner (tr.), *Hindu Scriptures*, Dent 1966, p. 12.
10. Sakuta Keiichi, *Haji no Bunka Saiko* (Rethinking on Culture of Shame),
Chikuma Shobo 1967, pp. 155–183.
11. Mircea Eliade, *Cosmos and History*, Harper & Row 1954, pp. 95–162.

7. To Dust You Shall Return

1. Gerhard Kittel (ed.), *Theological Dictionary of the New Testament*, Vol III.
Eerdmans 1965, article, 'kosmos'. Quotations from pp. 873, 874.
2. Kano Naoki, *Chugoku Tetsugaku Shi* (History of Chinese Philosophy),
Iwanami Shoten 1973, pp. 48–60.
3. The Nippon Gakujutsu Shinkokai (tr.) *The Manyoshu*, Columbia University
Press 1965, p. 28.
4. In writing this chapter I am indebted to Ienaga Saburo's *Nihon Shiso Shi ni
Okeru Hitei no Ronri no Hattatsu*, (Development of the logic of negation in the
history of Japanese thought) Shinsen Sha 1983, pp. 17–220.
5. Ibid., p. 126.

6. Ibid., p. 130.
7. Heinrich Zimmer, *Myths and Symbols in Indian Art and Civilization*, Bollingen Series, Princeton 1946, p. 152.
8. Ibid., p. 155.
9. Heinrich Zimmer, *The Art of Indian Asia, Its Mythology and Transformations*, Bollingen Series, Princeton 1955, Vol. I, p. 147.
10. Hans Schärer, *Ngaju Religion: The Conception of God among a South Borneo People*, (tr.) Rodney Needham, The Hague 1963, pp. 59–62, 65, 66.
11. R. S. Pine-Coffin (tr.), *Saint Augustine, Confessions*, Penguin Books 1961, p. 21.
12. Gerhard von Rad, *Genesis*, SCM Press and The Westminster Press 1972, p. 94.
13. Ibid.
14. Quoted in Hajime Nakamura's *Ways of Thinking of Eastern Peoples*, University of Hawaii Press 1974, p. 357.
15. Ienaga, op. cit., p. 213.
16. Ibid., pp. 82-86.
17. Ibid., p. 110.

8. Centre – Cosmological and Ideological

1. Mircea Eliade, *Patterns in Comparative Religion,* Sheed & Ward and Meridian Books 1963, p. 101.
2. Miyazaki Fumiko, 'Funi-Do no Rekishi Kan' (History View of Funi-Do) in *Sangaku Shukyo*, ed. Miyata Noboru and others, Shunju Sha 1981, pp. 121-138.
3. Ibid., p. 122.
4. Miyata Noboru, 'Noson no Fukko Undo to Minshu Shukyo no Tenkai' (Renewal Movement in the Rural Areas and the Development of the Popular Religion) in *Nihon Rekishi Koza* (Japanese History Lecture Series) Iwanami Shoten 1977, Vol. 13, pp. 210-45.
5. Ienaga Saburo (ed.), *Nihon Shukyo Shi Koza* (History of Japanese History Series) San Itsu Shobo 1971, Vol. 3, pp. 233f.
6. W. G. Aston, *Nihongi* (Chronicle of Japan), Tuttle 1972, p. 77 (part II, The Age of Gods).
7. Heinrich Zimmer, *Myths and Symbols in Indian Art and Civilization,* Bollingen Series, Princeton 1972, pp. 13-19; *krita* means 'accomplished, perfect', *treta*, 'triad or triplet', *dvapara*, 'two', *kali*, 'strife, quarrel'.
8. Brevard S. Childs, *Exodus*, SCM Press and The Westminster Press 1974, p. 596.
9. S. Radhakrishnan, *The Bhagavadgita*, Allen & Unwin 1971, p. 271.
10. Ibid., p. 273.
11. Philip P. Wiener (ed.), *Dictionary of the History of Ideas,* Scribner 1973, Vol. II, p. 558.
12. Frederic L. Bender (ed.), *Karl Marx, The Essential Writings*, Harper & Row 1972, pp. 241f.
13. Bob Jones III, in the *Washington Post*, 26 May 1983.

9. The Cauldron in Which a Spider Spins its Web

1. David J. Lu (ed.), *Sources of Japanese History*, McGraw-Hill 1974, Vol. I, pp. 39f.
2. Radhakrishnan, *The Principal Upanisads*, Taittiriya Upanisad, III.10,5,p. 562.

3. Gerhard Kittel, *Theological Dictionary of the New Testament*, article 'pleonexia'.
4. Emil Brunner, *The Divine Imperative*, The Westminster Press 1947, p. 423.
5. Anesaki, op. cit., p. 89.

10. Human Greed and Human History

1. *The Middle Length Sayings (Majjhima-Nikaya)*, Pali Text Society, Luzac & Company 1967, Vol. 1, p. 107.
2. Hisamatsu Shinichi, *Hisamatsu Shinichi Chosakushu* (Works of Hisamatsu Shinichi), Riso Sha 1972, Vol. 2, p. 409.
3. *The Middle Length Sayings* (Majjhima-Nikaya), Vol. 1, p. 28.
4. Mizuno Kogen, 'Shoki Butskyo no Enki Shiso' (Conditional Arising in the Early Buddhist Thought) in *Toyo Shiso*, (Oriental Thought), Tokyo University Press 1972, Vol. 5, p. 131.
5. *Kindred Sayings (Samyutta-Nikaya)*, Pali Text Society, Luzac & Company, Part II. p.45.
6. Ibid., p. 2.
7. Ibid.
8. Ibid., p. 21.
9. Winston L. King, *A Thousand Lives Away*, Bruno Cassirer, Oxford 1964, p. 18.
10. Quoted in Ananda K. Coomaraswamy, *Buddha and the Gospel of Buddhism* Harper & Row 1964, pp. 91f.
11. Masutani Fumio, *Butsu Kyo no Shiso* (Buddhist Thought Series), Kadokawa Shoten 1974, Vol. I, p. 107.
12. Mircea Eliade, *From Primitives to Zen*, Harper & Row 1967, p. 479. See *The Middle Length Sayings*, Vol. I, p. 212.
13. Eliade, *From Primitives to Zen*, p. 572.
14. Bhadragaka, *80 Inspiring Words of the Buddha*, Bangkok 1954, p. 9.
15. Eliade, *From Primitives to Zen*, pp. 572f.
16. Ui Hakuju, *Butsu Kyo Shiso Kenkyu* (Study in Buddhist Thought), Iwanami Shoten 1982, pp. 97–103. Professor Ui (1882–1963), one of the greatest of Japanese Buddhist scholars, describes lucidly the limitations encountered when we seek after information about the origin and early development of Buddhism.
17. Ibid., pp. 37–45
18. Narada Thera (tr.), *The Dhammapada*, John Murray 1959, p. 40 (Papavagga, 117).
19. W. Theodore De Bary (ed.), *Sources of Indian Tradition,* Columbia University Press 1958, Vol. 1, p. 140.
20. R. C. Zaehner (tr.), *Hindu Scriptures*, Dent 1966, p. 10.
21. Blaise Pascal, *Pensees*, 347.
22. *Kindred Sayings (Samyutta Nikaya)*, Part III, p. 175.
23. *Dialogues of the Buddha (Digha Nikaya)*, Pali Text Society, Luzac & Company 1966 (Maha Parinibbana Suttanta), p. 113.
24. Radhakrishnan, *The Principal Upanisads*, p. 392.
25. Ibid., p. 458.
26. *Book of the Discipline* (Sacred Books of the Buddhist Vol. XIV), Pali Text Society, Luzac & Company, Part, IV.I, Text 20.2, p. 45.
27. Francis Seeley (tr.), Thailand Theological Seminar, translation publication, 1965.

28. Marianne Katoppo, *Compassionate and Free*, Orbis Books, 1980, pp. 16–24.
29. The word 'Hinayana' is usually avoided since it carries a pejorative ring. The expression 'Theravada (of the Elders) Buddhism' is more acceptable.
30. Gerhard Kittel (ed.), *Theological Dictionary of the New Testament*, Vol. I, p. 32, article 'agapao'.
31. *Dialogues of the Buddha* (Maha Parinibbana Suttanta), pp. 108f.
32. Ibid., p. 173.
33. Quoted in *The Path of the Buddha*, ed. Kenneth W. Morgan, The Ronald Press 1956, p. 16.

11. Technology Occasions a Conflict between Efficiency and Meaning

1. Buddhadasa Bhikku, *Towards Buddha-Dhamma*, Wat Benjamabopit 1964, Bangkok, p. 48.
2. Ruth Leger Sivard, *World Military and Social Expenditures 1981*, p. 5.
3. Sivard, *World Military and Social Expenditures 1982*, p. 5.
4. Ibid., p. 6.

12. World of Spirits

1. Muraoka Tsunetsugu, *Nihon Shiso Shi Kenkyu* (Studies on History of Japanese Thoughts), Iwanami Shoten 1975, Vol. III, pp. 35f.
2. Ueda Masaaki 'Kodai No Saiki to Jirei' (Ancient Religious Practices and Rituals) in *Nihon Rekishi Koza* (Japanese History Lecture Series) Iwanami Shoten 1975, Vol. 1, pp. 324–357.
3. Ibid.
4. Motoori Norinaga writes; 'I do not yet understand the meaning of the term, *kami*. Speaking in general, however, it may be said that *kami* signifies, in the first place, the deities of heaven and earth that appear in the ancient records and also the spirits of the shrines where they are worshipped. It is hardly necessary to say that it includes human beings. It also includes such objects as birds, beasts, trees, plants, seas, mountains and so forth. In ancient usage, anything whatsoever which was outside the ordinary, which possessed superior power or which was awe-inspiring was called *kami*. Eminence here does not refer merely to the superiority of nobility, goodness or meritous deeds. Evil and mysterious things, if they are extraordinary and dreadful, are called *kami*.' Earhart, op. cit., pp.10f.
5. Ueda Masaaki, op. cit., pp. 334–36.

13. The Coming of Universal Civilization

1. Anesaki Masaharu, *History of Japanese Religion*, Tuttle 1963, p. 57.
2. Muraoka Tsunetsugu, *Nihon Shiso Shi Kenkyu* (Studies on History of Japanese Thoughts), Iwanami Shoten 1975, Vol. IV, p. 57.
3. W. T. De Bary (ed.), *Sources of Japanese Tradition*, Columbia University Press 1958, Vol. 1, p. 48.
4. Ibid., p. 50.
5. Ibid., p. 48.
6. Watsuji Tetsuro, *Nihon Rinri Shiso Shi* (History of Ethical Thoughts in Japan), Iwanami Shoten 1970, Vol. 1, pp. 138f.
7. W. T. De Bary, op. cit., p. 49.

8. Ibid.
9. Inoue Mitsusada, *Nihon Kodai No Kokka to Butskyo* (The Ancient State of Japan and Buddhism), Iwanami Shoten 1976, p. 14.
10. Japan Buddhist Academy, *Butsukyo no Ningen Kan* 1979 (Buddhist View of Man), carries an article by Okuda Jio; 'Shotoku Taishi No Ningen Kan' (Prince Shotoku's view on Man), p. 156.
11. Gerhard von Rad, *Genesis*, SCM Press and The Westminster Press 1972, p. 91.
12. Martin Luther, *Operationes in Psalmos*, 1519–21, WA 5, pp. 512–26.
13. Edward J. Thomas, *The History of Buddhist Thought*, Routledge & Kegan Paul 1971, pp. 16f.
14. H. Richard Niebuhr, *Radical Monotheism and Western Culture*, Harper & Row 1960, p. 37.
15. Watsuji Tetsuro, op. cit., Vol. 1, pp. 373f.
16. Tamura Yoshiro, 'Hongaku Shiso' (The Hongaku Thought) in *Butsukyo Shiso*, Riso Sha 1982, Vol. V, p. 457. See also *Nihon Butsukyo Shi Niu Mon* (Introduction to Japanese Buddhism), Kadokawa Shoten 1973, pp. 79–89.
17. Ibid., pp. 437–461.
18. Anesaki, op. cit., p. 174. Deeply impressed by the triumph of grace in the religious teaching of Honen and Shinran, Karl Barth writes; '... the Christian-Protestant religion of grace is not the true religion because it is a religion of grace. ... Only one thing is really decisive for the distinction of truth and error. And we call the existence of Yodoism a providential disposision because with what is relatively the greatest possible force it makes it clear that only one thing is decisive. That one thing is the name of Jesus Christ. Methodologically, it is to be recommended that in the fact of Yodoism, and at bottom, of all other religions, our first task is to concentrate wholly upon this distinction, provisionally setting aside whatever other deference we think we recognize. ... the truth of the Christian religion is in fact enclosed in the one name of Jesus Christ, and nothing else.' *Church Dogmatics*, T. & T. Clark 1956, I/2, p. 343.
19. Franklin Edgerton (tr.), *The Bhagavad Gita*, Harvard University Press 1972, p. 42.
20. Ishida Mizumaro, 'Honen' in *Butsukyo Shiso* (Buddhist Thought), Riso Sha 1982, Vol. VI, p. 139.
21. Anesaki, op. cit., p. 183.
22. *Tanisho*, chapter Three, the first paragraph.
23. Henry James Coleridge (tr.), *The Life and Letters of St Francis Xavier*, London, Burns Oates 1902, Vol. II, pp. 95f.
24. Ibid., pp. 227f., 11 Nov. 1549.
25. Ibid., pp. 228f.
26. Ibid., p. 252.
27. Ibid., p. 347.
28. Ibid., pp. 338f.
29. Ibid., p. 341.
30. Takase Kouichiro, 'Kirishitan to Toitsu Kenryoku' (Kirishitan and Unified Power) in *Nihon Rekishi Koza* (Japanese History Lecture Series), Vol. IX, p. 207.
31. Watsuji Tetsuro, *Sakoku* (Closed Nation), Chikuma Shobo 1974, pp. 1-3.

14. Amalgamation of Religions

1. Kawane Yoshiyasu 'Odo Shiso to Shinbutsu Shugo' (Idea of King's Land and

Amalgamation of Shinto and Buddhist Traditions), *Nihon Rekishi Koza* (Japanese History Series), Vol. IV, pp. 272–312. Quotation from p. 275.
2. Ibid.
3. Joseph M. Kitagawa, *Religion in Japanese History*, Columbia University Press 1966, p. 362.
4. Ibid.
5. Ishida Ichiro (ed.), *Shinto Shiso Shu* (Anthology of Shinto Thoughts), Chikuma Shobo 1975, pp. 3–37.
6. Muraoka Tsunetsugu, *Nihon Shiso Shi Kenkyu*, Vol. I, pp. 321–336. Quotation from pp. 327f.
7. Kim Young Bock (ed.), *Minjung Theology*, Christian Conference of Asia 1981, p. 54.
8. Ibid., p. 27.
9. Ibid., p. 58.
10. Ibid., p. 61.
11. Ibid.
12. Ibid.
13. Ibid.

15. Wealthy Nation Strong Army

1. Tahara Shiro, 'Kinsei Chuki no Seiji Shiso to Kokka Ishiki' (Political thought in the middle modern time and awareness of nationhood) in *Nihon Rekishi Koza* (Japanese History Lecture Series), Iwanami Shoten 1976, Vol. II, pp. 298–329.
2. Haraguchi Kiyoshi, 'Meiji Kempo Taisei no Setsuritsu' (The establishment of the Meiji Constitutional System) in *Nihon Rekishi Koza* (Japanese History Lecture Series), Iwanami Shoten 1976, Vol. 15, pp. 136–75.
3. Herman Roesler had been Professor of economics and law at the University of Rostock before he was invited to the influential position of adviser to the Japanese Government in preparation for the 1889 Constitution. Johannes Siemes, *Herman Roesler and the making of the Meiji State*, Sophia University, Tokyo 1966, p.44; Monumenta Nipponica Monographs, No. 24.
4. Iwai Tadakuma, 'Gunji and Keisatsu Kiko no Kakuritsu' (Establishment of Military and police Organization) in *Nihon Rekishi Koza* (Japanese History Lecture Series), Iwanami Shoten 1976, Vol. 15, pp. 185f.
5. See above, Chapter 2, note 9.

16. The Post-War Constitution

1. Kobayashi Naoki, *Kempo Kogi* (Lectures on Constitution), Tokyo University Press 1979, Vol. I, pp. 186–232, represents one of the most erudite and influential studies on Article Nine.
2. The Supreme Court took the position that to judge the Security Pact, an entity of such great political significance, was beyond the limit of the Judiciary so it passed the matter to the National Diet and the Cabinet to decide. Thus the Supreme Court of the nation avoided giving a verdict upon a most important legal question.
3. Kanamori Tokujiro, Minister of State, replied to questions addressed to him in the 90th National Diet (1946):
    Q. Should Japan be invaded by another nation, according to the principle set forth in the draft of the constitution we would not offer military resistance and

would at least for a time, allow our nation to be invaded. How do you think about this?

A. In certain cases what you say is unavoidable. Defence without force naturally has a limitation.

Q. Following the non-violent resistance of Gandhi, to let other nations invade us and trust in the sense of righteousness and justice of the world, believing that wrongs will be rectified. Until such a time comes to renounce the right to resist arms by arms. May I understand the spirit of Article Nine in this way?

A. We are not to take up arms and get into a war. We must defend ourselves by other means than war.

Kobayashi Naoki, op. cit., p. 221.

17. Limping Dance between God and Baal

1. M. J. Mulder, article 'ba'al' in G. J. Botterweck and H. Ringgren (eds), *Theological Dictionary of the Old Testament*, Eerdmans 1975, Vol. II, p. 200.
2. *Kojiki* 1.2.
3. Yasuda Naomichi 'Izanagi Izanami no Shinwa to Awa no Noko Girei' (Izanagi and Izanami Mythology and Agricultural Rites of Awa), in *Nihon Shinwa Kenkyu* (Studies on Japanese Mythologies), Gakusei Sha 1977, Vol. II, pp. 71–99.
4. George F. Kennan, *The Nuclear Delusion*, Pantheon Books 1983, p. 176.

18. Why Do All Who are Treacherous Thrive?

1. Wasin Indasara, *Theravada Buddhist Principles*, Mahamakut Buddhist University, Bangkok 1978, Book 2, pp. 1f.
2. Ibid., p. 24.
3. The Pali Text Society published the English translation of 547 Jataka tales in 1906 under the title *The Jataka*. The scenes taken from the Jataka tales have been painted on the walls of Buddhist temples in Thailand and Sri Lanka, for instance, and have become a centre of popular Buddhism.
4. J. S. Speyer (tr.), *The Jatakamala, Garland of Birth-Stories,* Motilal Banarsidass, Delhi 1971, pp. 8–19.
5. Chandogya Upanisad V.10.7. in *The Principal Upanisads* by Radhakrishnan (ed. tr.) op. cit. p. 433.
6. Quoted in Ananda K. Coomaraswamy, *Buddha and The Gospel of Buddhism*, Harper & Row 1964, pp. 35f.
7. Mahapadana Suttanta in *Dialogues of the Buddha*, tr. from the Pali of the *Digha Nikaya*, Pali Text Society 1966, Part II, pp. 36f.
8. Ui Hakuju, *Butskyo Shiso Kenkyu* (Studies on Buddhist Thoughts), Iwanami Shoten 1982, pp. 41f.
9. Irokawa Daikichi, *Meiji no Bunka* (The Meiji Culture), Iwanami Shoten 1976, pp. 3f.
10. See above Chapter 1, note 8.

19. Vanity of Vanities Says the Preacher

1. The Jewish Publication Society of America, Philadelphia 1982.
2. G. J. Botterweck and H. Ringgren (eds), *Theological Dictionary of the Old*

Testament, Eerdmans 1978, Vol. III, article 'hebhel', pp. 313–20. Isaiah quotation on p. 314.

3. Other words similar to *hebhel* used by the prophets are *riq*, 'empty' (Isa. 30.7), *tohu*, 'emptiness, vanity' (Isa. 49.4), *sheqer*, 'deceit, falsehood' (Jer. 10.14) *'aven*, 'deceit' or *shav'*, 'deceit, falsehood', (Zech. 10.2), *lo'ho'il*, 'to have no value, be good for nothing', (Isa. 30.6; Jer. 16.19). Botterweck and Ringgren, op. cit., pp. 314f.

4. Gerhard von Rad, *Old Testament Theology*, Oliver and Boyd 1968, Vol. I, p. 455.

5. *Sacred Book of the Buddhists*, tr. E. M. Hare, Pali Text Society, Colombo. Ceylon 1944, p. 120f. (804–807, 808, 811).

6. Narada Thera, *The Dhammapada*, John Murray 1959, p. 28.

7. Hisamatsu Shinichi, *Toyo Teki Mu* (Oriental Concept of *Mu*), Riso Sha 1982, p. 241.

8. Izutsu Toshihiko, *Ishiki to Honshitsu* (Consciousness and Essence), Iwanami Shoten 1983, pp. 123f.

9. A. A. MacDonell, *A Practical Sanskrit Dictionary*, Oxford University Press 1958, 'maya'.

10. John B. Alphonso-Karkala, *An Anthology of Indian Literature*, Penguin Books 1971, pp. 262f.

11. Heinrich Zimmer, *Myths and Symbols in Indian Art and Civilization*, Bollingen Series/Princeton 1963, pp. 32–34.

12. The Jewish Publication Society of America translation.

13. Ibid.

20. Theology of the Cross

1. The Commentary is called *Operationes in Psalmos, 1519–1521*. The last part of this commentary was written during the time he was almost on the way to hiding in Wartburg in 1521. During the time Luther wrote this commentary, we see his prolific writings. In 1520 alone, *Sermons on Good Works* (May), *The Papacy at Rome* (June) *The Address to the German Nobility* (August), *The Babylonian Captivity of the Church* (September) and *The Freedom of the Christian Man* (November). According to Heinrich Boehmer; 'That the Antichrist was ruling the Curia, he was already convinced by March or April, 1519'. (*Martin Luther; Road to Reformation,* p.265). Luther appeared in April, 1521 at Worms before the Emperor and refused to recant his theological position. In May 1521 Emperor Charles V adjudged Luther to be 'a limb cut off from the Church of God, an obstinate schismatic and manifest heretic'. (Kenneth Latourette, *A History of Christianity*, p.718). The *Operationes in Psalmos* was composed during these turbulent times.

2. Luther, *Operationes in Psalmos 1519–1521* WA 5, p.37/25. Translation from *Martin Luther's Complete Commentary on the First Twenty-Two Psalms*, Vols. I,II, by Henry Cole, London, Simpkin and Marshall 1826.

3. Ibid., p. 63/35.

4. Ibid., p. 394/24.

5. Ibid., p. 516/11.

6. Ibid., p. 99/23.

7. Ibid., p. 96/13.

8. Ibid., p. 204/26.

9. Roland Bainton, *Here I Stand, A Life of Martin Luther* Abingdon-Cokesbury

Press, New York 1940, p. 214.

10. The *New York Times*, 8 September 1983.

11. John F. Clarkson and others (tr. and ed.) *The Church Teaches*, Herder 1955, p. 172.

12. Quoted in Gordon Rupp, *The Old Reformation and the New*, Fortress Press 1967, p. 15.

    'Christians should be exhorted to be zealous to follow Christ, their Head, through penalties, deaths, and hells; and let them thus be more confident of entering heaven through many tribulations rather than through a false assurance of peace.' Quoted in Gerhard Ebeling, *Luther*, Collins, 1972, p.234.

13. Martin Buber, *Two Types of Faiths,* Harper & Row 1951, p. 164.

14. Alan Richardson, *An Introduction to the Theology of the New Testament*, SCM Press 1958, p. 222.

15. Ebeling, op. cit., p. 228.

16. The *New York Times*, 9 March 1983.

17. *Occasional Bulletin of the Commission on Theological Concerns*, Christian Conference of Asia, Vol. 2, No. 3, May 1981, p. 21.